CW00972149

Cultural Issues in Psychology

Does our cultural background influence the way we think and feel about ourselves and others? Does our culture affect how we choose our partners, how we define intelligence and abnormality and how we bring up our children? Psychologists have long pondered the relationship between culture and a range of psychological attributes. *Cultural Issues in Psychology* is an all-round student guide to the key studies, theories and controversies that seek to explore human behaviour in a global context.

The book explores key controversies in global psychology, such as:

- Culture: what does it mean and how has it been researched?
- Relativism and universalism: are they compatible approaches in global research?
- Ethnocentrism: is psychological research dominated by a few regions of the world?
- Indigenous psychologies: what are the diverse research traditions from around the world?
- Research methods and perspectives: how can we compare and contrast cross-cultural psychology and cultural psychology?

The book also includes detailed examinations of global research into mainstream areas of psychology, such as social, cognitive and developmental psychology, as well as abnormal psychology.

With insightful classroom activities and helpful pedagogical features, this detailed, yet accessibly written, book gives introductory-level psychology students access to a concise review of key research, issues, controversies and diverse approaches in the area of culture and psychology.

Andrew Stevenson has been teaching Psychology since 1990 at a variety of levels, including A-Level and undergraduate. He now divides his time between writing, freelance training and lecturing.

Cultural Issues in Psychology

A Student's Handbook

Andrew Stevenson

Routledge
Taylor & Francis Group

LONDON AND NEW YORK

First published 2010
by Routledge
2 Park Square, Milton Park, Abingdon, Oxon, OX14 4RN

Simultaneously published in the USA and Canada
by Routledge
711 Third Avenue, New York, NY 10017

Routledge is an imprint of the Taylor & Francis Group, an informa business

Copyright © 2010 Psychology Press

Typeset in Arial MT & Frutiger
by RefineCatch Limited, Bungay, Suffolk
Paperback cover design by Lisa Dynan

All rights reserved. No part of this book may be reprinted or
reproduced or utilised in any form or by any electronic,
mechanical, or other means, now known or hereafter
invented, including photocopying and recording, or in any
information storage or retrieval system, without permission in
writing from the publishers.

British Library Cataloguing in Publication Data
A catalogue record for this book is available from the British Library

Library of Congress Cataloging-in-Publication Data
Stevenson, Andrew.
  Cultural issues in psychology : a student's handbook / Andrew Stevenson.
    p. cm. – (Foundations of psychology.)
  Includes bibliographical references and index.
  1. Ethnopsychology. 2. Cognition and culture. 3. Cultural psychiatry. I. Title.
  GN502.S745 2009
  155.8′2—dc22—dc22
                                                    2009015151

ISBN: 978–0–415–42922–1 (hbk)
ISBN: 978–0–415–42923–8 (pbk)

Thanks to Ramsden

Contents

List of figures and tables

Figures

Tables

Series preface

The **Foundations of Psychology** series provides pre-undergraduate and first-year undergraduates with appealing and useful books that will enable the student to expand their knowledge of key areas in psychology. The books go beyond the detail and discussion provided by general introductory books but will still be accessible and appropriate for this level.

This series will bridge the gap between the all-encompassing general textbook and the currently available advanced topic-specific books which might be inaccessible to students who are studying such topics for the first time. Each book has a contemporary focus and fits into one of three main categories including:

- **Themes and Perspectives** (such as Theoretical Approaches or Ethics)
- **Specific Topics** (such as Memory or Relationships)
- **Applied Areas** (such as Psychology and Crime).

Series editors

Cara Flanagan is an experienced teacher and senior A-Level examiner.

Philip Banyard is Senior Lecturer in Psychology at Nottingham Trent University.

Preface

Does where we come from change the way we think? Does effective parenting take the same form the world over? Is schizophrenia
an international phenomenon?

Questions like these have unearthed many concepts and provoked
many controversies about how psychology should conduct itself on the
global stage. Part 1 of this book explores some of these controversies,
along with some of the concepts that enable us to understand and
participate in them. *Culture, relativism, ethnocentrism* and *race* are just
four of the concepts to figure in the first five chapters. In examining
these concepts from various perspectives a series of burning issues
from global psychology will be explored, including the following.

- Should global research aim to uncover human universals or should it
  investigate diversity in human behaviour and experience?
- Why does so much of the research we read about in our textbooks
  emerge from just a few regions in the world?
- Can research that is conceived in one region help us to understand
  behaviour in other regions?
- What is the history of global psychology?
- What is the difference between cross-cultural psychology and
  cultural psychology?
- What methods are used to conduct research in different cultures?

The issues and debates that feature in Part 1 have certainly spawned a
variety of views about how global research should be conducted and
what it is supposed to tell us. To anyone who's keen to really get to grips
with the aims, importance and relevance of all the key topics in Part 2
of this book, a firm grasp of the debates in Part 1 will be an invaluable
asset.

Research in global psychology investigates mainstream issues in
psychology from a global perspective, often reflecting diverse
research interests from around the world. Part 2 of this book explores

the contributions and insights of key classic and contemporary global research into four main areas of psychology. Specifically, research relating to the following areas is presented and analysed:

- culture, cognition and intellect
- culture, social cognition and social influence
- culture and child development
- culture and abnormality.

Within the field of global psychology researchers have approached these mainstream psychological topics from various angles and you will find in the following pages contributions from various global perspectives. The strength of debate relating to these topics will serve to illustrate that many questions remain to be answered in the global field, such as the following.

- Is intelligence defined differently in different parts of the world?
- Does my cultural background influence the way I perceive myself and others?
- Is childrearing the same the world over?
- Where do the most effective psychotherapies come from?

By placing mainstream issues from psychology in a global context and reviewing evidence from a diversity of backgrounds, it is intended that any student of psychology should be able to develop a more insightful, global *world*view of the study of human behaviour and experience.

Concepts and controversies

Searching for human universals

Introducing cross-cultural psychology

1

What this chapter will teach you

- What are **cultural universals**?
- What is **cross-cultural psychology**?
- What is meant by the terms **psychic unity** and **cultural equivalence**?
- How can we evaluate **cross-cultural psychology**?

Charles Darwin and the age-old search for cultural universals

Stop a random selection of passers-by anywhere on earth and a fair proportion of them will be able to tell you what John Lennon did for a living, that Mahatma Gandhi was a pacifist and that Charles Darwin wrote a famous book about evolution. A smaller proportion will be able to take you through the main arguments of *On the Origin of Species*. Fewer still will be able to reel off the names of Darwin's other bestsellers.

When he was researching one of these lesser-known works, *The Expression of the Emotions in Man and Animals* (1872), Darwin posed

KEY TERMS

Nature–nurture debate. Dispute about the relative contributions of biological inheritance (nature) and environmental influence (nurture) to our behavioural repertoire.

Cultural universals. Aspects of behaviour and experience that are common to all cultural settings.

Global psychology. A branch of psychology with a special interest in placing psychology in a global context.

a number of questions that still occupy psychologists today. These questions revealed Darwin as not only a biologist and natural historian, but also a student of the human mind. Notably, this was happening around 1850, twenty years before psychology itself set up its first laboratory to study mental life, in Leipzig.

One thing that interested Darwin about emotional expression was the question of its *universality*. He wondered whether pleasure, anger and confusion looked the same on the faces of Scots as on those of Egyptians. Take smiling, for example. Does this mouth-broadening, tooth-bearing contortion mean the same thing worldwide? If so, he reasoned, then perhaps emotional expression is a physiological response, universally shared among humans irrespective of upbringing. If, on the other hand, frowning in Jakarta and Kentucky mean two different things, then perhaps emotional expression is a learned response, determined by our cultural background. As you may recognise, this line of enquiry relates closely to what we now know as the **nature–nurture debate** (a dispute about the relative contributions of biological inheritance (nature) and environmental influence (nurture) to our behavioural repertoire).

By the turn of the twentieth century, when psychology had well and truly stirred itself into action, questions like Darwin's about the **cultural universals** of various aspects of human behaviour and psychological functioning were shooting up the agenda. In particular, for a branch of psychology with a special interest in placing psychology in a global context (known as **global psychology**), searching for human universals became a driving force for formulating research questions.

For example, in 1972 Deregowski asked:

Is the perception of three dimensions in drawings the same in different cultures?

In 1966 Piaget asked:

Does thinking develop in children at the same rate in different cultures?

Even into the twenty-first century the search for universals goes on. For instance, Van de Vliert (2006) asked:

Are autocratic leadership styles amongst managers equally effective in different countries and climates worldwide?

Many more examples of research inspired by the quest for cultural universals will feature during the course of this book.

Introducing cross-cultural psychology

Cultural universals are aspects of behaviour and experience that are common to all cultural settings. For example, Deregowski (1972) was interested in whether the ability to perceive drawings as representations of three-dimensional objects is common to all humans, irrespective of culture. Pursuing such questions requires you to uproot yourself and relocate (with laptops, cameras, notebooks, etc.) to various cultural locations. But searching for cultural universals isn't just about travelling into the field to conduct research (though this is part of it).

If you think universal psychological phenomena are out there waiting to be discovered, you're also likely to make certain assumptions about what global psychology is and how it should be carried out. These assumptions underpin an approach to global research known as **cross-cultural psychology**: a branch of global psychology that compares the behaviour and experience of people from different cultures in order to understand the extent of culture's influence on psychological functioning. In other words, cross-cultural psychologists try to find out what aspects of behaviour and experience are common to all human cultures – and thus what aspects are unique to certain places. Cross-cultural psychology is an approach that is favoured by a large proportion of global psychologists, though as we will learn it is not the only approach (see Chapter 5). As I have just hinted, cross-cultural investigations into cultural universality are underpinned by two key assumptions; one theoretical, one methodological.

KEY TERM

Cross-cultural psychology. A branch of global psychology that compares the behaviour and experience of people from different cultures in order to understand the extent of culture's influence on psychological functioning.

> ## REFLECTIVE EXERCISE 1
>
> 1. What's the difference between a *global psychologist* and a *cross-cultural psychologist*?
>
> 2. What kind of research finding might lead you to conclude that weeping at funerals is a *cultural universal*?

Assumption 1: psychic unity

Central to cross-cultural psychology's search for cultural universals is an assumption of **psychic unity** (Shweder, 1991). In everyday terms this dictum states that despite outward appearances, human diversity is only skin deep. Put more technically, it proposes that any differences in psychological functioning (personality traits, performance on perceptual and memory tests, and so forth) and in social behaviour

KEY TERM

Psychic unity. A set of psychic structures (mind, memory capacity, perceptual processes) that all humans share.

(courtship, attitudes, values, obedience levels) across cultures are limited by certain universal psychological capacities. So if children in Mozambique remember details from stories more accurately than Welsh children do, this is regarded as a 'local difference'. It doesn't mean that their underlying psychological capacities to remember and tell stories are different from each other.

According to the assumption of psychic unity, while researchers may report diverse behaviours in diverse cultural settings, these local differences are seen as no real challenge to the idea that deep down, all humans have an internal, global mind, or pure being, directing thoughts and actions (Shweder, 1991). In essence, psychic unity asserts that underlying our cultural variations is a set of psychic structures (mind, memory capacity, perceptual processes) that all humans share.

The assumption of psychic unity portrays a rather remote relationship between the human mind, on one hand, and behaviour in the outside world, on the other (Shweder, 1991). Mind and psychological capacities are seen as internal, universal, unaffected by culture. Meanwhile behaviour in the world is seen as external, diverse, under culture's influence. You could say that the cross-cultural psychologist's job is to work out how much of our behaviour is down to psychic unity (universals) and how much is down to our cultural background (variations).

Assumption 2: cultural equivalence

Cross-cultural research could be described as 'quasi-experimental' since in its basic form it mimics the experimental method in psychology. Two conditions of participants, separated by an independent variable (IV), are tested under otherwise equivalent conditions to find out whether the IV influences an aspect of their behaviour. In short, if participants in the two conditions behave differently it is assumed to be down to the IV.

Cross-cultural research simulates this scenario, where the IV is culture. Participants from differing cultural backgrounds are compared on a single, selected psychological ability or capacity. For example, Zambian adults might be compared with South African adults on their ability to perceive three dimensions in simple line drawings. Apart from the IV of cultural background, all other variables are held constant: this is the nub of **cultural equivalence**. So we have a research scenario where two (or more) groups are treated in an *equivalent* manner

KEY TERM

Cultural equivalence. Where two (or more) groups are treated in an *equivalent* manner throughout the study and are drawn from *equivalent* populations that differ only with respect to their cultural background.

throughout the study and are drawn from *equivalent* populations that differ only with respect for their cultural background. This is the basic research scenario used by cross-cultural research when investigating the possibility of cultural universals. As we will learn, it may not be the only type of research that is conducted cross-culturally, but it is the most popular.

As the definition in the previous paragraph implies, two kinds of equivalence are involved here. First, participants are exposed to equivalent testing conditions. Second, they are drawn from equivalent populations (in terms of factors like gender, age, income, literacy and numeracy levels) within their own culture (defined for the moment as a group with distinct *beliefs, opinions, customs and norms of behaviour* – though Chapter 3 discusses this concept in much more detail). This means avoiding situations where female Japanese graduates are compared with, say, male Israeli undergraduates. If cultural equivalence is achieved in these two ways, the groups in the study differ only in terms of their cultural background. Therefore, any differences in the groups' performance can be confidently attributed to cultural difference (where they come from). Equally, if little or no performance difference emerges, the ability in question can be more confidently declared culturally universal. After all, if participants from diverse cultures all perceive pictures in three dimensions, it would seem that three-dimensional picture perception is a capacity we all share.

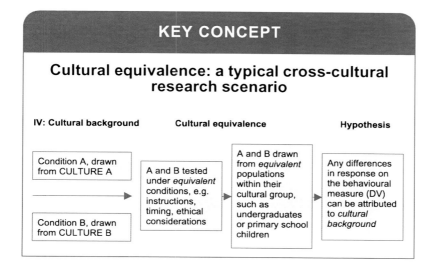

KEY CONCEPT

Cultural equivalence: a typical cross-cultural research scenario

IV: Cultural background | **Cultural equivalence** | **Hypothesis**

Condition A, drawn from CULTURE A

Condition B, drawn from CULTURE B

A and B tested under *equivalent* conditions, e.g. instructions, timing, ethical considerations

A and B drawn from *equivalent* populations within their cultural group, such as undergraduates or primary school children

Any differences in response on the behavioural measure (DV) can be attributed to *cultural background*

Searching for universals means 'transport and test'

KEY TERM

Cross-cultural replication research. An original study is replicated in different cultural settings to see if the same results emerge.

When researchers take the ideas of psychic unity and cultural equivalence out into the field to see how they fare in real life research settings, **cross-cultural replication research** is very often the result. This is a method of research that is well suited to anyone who is exploring the possibility of psychological universals. The thinking behind replication research is straightforward. An original study is replicated in different cultural settings to see if the same results emerge. For obvious reasons, this method has acquired the nickname of *transport and test*.

If, for example, girls in Cologne, Bradford and Taipei all show preferences for red pyjamas over blue, a 'red for girls' colour preference may be considered a potential cultural universal. To put this more broadly, such research aims to establish whether the knowledge and theories we have gathered from carrying out research in 'Culture A' hold true for 'Culture B' – and, by extension, for the majority of humanity that resides elsewhere. Though a simple rationale for guiding research into cultural universals, replication studies have produced some less than straightforward findings. Here are four examples.

Conformity: are we copy-cats?

Asch's (1955) conformity research was originally conducted in the US. In it, 35% of naïve participants went along with the clearly incorrect line-estimation judgements of a group of confederates. Yet cross-cultural conformity levels in Asch-like replications have revealed little by way of universal response levels. A **meta-analysis** (a review of findings from a large number of investigations into a similar research question) by Bond and Smith (1996) of 134 such studies, including 37 non-US ones, showed that susceptibility to group influence was significantly lower in Europe than in the US. Yet it was highest of all outside Europe and the US.

KEY TERM

Meta-analysis. A review of findings from a large number of investigations into a similar research question.

Familiarity preference: does familiarity breed contempt?

Zajonc (1968) repeatedly exposed US participants to nonsense words. They came to like them more the more they encountered them. This could lead us to dispute the maxim 'familiarity breeds contempt'. Findings like these may shed some light on how we form friendships, revealing a preference for what we know. Though these studies were replicated frequently in the US, with similar findings, Belgian and Brazilian studies showed scant support for Zajonc's results. Belgian participants preferred new objects to ones they'd seen two or three times (Vanbeselaere, 1983). Brazilians, though growing to prefer objects after repeated exposure, took significantly more trials than the US participants did to form their preferences (Rodrigues, 1982).

Social loafing: do many hands make light work?

Latané and colleagues looked at the trend towards easing off on a task when participating with others, known as *social loafing*. They measured how loudly participants would shout and clap in groups of differing sizes. They played the part of cheerleader, first in the US (Latané *et al.*, 1979), then in Indian, Thai, Taiwanese and Japanese replications (Gabrenya *et al.*, 1985). Social loafing reared its head in all these settings to varying extents, yet in another Japanese replication Shirikashi (1985) found Japanese students not to loaf. A further meta-analysis of social loafing studies found that for simple tasks loafing was common for both Pacific Asian and US participants. Complex tasks showed cultural differences; Pacific Asian participants, unlike North Americans, worked harder in groups (Karau & Williams, 1993). Earley's (1993) work was no more conclusive. Israeli and Chinese managers were found to be harder working when they thought they were part of a group, while US managers were harder working when they saw themselves as individuals.

Recognising facial expressions: does happiness look the same everywhere?

Ekman *et al.* (1987) gathered photographic portraits expressing happiness, sadness, surprise, disgust, fear and anger. Participants in the US, Japan, New Guinea and Indonesia all agreed when they were asked to say which expression corresponded to which emotion. This suggests that the facial expression of six emotional states is universally expressed and perceived across cultural settings.

But wait: These conclusions are not universally confirmed. Matsumoto (1992) found recognition of facial expressions to generate an agreement rate of just 70% on average (not as high as Ekman found, though still statistically significant). On closer scrutiny, Yrizarry *et al.* (1998) revealed cultural differences in the interpretation of 'angry' facial expressions between Japanese and US samples. The former labelled them 'sad', the latter favouring labels of 'disgust' or 'contempt'.

KEY TERM

Cultural differences. Behaviours or experiences that manifest themselves differently in different cultures.

Conclusions from replication research are far from straightforward

Where does all this evidence and counter-evidence lead us? These studies are only a drop in an ocean of evidence that has risen up from cross-cultural replication research. But this tiny selection hints at the diversity of findings from replication research in the search for universals of human behaviour. Generally speaking, some behaviours have been tentatively put forward as common to all cultures. Not surprisingly, these are often ones that are thought to have at least partly biological roots. Ekman *et al.*'s view that some basic emotions are expressed in the same way in all cultures is a good example of this. After all, the expression of fear and anger is arguably more instinctive (biological) than learned (cultural). Furthermore, our means for expressing these emotions are limited to our (biologically inherited) facial musculature.

Yet the picture is different if we consider behaviours thought to be more social in origin. These are less likely to be put forward as cultural universals, based on results from replication studies. Zajonc's (1968), Latané *et al.*'s (1979) and Yrizarry *et al.*'s (1998) findings are good indications of this. Ambiguous results such as these are not unusual. By and large, replicating studies in diverse settings has left global psychologists with the feeling that much of human behaviour doesn't travel too well. Huge slices of our behavioural repertoire, it seems, are influenced by local variations. In other words, there are behaviours or experiences that manifest themselves differently in different cultures, known as **cultural differences**. All of which offers only partial support for the view that we all share a universal human psychology.

In truth, replication research has unearthed as much ambiguity as it has universality. Results of quasi-experimental studies that seek to verify original findings have been inconclusive, even problematic (Smith *et al.*, 2006). Repeating original studies in diverse cultural settings has not always highlighted the existence of psychic unity.

So what are the reasons for the limited effectiveness of replication research in uncovering universal psychological phenomena? Well, let's look in detail at two possible answers to

---

REFLECTIVE EXERCISE 2

1. What's the difference between *cultural universals* and *cultural differences*?

2. Which of these behaviours are most likely to be culturally universal, and why?
   a. Crying at funerals
   b. Rapid eye movement during sleep
   c. Social loafing
   d. Obedience to authority

this question, which can serve as a two-pronged critique of cross-cultural replication research. The first of these would be the response most favoured from within cross-cultural psychology. The second emanates from global psychologists who advocate alternative approaches to investigating the relationship between culture, mind and behaviour.

Two types of evaluation of cross-cultural replication research

Evaluation type 1: from within cross-cultural psychology

Universal phenomena are out there but replication research hasn't consistently managed to uncover them

There is no suggestion here that there is anything wrong with searching for universals, only that replication research hasn't fully met the demands of the task. To put it another way, replication researchers have conspired in only a partially effective search for 'behaviour that everybody does' because of drawbacks with the research methods they have used. In particular, their methods have not always succeeded in comparing like with like.

As you will recognise from reading the first part of this chapter, what we have here is a problem of *cultural non-equivalence*. The doctrine of cultural equivalence, you will recall, requires that two (or more) groups be treated in an equivalent manner during a study and that they be drawn from equivalent populations that differ only with respect to their cultural background. Does replication research provide such a scenario? Fingers have been pointed at several features of the replication method to indicate that it may not. Here's why.

Why doesn't replication research guarantee cultural equivalence?

1 *Because culturally equivalent samples are hard to find.* Despite trying to ensure that samples are drawn from equivalent groups (students, the clergy, schoolchildren, doctors) within their own cultures, there's no escaping the likelihood that these labels have different connotations in different settings. For example, a priest in Melbourne (Australia) may have jumped through very different hoops from those set before priests in Cape Coast (Ghana).

2 *Because some researchers are more fastidious than others.* In all but a few rare cases, replications are not carried out by the same re-searchers that carried out the originals. So although all experimental

psychologists follow professional guidelines when doing research, it is likely that some are more fastidious than others when monitoring differences between conditions in their studies, or when allocating participants to groups and so forth (Segall *et al.*, 1990). In cross-cultural research it is reasonable to assume that inconsistencies between researchers are magnified since the tendency to control studies down to the last detail may vary across cultural settings.

3 *Because replications can lose something in translation.* In any controlled study it is vital that all participants receive standardised instructions. Typically, researchers either read out or distribute pre-prepared instructions so that everyone is equally clear about what is expected of them. In most cross-cultural replications these instructions have to be translated into different languages, so naturally some terms don't translate with perfect equivalence. For example, the requirement to 'say the first thing that comes into your head' has varying metaphoric resonances across different languages. The translation of participant responses faces just as many equivalence issues.

4 *Because for some of us, participation is second nature.* Filling in electronic questionnaires, answering telephone polls and being interviewed in the street are all part of the rich tapestry of urban living. For some of us it is hard to get through an entire day without spending at least a few minutes as a 'respondent'. Once you've done it a couple of times you get used to the requirements and dynamics of taking part in social research. You come to know how to behave, why your opinion is being sought and you take it for granted that whatever you say will remain confidential. Yet when research like this is replicated in settings where social research is a less familiar feature of everyday life, the strangeness and novelty of the social situation may well have an impact on the results. Extraordinary behaviour will, effectively, be compared with that which is wholly ordinary. Consequently, replication research methods can't be regarded as neutral tools that have the same meaning in all cultures.

5 *Because cultural similarity and difference are hard to measure.* One of the reasons why 'transport and test' experiments are hard to set up equivalently in different locations is that cross-cultural researchers themselves can't agree on how to measure certain behavioural variables in an internationally agreed manner. For example, in order to compare participants in Ho Chi Minh City (Vietnam) and Swansea (Wales) on measures of personality or intelligence, there have to be agreed, valid (measuring what they intend

to measure) and reliable (measuring the same thing on repeated occasions) scales for measuring such a construct. Furthermore, they have to be to the equal satisfaction of psychologists in the two locations. For many psychological concepts, no internationally agreed definitions of assessment methods exist.

Proponents of *type 1* evaluations would be unlikely to call off the search for cultural universals altogether. Nor would they favour abandoning cross-cultural replication research. Instead, they would prefer to hone the tools of replication so that greater levels of cultural equivalence could be achieved. In practical terms, this might involve paying greater attention to how participants are selected, to how research guidelines are translated, to ensuring more consistent standards of experimental control across cultures. Here are some of the ways in which cross-cultural researchers have worked at their methods in order to take them closer to that elusive goal of cultural equivalence.

Strategies for achieving better equivalence in replication research

1 *Select comparable, heterogeneous samples*. It is reasonable to set up a comparison of the behaviour of 50 Ghanaians with that of 50 Dutch people on a selected variable. But which sector of Ghanaian and Dutch society should the samples be drawn from? Opportunism may tempt a researcher to select from the most convenient source available. This may mean using undergraduates, executives or prison inmates from each of the two cultural settings. While selecting groups for such comparisons, it should be ensured that the sample selected from 'Culture A' actually has an equivalent in 'Culture B' and that the two samples are truly comparable. So for example, it needs to be established that 'undergraduates' or 'executives' from the two cultures being compared have similar qualifications or experiences behind them, or are from similar age and socio-economic groups.

There is a second consideration regarding samples selected for comparison. As well as being comparable, they should also be representative of their nation or culture as a whole. A student sample can hardly be regarded as representative of wider Ghanaian (or Dutch) society. Representative samples should include participants from various sectors; males as well as females; urban as well as rural dwellers; high and low income earners and so on. I would stress that such a level of heterogeneity is but an ideal and is

[handwritten margin notes: Properly represent their equivalent sample]

frequently not achieved. Nevertheless, for cross-cultural research findings to be confidently generalised from the sample studied to the population as a whole, samples being compared should be selected from comparable – and multiple – sites within that culture or nation.

[handwritten margin note: Careful translation]

2 *Issue standardised yet meaningful instructions to researchers.* In order to reduce problems associated with using different researchers in different cultural settings, it should be obvious that those administering the study in each replication are issued with instructions that mean the same thing in each case. The use of standardised instructions that have been carefully translated reduces the risk of researchers in one replication site 'taking matters into their own hands' and setting up testing conditions that are at odds with those used elsewhere.

3 *Use the 'back-translation' method.* The replication of instructions, survey or interview questions across two cultural settings – and therefore languages – needs to yield text that approximates equivalent meaning for the two samples. This is a tall order. Think of that phrase, for example: *a tall order*. Literally translated it would be fairly meaningless to most non-English speakers. As a partial defence against poorly translated text that can confound the equivalence of cross-cultural research, the **back-translation** method was devised (Brislin, 1970). This involves first translating the research text or instructions from the original language (A) to that of the comparison group (B), then translating it back from language B to language A to see if the original meaning is preserved. Try this with the phrase 'a tall order' from English to, say Mandarin, and the importance of back-translation might be aptly illustrated. By repeated use of this method with several translators, culturally specific and unhelpful phrases can be gradually whittled away and an approximation to equivalently meaningful text can be achieved.

[handwritten margin note: To be sure the meaning is clear to all anticipating people]

4 *Use meaningful data collection methods.* Replicating a set of questions that has been devised in urban and industrially/technologically developed regions in less technological, rural settings elsewhere may raise serious non-equivalence issues for the research project. If, for example, US respondents are asked to complete an electronic survey with which they are entirely comfortable, then other samples in the study should also be surveyed using a medium with which they are comfortable. If this means using pens and paper then so be it. Similarly, in a comparison of problem-solving, one sample may be asked to complete a culturally familiar crossword puzzle as a test of verbal reasoning. Yet for a cultural group that is unfamiliar with

KEY TERM

Back-translation. Translating the research text or instructions from the original language (A) to that of the comparison group (B), then translating it back from language B to language A to see if the original meaning is preserved.

[handwritten margin note: answer fits participants experience]

crossword puzzles, a more suitable means of assessing the equivalent skills would need to be researched and devised. This highlights
the methodological reality that 'equivalence' and 'standardisation'
are not the same thing.

5 *Use widely accepted dimensions of cultural variability*. For the
past quarter of a century cross-cultural psychologists have sought
psychometric measures of how attitudes, norms, values and
behaviours vary across cultures. Just as personality scales compare
factors such as extroversion at the individual level, these dimensions
assess average differences between groups of people at the
cultural level. They help us answer questions such as:

> *Are British people on average more individualistic than
> Colombians?*

To cross-cultural psychologists such dimensions are particularly
appealing, especially if they are acceptable to psychologists from
different continents. Several so-called **dimensions of cultural
variability** have been put forward over the years (Matsumoto &
Juang, 2004). Three of the most popular ones are outlined below.
Much of their popularity lies in their broad recognition among
cross-cultural psychologists worldwide.

- *The 'individualism–collectivism' (IC) dimension.* IC refers to how
  much a culture sanctions feelings of uniqueness or individualism
  on one hand, or collective belonging on the other. Cultures that
  emphasise 'I' over 'C' tend to engender and reward feelings of
  personal autonomy in their members. Those emphasising 'C'
  foster feelings of togetherness with other members of that culture
  (Markus & Kityama, 1991a). Hofstede (1980) used this dimension
  to assess IC tendencies among employees in a multinational
  organisation (IBM) across sites in 50 nations. Questionnaire
  responses showed widely differing levels of IC scores, with US
  participants revealing the most individualistic responses and
  Venezuela and Colombia among the most collectivist. IC is perhaps the most vaunted of all cultural variability scales, and is
  often incorporated in cross-cultural research.
- *The 'power–distance' (PD) dimension.* PD scores indicate average
  levels of inequality between higher and lower status individuals in
  a particular nation or culture (Hofstede, 1980). Among other
  things, the PD scale is a useful index of average employer–
  employee relations across cultures. It has been used to show that
  in some cultural settings, employees are more afraid of those in

KEY TERM

Dimensions of
cultural variability.
Psychometric
measures of how
attitudes, norms,
values and
behaviours vary
across cultures.

higher status, or are more tolerant of autocratic or non-consultative employers (Matsumoto, 1991). In one cross-cultural study, spanning 42 nations, it was found that closing the power-distance gap between employers and employees was associated with increased job satisfaction (Hui *et al.*, 2004).

- *The tight–loose (TL) dimension.* Initially put forward by Pelto (1968), this dimension distinguishes between cultures whose members typically observe its norms with gusto (tight societies) and those that tolerate a greater level of non-compliance (loose societies). Gelfand (2004) proposed that in cultural settings where there is overpopulation, a threat from neighbouring groups or a lack of natural resources, tight cultures are likely to thrive. Arguably, the keen observation of norms of behaviour fulfils a need in such cultures for structure and predictability in the lives of the members.

Figure 1.1 shows how the methodological measures outlined above represent the efforts of cross-cultural psychology to respond to perceived weaknesses in the basic idea of replication research.

Evaluation type 2: from beyond cross-cultural psychology

Universal phenomena may be 'out there', but replicating original research may not be the most effective use of global psychologists' time

According to this view the question of whether universal psychological phenomena are *out there waiting to be discovered* is not necessarily the most appropriate one for global psychologists to ask. Rather than simply looking for ways in which all humans are alike, the argument goes, perhaps we should concentrate more on what makes cultures different from each other. In other words, we should focus on investigating human cultural diversity rather than searching for universals (Shweder, 1991; Cole, 1998). To put this slightly differently, we should see differences between cultural groups as part of the findings of research, rather than as something to be controlled in the interests of achieving cultural equivalence (Poortinga, 1989).

Looking at the results from replication studies, proponents of this view might argue that the reason they are so mixed lies not in the research methods that have been used to collect them but in the simple, irrefutable extent of cultural diversity. In other words, obviously replicating original studies in diverse settings will reveal only moderate levels of cultural universality precisely because of the diversity of

Problem	Solution
Culturally equivalent samples are hard to find It is hard to establish cross-cultural comparisons between groups of people (such as undergraduates) with truly equivalent experiences or attributes. Also, a single group from one sector isn't representative of an entire culture	*Use comparable, heterogeneous samples* Try to ensure that samples selected for comparison actually are comparative in terms of their experiences and attributes, and are selected from multiple sites within each culture
Some researchers are more fastidious than others Researchers in different cultural locations may not apply experimental controls with equal rigour	*Use standardised, meaningful instructions* Issue standardised, carefully translated instructions to researchers
Research may lose something in translation Instructions to participants may contain terms or phrases that have different meanings when translated	*Use back-translation* Translate text from Language A to Language B, then independently back to A to see if original meaning is retained
In some cultures participation is second nature For participants in many cultures, survey and research participation is commonplace – not so for many others	*Use meaningful data collection methods* Find methods that are equally meaningful and commonplace for all participants
Culture is hard to measure Culture's influence on behaviour is difficult to measure in ways that are acceptable to researchers across cultures	*Use dimensions of cultural variability* Devise psychometric scales that can be used as indices of cultural similarity and variability, and that are internationally recognised

Figure 1.1 The cross-cultural replication research method: problems and solutions

the cultural contexts where these studies take place. Participants in Dunkirk and Durban are bound to think, talk and act differently, because they are from different cultures. Advocates of this type of evaluation would highlight three main reasons why replicating original studies cross-culturally might not be expected to uncover many human universals.

Why shouldn't we expect replication research to uncover many cultural universals?

1 *Because 'culture' is no ordinary independent variable.* When replicating original research cross-culturally, global psychologists

KEY TERM

**Culturally
constructed.** Having
different meanings in
different cultural
settings.

encounter social structures, norms and expectations that distinguish these cultures from the one where the study was originally carried out (Segall *et al.*, 1990/1999). For example, expected rules of conduct for particular roles (schoolchildren, undergraduates, healers, clergy) vary in different cultural settings. Degrees of social control and freedom vary too, as do class and ethnic divisions. What this tells us is that 'culture' is no ordinary independent variable. Groups of participants who differ according to cultural background actually have lots of factors to distinguish them. Culture, in short, is a bundle of variables (see Chapter 3). This seriously affects our ability to set up equivalent testing conditions in diverse cultural locations (Matsumoto & Juang, 2004).

2 *Because diverse settings mean diverse meanings.* It has already been suggested that some of the words used in replication research don't translate easily from one language to another. More fundamentally, some of the very concepts that are investigated in original research may lose their meaning once they are taken into other cultural settings (Enriquez, 1993; Smith *et al.*, 2006). Such concepts can be described as being **culturally constructed** (having different meanings in different cultural settings). Consider 'stress', for example. Its meaning arguably arose out of an industrialised, urban cultural context. If stress research is replicated in non-industrialised settings it is likely that the idea itself will either change its meaning or perhaps become meaningless altogether. 'Personality' is another example of a psychological phenomenon that you could say does not travel awfully well. Its meaning has been shown to vary in different cultures.

A central component of personality in China is known as Ren Qin. This refers to the degree to which individuals choose to participate in a series of social exchanges and reciprocal favour rituals (Cheung & Leung, 1998). Given the importance of this culturally specific aspect of personality in China, it would make little sense to compare, say, personality characteristics of Australian and Chinese participants solely by using Eysenck's Personality Questionnaire (Eysenck & Eysenck, 1975), which for the record does not measure Ren Qin.

Arguably then, many psychological concepts gain their meaning from the cultural context in which they are observed – or constructed (Nsamenang, 2000). The cultural construction of such key variables presents considerable theoretical difficulties to the global researcher who seeks to compare behaviour relating to those variables across cultures. Indeed, even though it has been demonstrated that some variables do hold their meanings across cultures (Aycicegi, 1993), the uncertainty associated with those that don't may undermine the confidence of the cross-cultural research project.

3 *Because cultural diversity could spell the end for psychic unity.* Looking for culturally universal behaviours that point towards the existence (deep down) of a universal mind structure is an approach that sits well with the doctrine of psychic unity. But if these replications do not provide evidence for the existence of psychic unity, arguably global psychologists should alter their view of what the mind is and where it is located. Instead of locating it internally, separate from cultural settings where behaviour is acted out, maybe we could 'bring it out into the open'. Maybe we could see the mind's major functions (thought, perception, attitude formation) as born out of, inseparable from, intermingled with, their cultural setting — in short, culturally constructed (Shweder, 1991). Taking this view, we should fully expect studies replicated in diverse settings to yield diverse findings, since the psychological activities of participants from diverse cultures would themselves be inseparable from culture. This shift in approach urges us to see thought as part of 'action in the world' rather than an activity that 'happens inside our heads'.

> ## REFLECTIVE EXERCISE 3
>
> Imagine yourself as a *cross-cultural psychologist* (with a belief in *psychic unity*) who has carried out replication research into body language across cultures. You have revealed only a moderate level of culturally universal behavioural responses. Suggest two changes that you make to your research strategy for your next study.

Beyond replication research: New directions for global psychology

So where do we go from here? What lies beyond the 'transport and test'-based search for cultural universals? Should cross-cultural psychology maintain its quest for the holy grail of psychic unity, honing its methods until it finally manages to establish cultural equivalence?

On the evidence of this chapter, it appears that other lines of enquiry should be contemplated in addition to established ones. Global psychology might profitably branch out from replication-based research in order to pursue additional, alternative truths about humans' diverse cultural contexts. Actually this, broadly, is what has happened. In reality global psychology is a little more complex, a little more interesting even, than this introductory chapter gives it credit for. Multiple, parallel lines of enquiry are currently being pursued, all straining to untangle the fascinating relationship between culture, mind and behaviour. Some of these lines of enquiry use replication research; some don't. You could say these approaches are complementary, since they add to our overall understanding of the field. You could say they are in conflict, since they reflect debates about what global psychology is and how it should be conducted. As outlined below, the remaining chapters of this book will introduce you to these parallel approaches, to the issues surrounding them and to the debates they have provoked. By the time you reach the end of the book you will be nicely placed to decide for yourself which approach has most to offer, and indeed whether it is desirable for several approaches to the same field to be asking different questions at the same time. One thing is certain: this multiplicity of approaches ensures that the field itself reflects the diverse nature of its subject matter.

Summary

Chapter 1 introduces the most widely used methodological and theoretical approach to the investigation of cultural issues in psychology: cross-cultural psychology. Originating from a desire to uncover cultural universals in human behaviour, mainstream cross-cultural psychology has spawned examples of human experience and action that seem common to all cultural groups. Several manifestations of such findings feature here, as does a detailed examination of the theoretical ideas that underlie cross-culturalism. In particular, we investigate the notion of psychic unity; the proposition that deep down, all humans, wherever they reside, share a core of common psychological characteristics that are only superficially modified by cultural interference.

Along with such theoretical concerns, this chapter presents an extensive overview and evaluation of the favoured research method in cross-cultural psychology – replication research. This paradigm involves testing established psychological theories in two or more cultural contexts to find out whether they hold true. This so-called 'transport and test' method has both loyal followers and harsh critics. Overall, Chapter 1 provides a detailed description and evaluation of cross-cultural psychology.

REFLECTIVE EXERCISE 4

Match up the definitions on the right with the terms on the left (see p. 221 for answers)

Translating the research text or instructions from the original language (A) to that of the comparison group (B), then translating it back from language B to language A to see if the original meaning is preserved

Cross-cultural psychology

Psychometric measures of how attitudes, norms, values and behaviours vary across cultures

'Transport and test' research

An original study is repeated, or replicated, in different cultural settings to see if the same results emerge

Global psychologists

Aspects of behaviour and experience common to all cultural settings

Back-translation

Where two cultural groups are treated in an equivalent manner throughout a study and are drawn from equivalent populations that differ only with respect to their cultural background

Dimensions of cultural variability

Cultural universals

Psychologists with a special interest in placing psychology in a global context

Cultural equivalence

Underlying our cultural variations is a set of psychic (memory, perceptual capacities) structures that all humans share

Cultural differences

Behaviours or experiences that manifest themselves differently in different cultures

Psychic unity

A branch of global psychology that compares the behaviour and experience of people from different cultures in order to understand the extent of culture's influence on psychological functioning

FURTHER READING

- Segall, M., Dasen, P., Berry, J. & Poortinga, Y. (1990) *Human Behaviour in Global Perspective*, Oxford, UK: Pergamon.
- Shweder, R. (1991) *Thinking through Cultures*, London: Harvard University Press.
- Smith, B., Bond, M. & Kagitcibasi, C. (2006) *Understanding Social Psychology across Cultures*, London: Sage.

How we got here

A short history of psychology across cultures

2

What this chapter will teach you

- What are the **philosophical roots** of psychology across cultures?

- How do **cultural anthropology** and psychology differ?

- Which were the **first major cross-cultural research projects**?

- What became of nineteenth-century **racial theories** of temperament?

- Who were the **twentieth-century pioneers** of research across cultures?

- What is **psychological anthropology**?

- What are the **Human Relations Area Files**?

- What of more **recent developments** in research across cultures?

KEY TERM

**Indigenous
psychologies.**
Diverse regional
traditions in
psychological
research, reflecting
differing cultural
concerns.

What this is (and isn't) a history of

Psychologists have been doing research *across cultures* for generations. They have also been busy establishing research traditions
within their own cultures for some time (Rus & Pecjak, 2004; Hwang,
2005; Stevens & Gielen, 2007). Of course, these are two quite different
things. The early history of psychology across cultures largely draws
on the ideas and journeys of thinkers, explorers and ultimately social
scientists from Europe who took it upon themselves to study people
from other continents. Meanwhile the history of psychological traditions
within cultures draws on what have become known as the **indigenous
psychologies**. You'll find an extended account of these in Chapter 5.
The history of psychology across cultures is our focus in this chapter.

Philosophical origins of psychology across cultures

The philosophical foundations of psychology across cultures are sunk
deep in the history of European thought. Distinct though merging
phases are decipherable in European philosophical traditions, and an
examination of these phases reveals an evolving fascination with
people from diverse places. Some aspects of this fascination have distinctly ethnocentric roots. This is unsurprising, as they are grounded in
a European view of the world. Many of these ideas emerged when
contact across continents was minimal and when communication with
those who did venture across the oceans was subject to hearsay, fear
of strangers and a distinct lack of methodological sophistication. Sadly,
echoes of this ethnocentrism in European and US writing lingered into
the twentieth century (Howit & Owusu-Bempah, 1995). This latent
cultural bias (ethnocentrism) in modern psychology will be discussed
at more length in Chapter 4. For now we'll concentrate on the historic
precursors of research across cultures.

Figure 2.1 outlines the philosophical origins of European psychology's adventures abroad. It also hints at the early exchanges between
the thinkers who argued for the universal constancy of the human mind
(universalists) and those who stressed the unique manifestation of the
mind in diverse cultures (relativists). First moves in the development of
cultural anthropology (a near neighbour of global psychology,
defined as the study of the complex social structures that make up
communities, societies and nations) are also indicated in Figure 2.1.
Such neighbouring disciplines share an interest in the relationship
between culture, experience and behaviour. As we shall see, though,

KEY TERM

**Cultural
anthropology.** The
study of the complex
social structures that
make up
communities,
societies and
nations.

Greeks, Romans and the Middle Ages *Cynocephali*, or 'human with dog's head' was the type of mythical creature used to illustrate descriptions of *barbarians*.	**Barbarians and bestial others** We owe the earliest examples of European writing about people from far-off places to the likes of Greek historian and traveller Heredotus (460–359 BC) and Roman philosopher and statesman Cicero (106–43 BC). Both made attempts to describe stages of civilisation among the peoples of the world, referring to differences in lifestyle between hunters, nomads and city dwellers. However, most early portrayals of 'the other' were not so level-headed. Non-inhabitants of Greek city-states and Roman civilisation were typically portrayed as uncivilised *barbarians* (defined as *one who is neither Greek nor Roman*). In a period that signalled the beginnings of European ethnocentrism, writers often drew and wrote about those encountered abroad as brutal, ugly creatures. Mythical caricatures such as the Cynocephali (literally, 'dog-head' from the Greek [see left]) were often used to embroider these descriptions. Chroniclers such as the Roman Plinius the Elder (AD 23–79) and Isodore of Seville (Archbishop and compiler of the first European encyclopaedia in AD 622) were among those who portrayed foreigners as monstrous subhumans. As the Roman Empire fell, the mythical portrayal of the bestial other was used to justify the spread of Christianity abroad, overriding much of the more moderate, learned writing of the time. In the Middle Ages, ignorance of foreigners abroad mirrored the persecution of 'aliens' in Europe, with Jews, 'gypsies' and other migrants persecuted, suppressed and periodically expelled (Winder, 2004). With a few exceptions, this was a period when accounts of foreigners were largely based on myth-making and caricature.
The Renaissance Cabinets of curiosity showcased (especially quirky and monstrous) artefacts gathered by travellers, for the consumption of Europeans.	**Conquest, contact and cabinets of curiosity** By the fifteenth century, conquests by European armies, explorers' voyages of discovery and the development of mercantilism all increased intercontinental contact and contributed to the wane of mythical accounts of diverse peoples. More sober stories emanated from abroad. These were informed more by observation than by religious dogma and caricature. Yet in an age of missionary zeal, religion still remained central to increased contact. In seeking to convert their hosts, many travelling missionaries dwelled for long periods with indigenous peoples. Favourable accounts were not uncommon, so long as the travellers themselves were well received. Typical of this more conciliatory approach to diversity were the writings of the sixteenth-century Spanish Dominican Bartholome De La Casas. He accompanied Christopher Columbus to Hispaniola and Cuba and sought to promote understanding, and even to raise moral concerns about universal human rights in the colonies. But no amount of increased contact could prevent a growing breed of popular travel writer from portraying diverse peoples as abnormal curiosities. Foreigners became exotic oddities to be marvelled at, exhibited and commoditised. The traveller Sebastian Munster (1544) expressed his curiosity for all things gathered abroad by building one of the first *cabinets de curiosité* (see left). These were showcases for Europeans to gaze at the customs and 'primitive' ways of the 'exotic other'. Though purely descriptive and exploitative, these curious cabinets were the forerunners of the modern ethnographic museum.
The Enlightenment 'It is universally acknowledged that there is a great uniformity among the actions of men, in all ages and nations, and that human nature still remains the same	**Reason, rationality and Rousseau** With the advent of scientific enquiry, the Enlightenment viewpoint was driven by a need to understand and analyse (rather than simply to gawp at) human diversity. David Hume's argument for the existence of a universal reason and rationality (see left) set the tone for a shift to a more inquisitive view of travel. This was reflected in writing on the subject. The search for universal reason signalled the notion of *psychic unity* (see Chapter 1). It also provided the theoretical spur for the later development of academia's own version of travel writing – *cultural anthropology*. This idea of universal rationality would ultimately preoccupy anthropologists in their assessment of the similarities and differences in the customs of people from diverse places. Meanwhile so-called *social evolutionists* and other thinkers, such as Condorcet (1794), saw diverse human societies as inevitably evolving toward a European *continued overleaf*

Figure 2.1 Philosophical roots of psychological research across cultures (based on Jahoda & Krewer, 1997)

. . . in all times and places' (David Hume, 1784/1894, p. 358).	ideal, and away from a natural, primitive state. Pure reason would, they surmised, eventually supersede the supernatural beliefs that were found in far-away places. But the argument about the universal desirability of European civilisation is two-sided. Jean-Jacques Rousseau (1755) argued that far from occupying a privileged stage of advancement, Europe lagged behind so-called 'primitive' societies, who adhered more closely to an unspoiled, compassionate, less artificial state of being. Transformation to complex, hierarchical social organisation, for Rousseau, brought out an undesirable side of humanity in which humans were forced to compete against others and take pride in their failures. Vico (1724) meanwhile cast doubt on the search for the universal, rational human. He argued that the human mind manifests itself differently in different socio-historical contexts. Accordingly, as adherents of Vico have since insisted (Shweder, 1991), studying the human mind across cultures requires us to study its unique differences in different contexts, rather than its culturally universal qualities. We can see here in the exchanges between Hume and Vico the beginnings of a debate between cultural universalists and cultural relativists that continues to enliven global psychology today.

Figure 2.1 (Continued)

researchers from these neighbouring fields have traditionally asked slightly different questions.

Early expeditions

The philosophical roots of research across cultures yielded their first large-scale empirical investigation in 1799. The Observateurs de l'Homme was an early attempt to compare different 'forms of collective life' (a loose definition for what would later be known as *culture*) based on objective observations, rather than on unsubstantiated conjecture. It was the brainchild of the newly formed Société des Observateurs (Hulme, 2001), a loose affiliation of scientists from various disciplines who were united in wanting to bring empirical rigour to the study of human behaviour, culture, morals, anatomy and physiology.

A first ever empirical, interdisciplinary, cross-cultural field expedition was duly arranged. It would go to Australia in 1800, led by Nicolas Baudin (1754–1803), who sadly died of tuberculosis on the return journey. Although the priorities of this expedition were not to explore psychological concepts, customs and behaviour were observed along with other facets of life. This (for Baudin at least) ill-fated expedition was perhaps the first example of research across cultures to be conducted according to prescribed methodological guidelines, which had been set down for the purpose by the philosopher Joseph-Marie Dégérando. His document, extravagantly titled *A Consideration of the Different Methods to be Followed in the Observation of Savage Peoples* (1800), amounted to a series of eminently sensible methodological 'dos and don'ts' for pioneering researchers working in other cultures. Dégérando's field manuals advised on which behaviours to observe and record (sensation, language, abnormal behaviour, problem-solving, opinions), and even alerted the potential fieldworker to the perils of ethnocentric observer bias and misinterpretation.

The Société itself turned out to be a short-lived affair, yielding few enduring data, though the work of two of its members deserves a mention. C.F. Volney (1804) travelled to North America essentially to study its soil, though he made some interesting observations of the language and lifestyles of North American Indians. Young anthropological pioneer François Péron survived Baudin's Australian trip to present a set of rather superficial data about the 'weak' and 'treacherous' temperament of the Tasmanians he encountered there (Hulme, 2001). Dégérando's field manuals are probably the most enduring outcome of the work of the Société des Observateurs. They can be justifiably regarded as the forerunners of contemporary ethical and methodological guidelines for those practising cross-cultural and anthropological research (Jahoda & Krewer, 1997).

> **REFLECTIVE EXERCISE 5**
>
> 1. What's the difference between *psychology across cultures* and *indigenous psychology*?
>
> 2. What was Jean-Jacques Rousseau's quarrel with the *social evolutionists*?

The nineteenth century and the coming of race

After the Baudin expedition and the demise of the Société des Observateurs, cross-cultural research as a serious endeavour lost its way for a spell. During the nineteenth century, explanations of temperament, behaviour and human diversity became entangled with a new concept that was beginning to find its way onto people's lips: **race**. Racial theories about mental abilities and character put differences between groups down to biological inheritance or ancestral lineage (Jahoda & Krewer, 1997). It was common at the time to regard racial difference as a greater influence on behaviour than differences in cultural background. This in part explains why expeditions to investigate lifestyles in diverse places – such as the earlier Baudin project – fell out of favour.

Figure 2.2 outlines some of the influential trains of thought that dominated arguments about race, temperament and behaviour in the early nineteenth century. Figure 2.3 reminds us of the unfortunate ways in which nineteenth-century racial explanations of difference and deficit in character and ability coloured the work of some influential psychologists for decades to come.

KEY TERM

Race. How groups with distinct ancestries differ from each other in terms of appearance, including skin colour, blood group, hair texture.

What is race?

Nowadays the term 'race' is used to invoke differences in appearance and ancestry, rather than in behaviour. When labels like 'black' or 'white' are applied to someone, this refers to their descent (African or European ancestry) or to their skin colour (Barfield, 1997). Contemporary definitions of race see it as

> A term used to distinguish a relatively large division of persons from another. It refers to how groups with distinct ancestries differ from each other in terms of appearance, including skin colour, blood groups, hair texture. (Fernando, 2002; Reber, 1997)

What's its history?

The term first entered the English language in the sixteenth century, to denote lineage (Banton, 1987). However, as this selection of early ideas on the subject (Gould, 1981) demonstrates, historically racial differences have also been used to explain differences in character and mental capacity.

- *Race c. 1758*. Linnaeus makes the earliest distinction between races. He deems *Homo sapiens afer* (African blacks) to be naturally 'capricious'. A more civilised character is attributed to *Homo sapiens europaeus* (European white), who is said to be motivated by 'custom'.
- *Race c. 1825*. Blumenbach's taxonomy of races is based on skull shape as well as skin colour. It features five 'races' – Caucasian, Mongolian, Ethiopian, American and Malayan. For Blumenbach the Caucasian skull-shape (widespread across North Africa, Europe and the Middle East) represents the 'classic' standard of humanity.
- *Race c. 1871*. Darwin sees different races as separate lineages that reproduce in different geographical regions. Yet despite being a fervent campaigner for the abolition of slavery, even Darwin joins the chorus of discrimination when he predicts the demise and extinction of 'savage' races who lack contact with more civilised races.

Views like these catch the mood of eighteenth- and nineteenth-century Europe. They reverberated through academic circles and wider society, reflecting a mindset that remained devoutly sceptical of outsiders. Mind you, they did not go unopposed. Anthropologist James Cowles Prichard (1843) was among those who argued that despite the division of humanity into races, inner mental (psychic) unity overrode such superficial differences.

Nineteenth-century race and social Darwinism

Much nineteenth-century writing on race assumed that 'the white European human' was a gold standard, with other versions of humanity paling by comparison in terms of intellect, conduct and custom. Non-European societies (and races) were seen by many as progressing towards the European ideal. Writing in the 1870s, Herbert Spencer epitomised this view when he pronounced some 'primitive' races to be intellectually comparable to European children. Spencer's espousal of *social Darwinism* reflected ideas contained in the then recently published *On the Origin of Species* (1859). In fact it was Spencer, not Darwin, who coined the term *survival of the fittest* to describe the idea that some societies grow stronger, more complex and are better at maintaining themselves over time, while others may fall by the wayside (Marshall, 1998). Echoes of social Darwinism are audible in the work of both Galton and Pearson (see Figure 2.3). Their eugenicist views fit snugly with the idea that some racial and cultural groups are naturally (biologically) more advanced than others. They saw it as the aim of psychology and the duty of eugenics to help discriminate between 'smart' races and their 'half-witted' or 'backward' inferiors (Fernando, 2002).

Criticisms of race-based theories

The use of race as an explanation for differences in abilities or character has, thankfully, more or less disappeared from contemporary psychology. Here are just two of the reasons why.

1 *The importance of race as a biological concept was greatly exaggerated*. Technology has revealed race to be of only moderate biological significance as a way of distinguishing between the behaviour of different people (Gould, 1981). Race, in fact, seems to contribute little to the overall genetic differences between individuals. On average, 84% of the genetic variation between two people is down to individual differences, irrespective of race, while 10% of variation is down to racial difference. It seems then that genetic difference between individuals within the same racial group is far more important than genetic differences across racial groups. You could conclude from this that race is a pretty good way of distinguishing between people physically, though it provides a less reliable basis for distinguishing between them biologically.

2 *While societies may become more complex, they do not necessarily move towards a white European ideal.* To say that societies change or develop throughout history is not especially controversial. But the assumption that such developments inevitably proceed towards a white European ideal is now widely regarded as ethnocentric. Writing about people from different racial or cultural groups as though they were not just different, but somehow less developed, is known as *evolutionary thinking.* This is *a brand of ethnocentrism which assumes that one's own group is the ideal towards which others will presently develop.* It thrived during a colonial period when European interests dominated African economies, when educated Africans in the then Belgian Congo were referred to as 'évolués', since they were thought to have made an evolutionary 'great leap forwards' towards European civilisation (Reader, 1998). Evolutionary thinking epitomised nineteenth-century European thought, both in psychology and in wider society, and is gradually disappearing from the radar of our subject.

Figure 2.2 Race-based theories in the nineteenth century

Francis Galton (1869) saw 'genius' as a hereditary perk of being upper class and well connected (being Charles Darwin's cousin, Galton was pretty well connected himself). He advocated sterilisation of the lower classes as a means of controlling the biological spread of genius. **Controlling inheritance by selective breeding** in this way is known as **eugenics**.

Karl Pearson (1901) founded the journal *Annals of Eugenics.* In its pages he linked the 'problem' of Jewish settlers in East London to lower intelligence levels and the spread of tuberculosis, heart disease and other conditions.

William McDougall (1908) was Cyril Burt's tutor at Oxford. He read intelligence test data from the First World War which showed white US servicemen outscoring blacks, and concluded that the only way to arrest the perceived downward trend in the intelligence of white Americans was a policy of racial segregation.

Cyril Burt (1937), whose father knew Galton personally, pursued the idea of heritable intelligence. He used twin studies to bolster this view. His data suggested that genetically identical twins reared apart still had very similar intelligence levels. However, following a *Sunday Times* exposé in 1976, he is now thought by many to have fabricated his results.

Arthur Jensen (1969) also offered hereditarian views on intelligence, this time directly relating to race. He ascribed black children's under-achievement in white-dominated schools to 'inferior genes'.

Hans Eysenck (1991), a student of Burt and supporter of Jensen, has over a long career supported the link between intelligence test scores, inheritance and race. Even his later writings tell how, despite his distaste for racism, he has 'little doubt that genetic factors were probably implicated in the observed differences between blacks and whites' (Eysenck, 1991b, p. 18).

Figure 2.3 Sadly, ideas about race and mental ability outlasted the nineteenth century

Rivers across cultures in the twentieth century

Preoccupations with biological and racial difference temporarily arrested the development of psychological research across cultures. But as the twentieth century dawned, another milestone in the development of field research was laid. The 1889 *Cambridge Anthropological Expedition to the Torres Straits* (between New Guinea and Australia) was seminal for the careers of several budding researchers and for the overall emergence of research across cultures (Hart, 1998). Cambridge anthropologist Alfred Haddon, who led the expedition, found room on board for a select band of researchers who are still considered to be among modern fieldwork's founders. They included the British psychologists William McDougall and Charles Myers, the anthropologist Charles Seligman, and W.H.R. Rivers, of whom we will soon learn more.

The trip was, to say the least, ambitious and wide-ranging. It sought knowledge on the language, society, folklore and cognitive abilities of the Torres Straits Islanders, who at the time were threatened by colonial expansionism (Hart, 1998). Although Haddon's Cambridge party set sail for the Pacific ostensibly in the name of anthropology (Stocking, 1995), it produced research that was methodologically groundbreaking for the newfangled field of cross-cultural psychology. W.H.R. Rivers was the main reason.

Rivers' background was in experimental psychology at Cambridge, and he brought much-needed empirical rigour to the cross-cultural scenario. As well as carrying out pioneering psychological research, he was a founder of anthropology in Britain (and uniquely among his colleagues, he eventually metamorphosed into a central character in a Booker Prize winning trilogy of novels (Barker, 1996)). True to his varied background, Rivers combined the empirical method of (psychological) experimentation with an anthropologically inspired belief in the efficacy of lengthy immersion in the cultural group being studied (Hart, 1998). He was among the first to recognise that reliable field data needed to be gathered first-hand by expert social scientists, and not borrowed from potentially less rigorous secondary sources such as explorers or missionaries (Kuper, 1994). To complement his experiments Rivers gathered extensive contextual details about the demographics and everyday practices of his informants. Such preparatory work is now common practice in cross-cultural research.

In the Torres Straits, Rivers set out to test the theory, popular at the time, that non-Europeans possessed extraordinary visual acuity and perceptual abilities (Jahoda & Krewer, 1997; Berry et al., 2002), at the expense of higher cognitive functioning. In other words, so-called 'primitives' were seen as devoting a higher proportion of mental energy to seeing and perceiving, and less to more elevated intellectual pursuits. Uniquely for his era, Rivers triangulated everyday participant observation with controlled, experimental tests of ability. Unlike many of his contemporaries, he was concerned as to how well his procedures were understood by participants, and would modify them if he thought they were not well understood. Such devotion to objective experimentation and transparency had not figured before in cross-cultural psychology. Rivers concluded that claims about the extraordinary visual acuity of non-Europeans were exaggerated, and that they had arisen out of

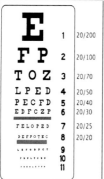

On the Cambridge Anthropological Expedition to the Torres Straits, W.H.R. Rivers broke new methodological ground by designing research procedures that sought to take account of the viewpoint of his participants. Yet even though repeated experimental trials using the Snellen chart (left) showed little difference between European and Torres Straits Islanders in terms of visual acuity, Rivers wrote that:

the acuity of savage and half-civilized people, though superior to that of the normal European, is not so in any marked degree. (1901, p. 42)

If too much energy is expended on the sensory foundations, it is natural that the intellectual super-structure should suffer. (1901, pp. 44–45).

Figure 2.4 W.H.R. Rivers: through the eyes of the Torres Straits Islanders

casual observation. Yet as Figure 2.4 shows, he was not entirely immune to the beliefs of his contemporaries.

The Rivers Torres Straits adventure undoubtedly left its mark, yet it didn't take long for critics to recognise the inherent problems involved in trying to set up controlled experiments in what were then regarded as exotic places. Clearly, no two cross-cultural controlled settings are ever the same, so an essential problem of replicability is unavoidable (Titchener, 1916). But the die was cast for the future direction of cross-cultural psychology.

The early part of the twentieth century spawned several Rivers-like studies; empirical cross-cultural comparisons of the sensory abilities of Europeans and non-Europeans (Bruner, 1908; Woodworth, 1910; Oliver, 1932; Thouless, 1933; Beveridge, 1935). Researchers variously explored differences in hearing (Bruner, Woodworth), visual (Beveridge) and musical (Oliver) perception. While race-related interpretations of findings didn't disappear, they receded as the archives of cross-cultural data were about to be systematically collated for the first time.

REFLECTIVE EXERCISE 6

1. Suggest one difference between eighteenth-/nineteenth-century and contemporary ideas about *race*.

2. You study the complex social structures that make up communities, societies and nations. Which of these are you?
   a. Evolutionist
   b. Cultural anthropologist
   c. Social Darwinist
   d. Eugenicist

HRAF: A who's who and what's where of psychology across cultures

With any unruly body of knowledge about a new topic, a moment usually comes when someone sits down and tries to organise and classify it. For the emerging enterprise of cross-cultural psychology, this moment came in 1936. The idea behind establishing the *Human Relations Area Files* (HRAF) was to provide a rich seam of data for the use of researchers intending to work in diverse places. Since its beginning in the 1930s and its formal establishment (under the auspices of the University of Yale) in 1949, the HRAF has provided an ever-swelling knowledge resource based around two themes.

1 The *Outline of World Cultures* (Murdock, 1975) is as comprehensive as possible a list of the world's cultural groups.
2 The *Outline of Cultural Materials* (Murdock *et al.*, 1971) is a classification of topics that are considered eligible for study worldwide, due to their universal applicability.

This second classification is organised around eight sections, including *food and clothing*; *economy and transport*; *welfare*; *religion*; *science*. Both archives appear in updated form on the HRAF website. Together they help researchers select who and what to study, without having to trawl through innumerable, disparate sources before entering the field. HRAF is as much a labour-saving device as an archive. Yet despite its obvious uses, it has limitations.

Limitations of the HRAF

1 *Though centrally located, data are drawn from diverse sources.* The data in the HRAF may be conveniently drawn together in a single bank, yet the reliability of its original sources is far from uniform. Some of the data stem from social science, others are from journalists, missionaries and merchants. Despite efforts at quality control (Narroll *et al.*, 1980), such variable reliability needs to be taken into account by users.
2 *'World cultures' are not easily defined.* The 'outline of world cultures' is an attempt to classify and list hundreds of cultural groups worldwide. Yet unlike, say, football teams or brands of chewing gum, 'cultures' are not discrete entities that lend themselves easily to classification. For example, membership of one group does not exclude a person from membership of another. Such

lack of mutual exclusivity arguably hampers any attempt at classification.

Despite these drawbacks, the HRAF represents a useful resource and a milestone for the enterprise of psychological research across cultures. While what it offers is certainly no substitute for data gathered first-hand in the field, it has had plenty to offer cross-cultural practitioners who are at the planning and contemplation stage.

Psychology, anthropology – and psychological anthropology

Since the 1930s the HRAF has served as a useful archive for psycho-logists and anthropologists, both to contribute to and to borrow from. At around the same time, with the efforts of some notable twentieth-century pioneers, the neighbouring fields of global psychology and cultural anthropology were making great steps forward. Soon they were both firmly established as academic disciplines in their own right. Indeed, during this period even the space between psychology and anthropology acquired a label of its own. Unimaginatively, it was known as **psychological anthropology**. All of which raises three questions:

- What's the difference between psychology and anthropology?
- What is psychological anthropology?
- Who were the twentieth-century pioneers of these neighbouring disciplines?

Let us answer these questions in reverse order. Figure 2.5 rounds up the most influential pioneers of twentieth-century research across cultures. The contribution of the early twentieth-century school of thought known as psychological anthropology is a key concept. This leaves us with our first question. How do psychology and anthropology differ? Well, nowadays psychologists and cultural anthropologists tend to occupy different departments in most universities (when they are not actively engaged in the field, that is). Psychologists with a particular interest in cultural issues are usually part of a general psychology department, while cultural anthropologists can be traced to a separate department of their own, or to part of a larger cultural studies or sociology department. Yet such segregation belies historical and the-oretical commonalities (Jahoda & Krewer, 1997). Early adventures such as the Torres Straits expedition (outlined above) yielded findings

KEY TERM

Psychological anthropology. Anthropological investigations that make use of psychological concepts and methods.

Franz Boas (1911) had more say than anyone else in the emergence of twentieth-century cultural anthropology. In his fieldwork along the coast of British Columbia he recorded the linguistic and cultural practices of native people. His methodical approach superseded the casual observation and impressionistic writing that dominated the work of nineteenth-century missionaries and explorers. Boas railed against social Darwinism, which explained away cultural differences by using crude racial and evolutionary arguments. He saw the more subtle notion of culture itself as instrumental in shaping the psychological worlds of those who formed them (Barfield, 1997). Boas encouraged fieldworkers to investigate cultures in their own unique contexts, rather than looking for grand racial or evolutionary models to try to explain behavioural differences. Though he was a founder of anthropology, his teaching and writing had a direct effect on those who carried the torch of cross-cultural psychology into the twentieth century.

Richard Thurnwald (1913) was an Austrian-born ethnographer who contributed to psychological research 'on the side'. Like W.H.R. Rivers, Thurnwald worked the space between anthropology and psychology. He did fieldwork in Bosnia at the end of the nineteenth century and in Pacific Melanesia between 1906 and 1909. There he conducted small-scale studies into what he called *ethno-psychology*. He was probably the first fieldworker to employ a technique known as *serial reproduction* (which mimics the parlour game *Chinese whispers* and is usually associated with the memory research of Frederic Bartlett) to investigate creative aspects of thinking. Though he is mainly remembered as an ethnographer, Thurnwald's contribution to the exploration of cognitive functioning across cultures is undersold outside Germany and Austria (Jahoda & Krewer, 1997).

Margaret Mead (1928) was a student of Boas and associate of Sapir and Benedict (see below), yet ultimately she outstripped them all in the popular imagination of anthropology and psychology. Her 1928 field trip to Samoa made her one of the first women to conduct prolonged cross-cultural research (Barfield, 1997; Kuper, 1994). Like Boas she stressed the importance of culture as a formative influence on development. She argued for the cultural construction of gender roles, and of adolescence. The latter, she claimed, was present in her native US yet absent in Samoa. Mead popularised the study of diverse cultures. Her accessible writing brought her celebrity status beyond academia. However, after her death her work was criticised for lacking objectivity, when Freeman (1983) famously claimed that her conclusions were skewed by her own belief in the primacy of culture over nature. This so-called 'Mead–Freeman' dispute still rumbles.

Edward Sapir (1929), another student of Boas, made his mark by studying the hotly debated relationship between language, culture and psychology. He applied his classical linguistic training to his fieldwork on North American Indian languages of California. As well as subscribing to the ideas of *psychological anthropology*, Sapir is best known for his advocacy of the so-called *linguistic relativity theory* (Sapir, 1929). This suggests that the languages we speak in particular, and our linguistic habits in general, determine – or at least heavily influence – how we think. Thus, learning a new language involves learning a second, unique framework for thought and perception. Linguistic relativity has spawned various cross-cultural research projects, yielding both supporting evidence and counter-evidence (Berry *et al.*, 2002).

Frederic Bartlett (1932) studied under W.H.R. Rivers and rebelled against what he saw as ethnocentric methods for conducting research across cultures. He disliked the imposition of alien, artificial experimental scenarios on indigenous participants. In Swaziland he did innovative research to contend that remembering is not just a cognitive concept, but a social one too. Our ability to bring details to mind, this argument goes, is partly down to the distinct values and beliefs and temperament of the social groups we belong to. So for his Swazi participants, for example, material relating to their day-to-day livelihoods (which revolved around cattle) was remembered more efficiently than other, less pertinent material. Bartlett's Swazi research is perhaps most innovative for its positioning of the study of memory in the dual arenas of social and cognitive psychology.

Figure 2.5 Twentieth-century pioneers of research across cultures

KEY CONCEPT

Psychological anthropology

Between the spheres of psychology and anthropology, there is today a no-man's land . . . it must for the present be filled by workers in either field making excursions towards the other's province (Bronislaw Malinowksi, 1931, p. xi).

The influence of *psychological anthropology* (Hsu, 1961), also known as the *culture and personality* approach to research across cultures, peaked in the 1920s and 1930s and has diminished more recently. Something of a theoretical hybrid, psychological anthropology occupied Malinowski's no-man's land between psychology and anthropology. The approach can be adequately defined as *anthropological investigations that make use of psychological concepts and methods* (Bock, 1980, p. 1).

Psychological anthropology's subject matter

The so-called *culture and personality theorists* approached their subject matter at a population, rather than an individual, level. Culture, experience and behaviour were deemed interesting insomuch as they manifested themselves differently in different populations. Thus, from this perspective one might ask

Do Germans have distinctly authoritarian personalities? (Fromm, 1941)
Is there such a thing as 'Japanese character'? (Benedict, 1946)

Ruth Benedict was a prime mover in the heyday of the culture and personality school. She maintained that *each culture fosters a specific personality type* (cited in Kuper, 1994, p. 188). To support such assertions, explanations were sought in the differing childrearing practices across cultures. So, for instance, the Russian practice of intermittent baby swaddling was seen as a contributory factor in Russian adults' alleged national propensity for mood swings; one moment introspective, another intensely sociable (Gorer & Rickman, 1949). In *Patterns of Culture* (1934) Benedict cast culture as personality writ large. Cultures were portrayed as distinct systems, embodying the typical personality configurations of their inhabitants. North American Kwakiutl Indians, for instance, were labelled as a 'megalomaniacal culture' on the basis of the (alleged) typically attention-seeking competitive behaviour patterns of its inhabitants. Resonances of psychological anthropology continued after the Second World War, when some renowned research continued to entertain the idea of 'national character'. Hofstede, comparing the typical personality profiles of IBM employees from forty nation states, wrote that *mental programs of members of the same nations tend to contain common components* (1980, p. 38).

Psychological anthropology's method

A combination of complementary research methods was used by the culture and personality school, reflecting the influences of its parent disciplines. An anthropological footprint is clear to see in the use of naturalistic *ethnographies*, involving *the collection of data for descriptive purposes by using fieldwork techniques, focusing on a single cultural setting.* Benedict herself, a student of the anthropologist Franz Boas, did field-work among North American Zuni Indians (Benedict, 1934). Ethnographies centre the attention of the researcher on a detailed description of a single cultural group. The accent is on uncovering diversity in cultural practices, with relatively little energy chan-nelled into generalising findings to those gathered in other settings. Psychological anthropology also used more traditionally psychological *projective techniques*. These are *tests designed to provide insight about personality traits*. These can be pen-and-paper or interview-based, and provide data that, when set alongside qualitative ethno-graphic findings, can shed light on the typical characteristics of a population. An example from the archives of psychological anthropology illustrates the use of project-ive techniques.

The people of Alor

In 1944 Cora DuBois studied an Indonesian island population, the Alorese, using the 'inkblot' or *Rorschach test*. This, 'the grandfather of all projective tests' (Reber, 1997, p. 675), is *a clinical technique by which an analyst uncovers aspects of a client's personality from their perception of a series of ambiguous black and coloured shapes (inkblots)*. DuBois had 50 Alorese tested and from her data claimed to derive the essential personal-ity configurations of the population. They included 'fearlessness', 'suspiciousness', 'greed' and 'shallowness'. Yet they were said to be burdened with few neuroses.

The influence of psychological anthropology owed much of its appeal to a fascination with the idea of *national character*. This is *the notion that people from the same nation share certain personality traits*. More recently, as the importance of nationality has itself been questioned as a primary source of identity, the appeal and distinctiveness of psy-chological anthropology has waned.

Evaluating psychological anthropology

Psychological anthropology helped bridge the 'no-man's land' between psychology and cultural anthropology. By opening up channels of communication between the two disciplines the approach highlighted the value, to psychologists, of anthropological enquiry. In particular, it stressed the contribution of ethnography as a research method.

Problematically though, culture and personality theory habitually homogenised whole populations of individuals by characterising them as being in possession of the same personality traits (Berry *et al.*, 2002). This approach emphasises variations between cul-tures while ignoring what may well be equally diverse personality variations within cultures. Methods favoured by culture and personality researchers are problematic too. Many of these projective techniques (such as the Rorschach test) were originally designed for clinical use. Therefore when they are applied outside the consulting room they tend to yield data that are couched in the language of pathology. Resulting per-sonality profiles sound like syndromes or illnesses. This is a problem with transferring clinical techniques, unadapted, to non-clinical settings.

that were of both psychological and anthropological interest. Rivers and colleagues revealed something about human perception at the *individual* level, and about how Torres Islanders organised themselves at a *group* level. It is these differences in levels of explanation that are the crux of the differing orientations of global psychology and cultural anthropology (Berry *et al.*, 2002).

Cultural anthropology (also known as *social* anthropology) is the study of the complex social structures that make up communities, societies and nations (Reber, 1997). True, psychologists regularly collect this kind of social or community-based data about the people they study, but their main interest focuses on the investigation of certain prescribed behaviours or cognitive abilities that reveal themselves in individuals from different backgrounds. A psychologist is more likely to study perception, problem-solving or conformity among the individuals who make up groups. A cultural anthropologist is likely to dwell on the complex relationships and beliefs or norms of the group as a whole. Put another way, a typical psychologist's question might be:

How does visual perception manifest itself differently in individuals from different cultural backgrounds?

A cultural anthropologist might ask:

What are the characteristic norms, beliefs and customs of the cultural group I am studying?

There is a second, methodological difference between the work of psychologists and cultural anthropologists. In general, psychologists are more interventionist and anthropologists more naturalistic in the way they conduct research (Edgerton, 1974). So while a psychological approach might involve setting up replicable experiments under controlled conditions across different cultural settings, an anthropologist would prefer a more 'hands-off' method. This would involve observing conduct as it happens in the natural course of things, without tasks or experimental procedures being imposed by the researcher. The anthropological method is typified by the use of **ethnographies** (see key concept), which tend to yield data of a qualitative nature. The replication research method (see Chapter 1) that psychologists commonly use tends to yield quantitative data.

Differences in approach between the practitioners in these two neighbouring fields are subtle rather than stark. Separating 'typically

KEY TERM

Ethnographies. The collection of data for descriptive purposes by using fieldwork techniques, focusing on a single cultural setting.

REFLECTIVE EXERCISE 7

Imagine you are planning to conduct some research across cultures. You are keen to combine the strengths of psychology and cultural anthropology in the design of your research. What two methodological strategies might you incorporate to help you combine the strengths of an anthropological approach with those of a more psychological approach?

---

psychological' approaches from 'typically anthropological' approaches is a delicate operation requiring a steady hand, because what we're talking about here is differences of emphasis, not opposing approaches. Indeed, as the achievements of the pioneers who feature in Figure 2.5 bear out, the early twentieth century spawned several examples of psychologists who were happy to combine experimental approaches with more naturalistic, anthropological ones.

Later trends: Cross-cultural psychology or cultural psychology?

The end of the twentieth century saw psychology and anthropology go their separate ways and psychological anthropology fall out of favour. The study of psychology across cultures expanded and developed in several directions and along numerous pathways. The most well-worn of these paths led to the emergence of *cross-cultural psychology* (see Chapter 1). The publication of books and articles written from a cross-cultural viewpoint snowballed during the 1960s and 1970s. These included a manual discussing the problems of cross-cultural testing (Biesheuvel, 1969). Many of what are now regarded as 'classic' cross-cultural studies in the areas of cognitive (Segall *et al.*, 1966) and developmental (Dasen, 1972) psychology were conducted during this period and will be revisited in subsequent chapters. That this was a period of growing institutional acceptance for cross-cultural psychology was confirmed by the formation of several cross-cultural journals and associations, and by the invention of several accompanying acronyms:

- 1966 – IJC: *International Journal of Psychology*
- 1970 – JCCP: *Journal of Cross-cultural Psychology*
- 1972 – IACCP: International Association for Cross-Cultural Psychology
- 1984 – ARIC: Association pour la recherché interculturelle.

Yet to be fully accepted into the mainstream of psychology, the cross-cultural approach still had (and has) work to do. Arguably, the reason for its continued peripheral position in most psychology undergraduate courses is that its emphasis on cultural influence on behaviour poses a threat to the formulation of universal psychological laws (Jahoda & Krewer, 1997). Indeed, during the 1970s some researchers with an interest in culture's influence began to reject the core ideas behind cross-cultural psychology, which are largely based on the search for human universals (see Chapter 1).

Influenced by Vygotsky (1978) and Luria (1976), a group of researchers led by Cole (1978) decided to rethink the rationale for doing psychology across cultures. Questioning the existence of a culturally universal, inner core of psychological structures (psychic unity – see Chapter 1), they portrayed the human mind not as a universal, internal entity but as being inseparable from the diverse cultural contexts we inhabit. According to this view, the mind is wide open to cultural influence and all biological and environmental influences on our development are mediated by cultural context. In short, all human behaviour is *culturally mediated*.

Proponents of these views set in motion a new approach to studying psychology and culture – known as cultural psychology. For cultural psychologists, culture's role in human development (throughout history and during the life-cycle) is even more prominent than it is for cross-cultural psychologists (Berry *et al.*, 2002). Cultural psychology is further explored in Chapter 5.

This short history of psychology across cultures has focused on its European origins, since this is where empirical psychology began. Yet in the twentieth century psychology became a global enterprise (Stevens & Gielen, 2007), as demonstrated by an unprecedented rise in the number of international psychologists' associations. The creation of these forums empowered psychologists from different nations to exchange ideas, work collaboratively – and of course, create acronyms:

- 1951 – IUSP: International Union of Scientific Psychology
- 1962 – ICP: International Council of Psychologists
- 1965 – IUPsyS: International Union of Psychological Science

As well as the development of these international associations, another relatively recent trend has been the emergence of several psychological traditions originating in diverse regions of the world, known as indigenous psychologies. Psychologists from Latin America, Africa, India and elsewhere have now come to the fore to challenge the global hegemony of US/European psychology, and to conduct research in response to indigenous concerns. The growth of indigenous psychologies (also known as psychological traditions within diverse cultures) is arguably the most exciting recent development in the field of global psychology, and will be discussed in detail in Chapter 4.

Meanwhile, to ensure that you have understood the ideas contained in this overview of the history of psychology across cultures, try the reflective exercise opposite.

Summary

Chapter 2 is a potted history of psychology's tradition of studying human behaviour in different cultures. It begins with an overview of the European philosophical ideas regarding the study of inhabitants overseas, including the demonising and romanticising in equal measure of 'the exotic other' by Greeks, Romans and Renaissance thinkers. More recent historical precursors of global psychology include investigations of behaviour and temperament that formed part of the great scientific expeditions of the nineteenth century. These adventures included Baudin's expedition to Australia in 1799 to study 'customs and behaviour', and the Cambridge Anthropological Expedition's pioneering field research into 'visual acuity' among Torres Straits Islanders in 1889.

Yet the history of global psychology is also one of racism, ethnocentrism and controversy. We read here of questionable attempts to unearth the behavioural implications of race, for example in relation to intelligence levels. More systematic, even-handed attempts to study humans across cultures are however reflected in the work of twentieth-century pioneers of both psychology and anthropology. These include investigations into linguistic diversity by Francis Boas and into gender and adolescence by Margaret Mead, both of whom left their legacy in the development of psychological anthropology, whose advocates sought the link between culture and temperament. Coming more up to date, this chapter also plots the development of contemporary approaches to cultural issues in psychology, including the distinction between cross-cultural psychology (see Chapter 1) and cultural psychology (see Chapter 5).

REFLECTIVE EXERCISE 8

Match up the definitions on the right with the terms on the left (see p. 222 for answers)

A brand of ethnocentrism which assumes that one's own group is the ideal towards which others will presently develop

The notion that people from the same nation share certain personality traits

Projective test

The idea that some societies grow stronger, more complex and are better at maintaining themselves over time, while others may fall by the wayside

Cultural anthropology

Indigenous psychologies

The collection of data for descriptive purposes by using fieldwork techniques, focusing on a single cultural setting

Race

Controlling inheritance by selective breeding

Social Darwinism

A term used to distinguish a relatively large division of persons from another. It refers to how groups with distinct ancestries differ from each other in terms of appearance

Evolutionary thinking

Eugenics

Psychological traditions within cultures

Psychological anthropology

Anthropological investigations that make use of psychological concepts and methods

National character

Test designed to provide insight about personality traits

Ethnography

The study of the complex social structures that make up communities, societies and nations

FURTHER READING

- Hart, K. (1998) *The place of the 1898 Cambridge Anthropological Expedition to the Torres Straits (CAETS) in the history of British social anthropology*, lecture given in the opening session of a conference held at St John's College, Cambridge, UK, 'Anthropology and psychology: the legacy of the Torres Straits expedition, 1898–1998', 10–12 August 1998.
- Jahoda, G. & Krewer, B. (1997) History of cross-cultural psychology and cultural psychology, in Berry, J., Poortinga, Y. & Panday, J. (eds.), *Handbook of Cross-Cultural Psychology. Vol. 1: Theory and method*, Boston: Allyn & Bacon.
- Kuper, A. (1994) *The Chosen Primate*, Cambridge, MA: Harvard University Press.

Culture and its influence

3

Exploring a key concept in global psychology

What this chapter will teach you

- What is **culture**?
- What's the difference between **culture, nation, ethnicity** and **race**?
- How is culture transmitted?
- What is the validity of analysing behaviour at the cultural level?
- What is the **ecological fallacy** and how can we minimise it?

What do we talk about when we talk about culture?

Culture: the people around us and the things emanating from them (encompassing objects, institutions, beliefs, opinions, customs, norms of behaviour)

(Segall *et al.*, 1990)

Along with *mind, normality* and *consciousness,* **culture** is one of the most disputed words in your psychology dictionary. Indeed, it hardly seems appropriate that words like these find themselves into dictionaries at all, since such volumes are meant to offer definitive meanings. The truth is that culture has no single agreed definition. Segall *et al.* are neither the first nor the last to attempt to coin a workable definition. We'll look at several others presently.

First though, rather than striving for a once-and-for-all definition, to help gain a broader understanding of culture, let us look at how the word is used in everyday discourse (Eagleton, 2000; Matsumoto & Juang, 2004). As Figure 3.1 shows, it comes up in conversation under various guises. *Entry 1* certainly overlaps with Segall *et al.*'s definition. Seeing culture as art means recognising it as a creative force 'emanating from people around us'. Yet *entry 3* has most in common with Segall *et al.*'s idea. To speak about culture as a distinct way of life refers to those aspects of the human-made part of our environment (norms, traditions, architecture, art (Herskovits, 1948)) that distinguish one social group from another. Whatever culture is, then, it is certainly what renders one group different from others.

1 **Culture as art**. Culture can refer to those activities one might take part in (theatre, reading, opera) in the interests of self-improvement.
2 **Culture as cultivation**. As a verb with biological connotations, culture (derived from cultivation) is used to describe a process by which organisms, for example pearls, are grown (cultured) under laboratory conditions.
3 **Culture as a distinct way of life**. Culture is used as a noun to refer to a unique way of living (involving attitudes, norms, behaviours, traditions) shared by a social group with a particular origin or shared interest, distinct from that of other social groups, often associated with a particular location. We may, for instance, talk about 'Western culture', 'Japanese culture' or 'the drug culture'.

Figure 3.1 Everyday ways of talking about 'culture'

Short of striving for a once-and-for-all definition of culture, Berry *et al.* (2002) aid our understanding of the term by arguing that it is an idea that seeps into six areas of our lives. For them, when I talk about my culture I speak of my social group's:

● History and traditions – *Mid-winter celebrations are a tradition in my culture*
● Conventions and norms – *It's conventional here to kiss both cheeks when greeting*
● Activities and behaviours – *Music, dancing and sport are some of our favourite pastimes*

- Institutions and organisational infrastructure – *The separation of Church and state is part of our culture*
- Biological ancestry – *Our ancestry dates back centuries*
- Psychological characteristics – *Modesty, pride and co-operation are part of our mentality.*

It is interesting to note how these six contexts for culture encompass elements of both ethnicity (shared identity) and race (biological ancestry), as they are described in Table 3.1. This highlights the overlapping nature of all these concepts. Part of the reason why it is so hard to see where culture ends and nation and ethnicity begin is that these labels refer to phenomena that are partly intangible and unobservable, such as 'feelings of belonging' or 'the psychological dispositions of different groups'. Triandis (2002) acknowledges this when distinguishing between material and subjective aspects of culture. The former refers to the visible, shared characteristics of my group: how we dress, our defining technologies, our favourite cuisine. Subjective culture encompasses the invisible yet influential ideas and values that my social group deems sufficiently valuable to pass on to future generations (through a process known as *cultural transmission*). These may include moral codes, religious doctrines and social etiquette. According to this formulation, when most people in a social group (from a

TABLE 3.1
My culture, my nation, my ethnicity, my race

My culture	My nation	My ethnicity	My race
How my social group is distinctive in terms of its **values, institutions, norms and behaviours** (Segall *et al.*, 1990), as well as the shared meaning it attaches to events (Rohner, 1984). My culture can be changed by **acculturation – a process whereby a member of one cultural group is integrated into another** (Marshall, 1998).	**My status as a citizen of a sovereign nation state**, with precise geographical boundaries that are internationally recognised, if subject to change. The equation between my culture and my nation is unreliable, as within nations many cultural groups coexist.	**My sense of belonging to my social group**. We are bound together by a shared history, language, place of origin. My ethnicity reveals the subjective experience of feeling different from people from other groups. Within nations, numerous ethnic groups coexist, such as Latinos or Native Americans in the US (Matsumoto & Juang, 2004), Tutsis and Hutus in Rwanda (Reader, 1998).	How groups with distinct **ancestries** differ from each other, often in terms of **appearance**, usually their skin colour. Unlike culture, nation or ethnicity, race is generally seen as being permanent and inflexible, if relatively insignificant in terms of genetic underpinning (Gould, 1981; Fernando, 2002).

KEY TERMS

Nation. Sovereign state, with geographical boundaries, which incorporates many cultures and ethnicities.

Ethnicity. A sense of belonging to a social group, the subjective experience of feeling different from other groups.

particular region or time period) share these material and subjective elements, we have what is known as a cultural group, or **culture**. Such a group may or may not also share a national identity (*Japanese culture*), an ethnic identity (*Latino culture*) or even a particular occupation or interest (*student culture, drug culture, counter-culture*).

Lines denoting the limits of one culture and the beginning of another are invisible to the naked eye. They are not plotted on maps, like national boundaries. Furthermore, the precise meaning of culture is arguably more difficult to arrive at than is a definition of a nation. We can, though, agree that 'culture' is a term that distinguishes between groups of people. Yet there are other terms that perform a similar function. 'Nation', 'ethnicity' and 'race' are all labels that divide us into groups. This can be a little confusing, since such labels are frequently used interchangeably (Matsumoto & Juang, 2004). Nevertheless, as Table 3.1 shows, several writers have argued that when I use phrases like 'my nation', 'my culture', 'my ethnicity' and 'my race', I am emphasising meaningfully distinct aspects of my identity. While there is a degree of overlap between these four labels, they all refer to a different piece of me.

As a conceptual tool for distinguishing between groups, culture is a Swiss Army knife of a concept. It is multi-functional. At a simple level it serves as a means of describing and categorising people. At a more complex level it is used to explain (cultural) variations in behaviours in different places (Matsumoto & Juang, 2004). Just as the use of culture as a descriptive and explanatory device in psychology has a long tradition, so does the race to find a satisfactory definition of the word itself. Let us now see how some of these attempts have changed over the years.

REFLECTIVE EXERCISE 9

1. What is the difference between a *culture* and a *nation*?

2. Can you think of an example of a *material* aspect of your culture, and an example of one of its *subjective* aspects?

The race to define culture

In a painstaking literature review, Soudijn *et al.* (1990) found 128 different definitions of culture. As the key concept shows, successive definitions down the years have grown more sophisticated – and longer. Inevitably, some of these definitions reflect various authors' theoretical interpretations, with a number emphasising material aspects, and others more intangible, subjective ones. Rohner (1984) can be counted among the latter. For Rohner culture amounts to shared meanings and

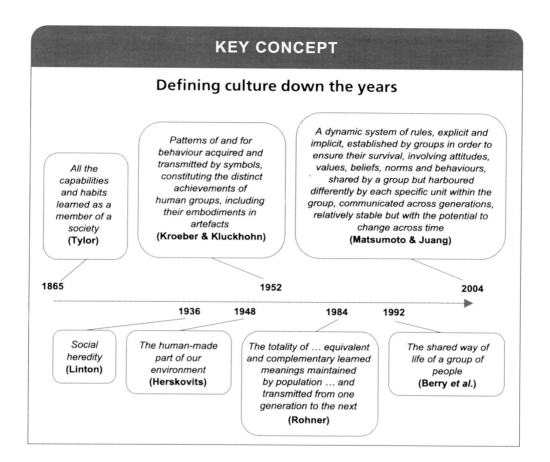

KEY CONCEPT

Defining culture down the years

All the capabilities and habits learned as a member of a society
(Tylor)

Patterns of and for behaviour acquired and transmitted by symbols, constituting the distinct achievements of human groups, including their embodiments in artefacts
(Kroeber & Kluckhohn)

A dynamic system of rules, explicit and implicit, established by groups in order to ensure their survival, involving attitudes, values, beliefs, norms and behaviours, shared by a group but harboured differently by each specific unit within the group, communicated across generations, relatively stable but with the potential to change across time
(Matsumoto & Juang)

1865   1952   2004

1936   1948   1984   1992

Social heredity **(Linton)**

The human-made part of our environment **(Herskovits)**

The totality of ... equivalent and complementary learned meanings maintained by population ... and transmitted from one generation to the next **(Rohner)**

The shared way of life of a group of people **(Berry et al.)**

interpretations of events, rather than the material actions or products that figure in the definitions of Segall *et al.*, Matsumoto & Juang and Kroeber & Kluckhohn (1952). Rohner's has been termed a relational definition since it emphasises the shared spaces between people, rather than their material actions or products (Smith *et al.*, 2006). It dwells on the 'glue' of ideas that binds us together, rather than on similarities in our behaviour patterns.

This theoretical separation of ideas (meanings) from actions (behaviour) is insightful since it acknowledges that in reality the two often operate independently (LaPiere, 1934). After all, interpretations of events are not always translated into action. Yet portraying culture as a community's shared meanings alone, separate from *what people actually do out there in the world*, does rather underplay the role of attitudes and beliefs in predicting behaviour (Smith & Bond, 1993). Jahoda (1984) uses a game-playing analogy to illustrate this criticism of Rohner. He suggests that while the rules of, say, basketball, don't give an exact guide to how the game is played, they do provide a 'probabilistic' guide to what happens in play. Similarly, the idea of culture provides a useful, probabilistic guide to how we act in life's field of play.

Whether we define it as predominantly meanings, actions or arte- facts, culture represents something that is generated by certain groups who occupy a particular time, space or occupation, or who have a particular interest. However, not only are cultures generated by group members, they are perpetuated by a process of transmission that ensures their survival (see the definitions of Kroeber & Kluckholn; Rohner; Matsumoto & Juang). They are, in this sense, self- perpetuating. It is to the processes of cultural transmission and per- petuation that we are about to turn. First, though, we might reflect that while we have no single, agreed definition of culture, the definitions we have looked at do seem to point to half a dozen agreed characteristics of culture. These are summarised in the key concept.

KEY CONCEPT

Characteristics of culture

1 It is a descriptive label that *distinguishes one social group from another*.
2 It refers to aspects of identity that overlap with (though emphasising different elements from) national, ethnic and racial identity.
3 It encompasses both material and subjective elements.
4 It is an explanatory label that is used to account for variations in behaviour between different groups.
5 It is reciprocal: it is generated by its members, yet influences their behaviour.
6 It is transmitted from members of one group to those of others.

The dynamic process of cultural transmission

How does culture perpetuate itself? Or, to put it another way, by what means do cultures manage to survive? A glib one-word answer to both of these questions would be – 'dynamically'. Dynamically because as any history book will tell you, though 'attitudes, norms and behaviours' may be passed down through generations, they change (or adapt) in the process. A twenty-first-century European may think and act similarly to a nineteenth-century European, but there are plenty of differences too. Matsumoto and Juang's (2004) definition of culture captures this dynamism. It is also compatible with a widely held view that the dynamic process by which cultures perpetuate themselves (survive) is analogous to the way species adapt biologically to their environments. Several authors regard cultural and biological adaptation as parallel processes that exert a **dual influence** on human development and diversity (Boyd & Richerson, 1985; Berry *et al.*, 1992/2002; Matsumoto & Juang, 2004).

Dual influence: cultural and biological adaptation

The conceptual tool of dual influence offers a model for understanding two influences on who we are. It portrays biological and cultural influence as adaptive processes that are similar in some ways yet dissimilar in others (Table 3.2). We can use dual influence to provide a bird's-eye view of the role biology and culture play in the spread of human diversity through time and space. In a sentence, the idea of dual influence states that:

> Biology and culture are *similar* in that they both work according to evolutionary principles of selection and adaptation, yet they *differ* in that instinct draws humans towards *universality*, while culture draws us towards *diversity* (see Table 3.2).

Furnished with this overview we can now give more detailed consideration to the nitty-gritty of why some aspects of culture (ideas, norms and behaviours) survive as good adaptations, while others don't. For example – *Why did cities develop? Why do people in some regions fish for food? Why did the (Guatemalan) Xinca language die out?* These are all questions about cultural transmission. Their answers reside in the diverse influences of several **circumstantial variables** (Segall *et al.*, 1990; Berry *et al.*, 2002). It is generally accepted that in the case of certain biological predispositions to act (known as **instincts**), though they are present at birth, their expression in behaviour depends on circumstances that prevail to a greater or lesser extent out there in the world (known as circumstantial variables). Likewise, in the case of ideas, norms and behaviours that are created and maintained by

KEY TERMS

Circumstantial variables. Circumstances that prevail to a greater or lesser extent.

Instincts. Biological predispositions to act.

TABLE 3.2
Biological and cultural influence: adaptive processes with similarities and differences

Similarities	Differences
Biology and culture operate according to Darwinian, evolutionary principles of **selection** and **adaptation** (Segall et al., 1990).	While biological influence takes place between parents and offspring who are genetically related, cultural influence also occurs between people who are not related to one another.
To understand how, first consider **biological inheritance**. Biological predispositions to certain behaviours (instincts) that survive in a population are passed (genetically) from one generation to another. They are selected because they help species adapt to and thrive in whatever circumstances prevail in our environment. For example, the instinct to stake out territories in the face of predators works because it helps to avoid capture, enabling genes to live on through subsequent generations (Ardrey, 1966). In short, being territorial works as a behavioural strategy because it is an effective **adaptation** to dangerous, predator-ridden landscapes.	Biological adaptation is more gradual and homogenising (it makes humans more similar to each other) than cultural adaptation. While both biology and culture influence the way we behave, the changes brought about by culture are much more rapid and varied than those ushered in by instinct.
Now consider **cultural influence**. Ideas, norms and behaviours that survive in a culture (passed from parent to child, from teacher to learner, from nephew to uncle – yes, they can be passed from the young to the older) are selected because they are effective **adaptations** to changing cultural circumstances. They are 'in tune' with ways of thinking that prevail at a particular time and place. Other ideas, norms and behaviours grow obsolete in certain cultural settings. In some European countries, at the beginning of the twenty-first century, the practice of smacking children is an example of this.	To understand how, first consider **biological inheritance**. Innate predispositions for behaviour (instincts) which are selected as effective adaptations to environmental circumstances are relatively **unchanging**, **inflexible** and **widespread**. They are not fashions for behaviour that come and go in a few years (or even in a few thousand years). Generally speaking, if instinctive predispositions have been selected for their survival value, they're here to stay. They also tend to be present in virtually all cultural settings. For example, the instinctive predisposition to care for offspring (which is an effective way for our genes to propagate themselves) is culturally universal.
Culture and instinct operate in parallel, according to evolutionary principles. Selected behaviours, norms, ideas, adapt to their circumstances.	Now consider **cultural influence**. Ideas, behaviours and norms that are effective adaptations to our person-made environment are comparatively **transient** and **prone to cultural variation**. They come and go, often in the space of a few months or a few hundred years. Also, the form they survive in tends to vary from one cultural setting to another. Think of examples such as democracy, marriage, or particular childcare practices. Manifestations of all these vary throughout history and from one cultural setting to another.
	Culture and instinct exert rather different influences on human behaviour. Innate predispositions (instincts) are adaptations that proceed very slowly, and have a unifying effect on humans. Ideas, norms and behaviours that are selected culturally live and die by a much faster timescale, with the effect of producing a variety of behaviours across cultural settings.

cultural means, how they express themselves and which ones are selected will again depend on circumstantial variables. Some of these variables are naturally present in some cultural settings; others are human-made. They either inhibit or promote ideas, norms, behaviours and predispositions. Furthermore, they come in several varieties, including the following.

- *Ecological variables*: weather systems, climatic changes, predators, diseases, pests, the availability of foods. For example, a harsh climate might inhibit the instinct to behave territorially as it may force a species to keep on the move.
- *Socio-political variables*: changes in governments, war, religious conflicts. For example, a new government may legislate to make society less tolerant of corporal punishment.
- *Individual–psychological variables*: actions, values and personalities of certain individuals or groups. For example, hunting animals for sport might die out due to campaigns staged by pressure groups or charismatic individuals.

Thus, how instincts (say, aggression) are expressed in behaviour and how well certain ideas, norms and behaviours (go-karting, circumcision or monogamous marriage) survive and adapt in particular times or places depend on a combination of circumstances in the natural and political world, as well as on the actions of certain charismatic individuals or groups. Berry *et al.* (2002) represent these influences diagrammatically in their *eco-cultural model* (Figure 3.2). This is an overarching description of the complex process of cultural adaptation and transmission. It operates according to several key principles and concepts.

- *Adaptation*. Culture and biology are engaged in a dual process that increases the 'fit' between members of groups and their diverse environments. This process yields diversity in cultures, as well as sustainable biological responses to diverse ecologies. Certain behaviours and psychological characteristics are selected (by both individuals and populations) as best adaptations to changing environmental contexts (Buss, 1989).
- *Bidirectionality*. Several aspects of the model reflect what you might call two-way interactions (as opposed to one-way traffic). They are mutually influential, in other words. Ecological conditions affect – and are affected by – cultural and biological adaptations. For example, the way of life of a social group (hunting, fishing or

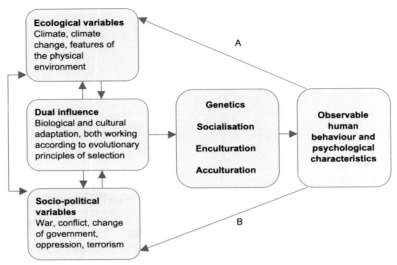

Figure 3.2 The eco-cultural model of cultural transmission (based on Berry *et al.*, 2002; Matsumoto & Juang, 2004)

logging) is influenced by its ecology, yet also influences its ecological circumstances (think of deforestation).

Another bidirectional dynamic is illustrated by feedback arrows 'A' and 'B' in Figure 3.2. The actions of individuals and groups can have agency over their ecological and socio-political circumstances (Berry *et al.*, 2002). In other words, the model refrains from **cultural determinism** (the view that human behaviour is primarily shaped by cultural factors (Reber, 1997)). Rather, it acknowledges that individuals are not passively shaped by their context, but also have a role in its formation.

- *Transmission*. The way biology, culture, ecology and socio-politics manifest themselves in human behaviour depends on a raft of supplementary concepts: genetics, socialisation, enculturation and acculturation. These can each be understood separately, though they are all vehicles of transmission.

KEY TERM

Cultural determinism. The view that human behaviour is primarily shaped by cultural factors.

  - *Genetics*. Genetic information (predispositions to behave in certain adaptive ways) is passed from generation to generation from biological parents (known as *vertical* transmission).
  - *Socialisation*. Norms, values, behaviours and other psychological characteristics are passed on via a variety of agencies (family, media, peers, church), often by formal instruction. This can operate *vertically* (biological parent → child), though it also uses

horizontal (peer ↔ peer) as well as *oblique* transmission – via non-related adults (*My friend's Dad taught me this*).

- ○ *Enculturation*. This is a less formal version of socialisation. Individuals are 'encultured' as they adopt the norms, values and behaviours of their cultural group into their repertoires. As with socialisation, this can work horizontally, vertically or obliquely.
- ○ *Acculturation*. This is cultural transmission by contact with other groups. Direct or indirect interaction between people from different cultural groups (through travel, migration or exposure to the mass media) leads to the spreading and changing of attitudes and behaviours. This can be creative, producing new mixes of cultural forms (analogous to the emergence of reggae music out of disparate Jamaican, British and American musical styles (Bradley, 2000)). It can also be stressful, as in cases of forced migration from one culture to another (Al-Issa & Tousignant, 1997).

The eco-cultural model juxtaposes biological and cultural adaptation as responses to new ecologies and other circumstantial variables. One question that arises from this is whether we therefore regard cultures – or indeed the human species as a biological entity – as *getting better*, or at least more sophisticated. It is debatable whether cultural and biological adaptations ought to be regarded as 'improvements' (Sahlins & Service, 1960; Hallpike, 1986). While the transition from fishing or hunting lifestyles to city-dwelling may be regarded as an adaptive response to circumstantial variables, the question of whether this amounts to an improvement is really a value judgement, so not something to be decided in a psychology textbook. Berry *et al.* (2002) distance themselves from those wishing to interpret their model as an explanation for 'how cultures evolve into something more advanced'.

The eco-cultural model attempts to represent, theoretically and pictorially, dynamic relationships between organisms and their environmental, biological and political contexts. It demonstrates the dual and inseparable influences of biology and culture as working evolutionary adaptations to circumstantial variables. It also reflects the mutually influential nature of our behaviour with our surroundings. Yet despite (or perhaps because of) attempting to represent so many facets of behaviour and diversity, the model arguably has some limitations.

Limitations of the eco-cultural model

1 *Overarching models may overlook individual differences.* Such an all-encompassing model is strong on advancing a top-down view of how cultural and biological adaptation is manifest in human behaviour and psychological characteristics. Yet such a generalised picture struggles to explain why some members of cultural groups are more willing to adopt apparently adaptive cultural norms – norms which, after all, enable their cultural group to survive. Such differences in willingness perhaps need to be analysed at more of an individual level, rather than by using a top-down model.

2 *Some cultural groups are more tolerant of deviation than others.* The eco-cultural model suggests that the actions of individuals or concerted groups can have an effect on the norms and values of their cultural group. Yet it stops short of explaining why different cultural groups are variously tolerant of deviation from their norms (Pelto, 1968). To put this another way, some cultures are more likely to embrace adaptations to new circumstances than others. As to why this is, again a closer analysis of the characteristics of different groups would be required.

REFLECTIVE EXERCISE 10

1. Suggest one difference between cultural and biological adaptation.

2. As a migrant from one nation to another, you are faced with a number of new ideas and norms as you adapt to a new culture. Which of these words most accurately describes the process you are undergoing?
   a. Enculturation
   b. Socialisation
   c. Acculturation

Arguably, the limitations of the eco-cultural model are a consequence of its all-encompassing, 'top-down' nature. Yet the model does allow for the transformative effect that the actions of individuals and groups have. It illustrates not only how culture influences the behaviour of large groups of people *at the population level*, but also how people operating *at an individual level* can influence their cultural context. To conclude this chapter we will now further explore the distinction between so-called culture-level analyses of behaviour on one hand, and individual-level analyses on the other.

Culture and individual levels of analysis

A recurring debate in global psychology concerns the use of culture as a level for analysing behaviour. Specifically, the debate revolves around the validity of analysing actions at what has been termed the *culture* level, rather than at the *individual* level (Smith *et al.*, 2006). To grasp how these two levels differ, consider one of the quirks of global psychology. Unlike most types of psychologist, global researchers often ask questions about how whole cultural (or national) groups differ from each other in relation to selected behaviours – rather than asking about how individuals differ from each other on those same variables. In this regard they treat cultures as single, discrete sources of data, while the rest of psychology sees individuals as discrete units for yielding data (Smith *et al.*, 2006). This is the key distinction between culture and individual levels of analysis.

Actually, Berry *et al.*'s (1992) eco-cultural model allows for such so-called **culture-level analyses**, wherein the actions and psychological characteristics of individuals are deemed to vary according to their membership of one cultural group or another. For example, individuals from one culture might act differently from those from another in a given situation due to the differing effects of enculturation and socialisation in those two cultures.

To illustrate the distinction between culture and individual analyses, let us examine the relationship between two frequently studied variables: wealth and happiness. Does the former bring the latter? This is a reasonable question that can be analysed at two levels. At the culture level we might ask:

Do people from wealthy cultural groups (or nations) generally report higher levels of subjective well-being (happiness) than those from less wealthy nations?

A study that asks this question would typically compare respondents from two or more cultural groups and would yield interpretations that might be phrased in the form:

People from wealthier nations generally report higher levels of subjective well-being.

At the individual level we might ask:

Do wealthy individuals generally report higher levels of subjective well-being than less wealthy ones?

Research that poses this question would tend to take place *within* a cultural group, and would typically spawn interpretations such as:

KEY TERM

Culture-level analyses. The actions and psychological characteristics of individuals are deemed to vary according to their membership of one cultural group or another.

Wealthier people are generally happier than people with low incomes.

Global, and especially cross-cultural (see Chapter 1), psychology frequently operates at the culture level of analysis. In a typical culture-level scenario, data are collected from samples of participants who are taken to represent certain regions, enabling conclusions to be made about the relationship between (1) cultural background and (2) psychological characteristics *(North Americans are generally more individualistic in their attitudes than South Asians)*.

A key motivation for pitching analyses at the culture level is that it yields research findings that emphasise the influence of contextual (environmental, social, cultural) factors on our thoughts and behaviour. Conversely, individual-level analyses stress internal (genetic, personality, information-processing), or context-*less*, influences on behaviour (Smith *et al.*, 2006). Yet while they do allow for the considerable influence of context variables, are culture-level analyses wholly reliable explanations of behavioural differences? In other words, do they yield explanations that can be generalised to other levels of analysis (like the individual level)?

The reliability of culture-level analyses

Personal experience tells us that some people are more susceptible to the norms and values of their culture than others. In other words, the vicissitudes of socialisation and enculturation affect us to differing degrees. So while membership of 'my culture' may partly explain why I act differently from you on certain behavioural measures (such as individualism, conformity, depth perception), common sense dictates that culture-level analyses can provide only some of the explanation for these differences.

Smith *et al.* (2006) raise a deeper concern about culture-level analyses. They argue that just because an interesting relationship between two variables emerges at the culture level, we shouldn't assume it will hold true at the individual level. In other words, findings unearthed at the culture level don't necessarily apply across the board.

To illustrate this, consider again the link between wealth and happiness. Culture-level research has suggested that they are indeed correlated. Participants from nations with relatively high average incomes have reported higher levels of subjective well-being (Diener *et al.*, 1995). Yet analysis of the same variables within cultural groups yields rather different findings. Particularly in richer nations, personal wealth shows up as a poor predictor of well-being (Oishi *et al.*, 1999). For the record, home-life satisfaction was shown to be more closely associated with happiness.

A similar mismatch emerges in findings about the relationship between job satisfaction and individualistic attitudes. Culture-level analyses found that participants from nations that are categorised as *individualistic* (Hofstede, 1980) reported higher work satisfaction. Meanwhile in individual-level analyses, within specific cultural groups such as Hong Kong, attitudes of collectivism, not individualism, were predictive of work satisfaction (Hui *et al.*, 1995). All this indicates that very often, findings gleaned at the cultural level are not supported when the same variables are analysed at the individual level.

The ecological fallacy – and how to minimise it

We can learn a number of things from these inconsistencies. First, while there are plenty of examples of research findings that do uncover consistent relationships between variables at the cultural and individual levels of analysis (Earley, 1993; Singelis *et al.*, 1999), there is no reason to assume that this should always be the case (Smith *et al.*, 2006). Second, we should beware of making the assumption that findings that are demonstrated at the culture level of analysis will be replicated within cultural groups. As we have seen, it would be wrong for us to assume that high income and happiness coexist within cultures, just because they do across cultures. This kind of misguided assumption is known as the **ecological fallacy** (Hofstede, 1980). It serves as a warning against over-generalising from cross-cultural research findings. It tells us that interesting findings about human behaviour do not always trickle down from one level of analysis to another.

However misguided and debilitating, Hofstede's fallacy is not incurable. By taking care when selecting variables to be studied, researchers can minimise its chances of blighting their conclusions (Smith *et al.*, 2006). Specifically, a strategy to ensure that concepts and variables that are used in culture-level analyses are meaningful to all the groups involved can help reduce the likelihood of making fallacious generalisations. In other words, before doing culture-level analyses of particular variables (such as happiness, wealth or freedom) these can first be subjected to individual-level analyses within each cultural group, simply to ensure that they have comparable, replicable meanings.

Schwartz (1992) adopted precisely such a strategy, calling it a **parallel individual analysis**. Respondents in over 60 nations were asked to rate 56 values (such as happiness, wealth and freedom) in terms of

KEY TERMS

Ecological fallacy. The assumption that findings which are demonstrated at the culture level of analysis will be replicated within cultural groups.

Parallel individual analysis. A strategy to ensure that concepts and variables which are used in culture-level analyses are meaningful to all the groups involved.

their importance in their own lives. The values used for the study were drawn from various cultural settings (Smith *et al.*, 2006). Within each national sample the degree to which each value correlated (or clustered) with others was taken to indicate whether they had approximately equivalent meanings across national groups. For example, if all representatives from all national groups repeatedly rated values x and y similarly, yet saw value z as diametrically opposed, their meanings were regarded as relatively stable and replicable.

In this ongoing research project forty-four of the original fifty-six values have been shown to have relatively replicable and equivalent meanings (Schwartz *et al.*, 2001). Arguably, on the basis of this individual-level scaffolding exercise, these values have been 'cleared for use' in more valid culture-level analyses. Valid culture-level analyses of behaviour can thus arise out of parallel individual analyses, minimising the likelihood of the dreaded ecological fallacy.

REFLECTIVE EXERCISE 11

Imagine you are planning to conduct some research across cultures, into the proposed relationship between subjective well-being (happiness) and 'freedom'. Outline what steps you might take to avoid the ecological fallacy.

In their study Schwartz *et al.* used values and variables gathered from various regions. They also made strenuous efforts to ensure the widespread meaningfulness of these values within each cultural group. Such measures reflect a desire to avoid the ethnocentric importing of potentially meaningless variables from one culture to another in global research.

Having given lengthy consideration to the concept of culture itself in this chapter, it is to this knotty issue of ethnocentrism (culture bias) that we now turn. First, though, to consolidate your understanding of culture and its related concepts, try the reflective exercise on p. 60.

Summary

Chapter 3 investigates the concept of culture in close detail. Definitions of culture abound, both colloquially and in learned circles. Various definitions are examined here, as are the much disputed distinctions between culture, nation, ethnicity and race. You may think you know the difference, but it is far from straightforward and indeed laced with controversy. In a related debate we learn how culture, like biological inheritance, has a deep influence on the way we behave. The similarities between these 'dual influences' are also examined in detail here.

Segall *et al.*'s (1990) 'eco-cultural' theory of cultural and biological inheritance is discussed, setting the influence of culture in an evolutionary context. This enables us to see how cultures, like individual organisms, are subject to the vicissitudes of evolution and adaptation. In other words, just as biological predispositions to behave in certain ways (instincts) are subject to Darwinian principles, so are the ideas and norms that separate cultural groups from one another.

We see how environmental and climatic variables also contribute to cultural diversity across the globe and perhaps go some way to explaining cultural diversity in human behaviour. The chapter culminates with an examination of how useful culture is as an explanation for differences in behaviour between individuals and groups, especially when we consider that some of us are more susceptible to the norms and influences of our culture than others.

FURTHER READING

* Hofstede, G. (1980) *Culture's Consequences*, Beverly Hills, CA: Sage.
* Pelto, P. (1968) The differences between 'tight' and 'loose' societies, *Trans-action*, April, 37–40.
* Smith, P. (2002) Levels of analysis in cross-cultural psychology, in Lonner, W., Dinnel, D., Hayes, S. & Sattler, D. (eds.), *Online Readings in Psychology and Culture* (Unit 2, Chapter 7), Bellingham, WA: Center for Cross-Cultural Research, Western Washington University.

REFLECTIVE EXERCISE 12

Match up the definitions on the right with the terms on the left (see p. 223 for answers)

Assumption that findings that are demonstrated at the culture level of analysis will be replicated within cultural groups

Norms, values, behaviours and other psychological characteristics are passed on via a variety of agencies (family, media, peers, church), often by formal instruction

Cultural determinism

Actions and psychological characteristics of individuals are deemed to vary according to their membership of one cultural group

Socialisation

Circumstantial variables

Sovereign state, with precise geographical boundaries that are internationally recognised, if subject to change

Dual influence

The people around us and the things emanating from them (encompassing objects, institutions, beliefs, opinions, customs, norms of behaviour)

Culture-level analysis

Enculturation

Circumstances that prevail to a greater or lesser extent out there in the world

Ethnicity

Informal process wherein individuals adopt the norms, values and behaviours of their cultural group into their repertoires

Culture

Parallel individual analyses

The view that human behaviour is primarily shaped by cultural factors

Ecological fallacy

The subjective experience of feeling different from people from other social groups

Acculturation

Cultural transmission by contact with other groups

Nation

The notion that biology and culture both work according to the evolutionary principles of selection and adaptation

Strategy to ensure that concepts and variables which are used in culture-level analyses are meaningful to all the cultural groups involved

Is psychology ethnocentric?

Imposed etics, culture bias and indigenous psychologies

4

What this chapter will teach you

- Where does most published psychological research originate from?
- Where are most psychology textbooks written?
- What is the dominant language of psychology?
- Where do psychology's practitioners predominantly practise?
- What are etic and emic approaches to research?
- What are derived and imposed etics?
- What is the indigenous psychology movement?

Where is psychology?

Ethnocentrism: seeing other cultural groups solely from the point of view of one's own culture.

Psychology students traditionally begin their studies by asking – *what is psychology?* It may take the entire course to find a satisfactory answer, but as a rite of passage for students of human behaviour, tackling this question is more or less mandatory. But what about a second question, concerning psychology's whereabouts? *Where is psychology?* This question is less common on mainstream psychology courses, yet we are duty-bound to ask it if we are interested in whether psychology should stand accused of being an ethnocentric (culturally biased) science that is dominated by the interests of one or two regions of the world. After all, if psychology professes to be the study of all human behaviour and experience – wherever it may occur – its students really ought to be curious about where in the world most of its research actually takes place.

The whereabouts of the written word in psychology

Lean over and reach for your nearest psychology textbook. Turn to the bibliography. Is most of the research featured there published in the US, with perhaps a smaller proportion from Europe? Is there much from Cameroon, India or Finland? Are your answers to these questions *yes* and *no* by any chance? It is likely that most of the books and articles featured in your textbook derive from research carried out by North American (and a smaller proportion of European) researchers, using North American (and a smaller proportion of European) participants.

There is nothing unusual about your textbook. Psychology textbooks reflect the accumulated knowledge and efforts of writers, researchers and participants who are unevenly distributed around the world. Moghaddam (1987) has provocatively suggested that this unevenness reflects psychology's own stratification into three geographical regions, each with varying levels of influence over the discipline. He identifies a tendency for mainstream psychology to gather and publish a disproportionate segment of data from selected geographical and cultural locations, mostly concentrated in North America (known as psychology's first world) and to generalise these data worldwide. You could call this a **sampling error** (an error involving taking results from a restricted sample of participants and mistakenly applying them to the population as a whole) which jeopardises psychology's claim to be the study of all human behaviour and experience, wherever it may occur. Between psychology's first and third (i.e. the developing) worlds, Moghaddam identifies a 'second world'. This encompasses industrially and techno-logically developed 'middleweight' nations such as Britain, Russia and Germany. Second-world states are materially better equipped for psychological research than those in the developing world, though they have tended to lag behind the US in terms of libraries, laboratories, publishing facilities, trained personnel and all the other paraphernalia of the psychology industry. Moghaddam points out that traditionally psychology's first world has claimed the greatest concentration of material resources for producing research data, leaving the discipline vulnerable to accusations of ethnocentric 'western' bias. So, is the production of psychology's printed word (books and journal articles) over-concentrated in 'the west'? Figure 4.1 does suggest a pronounced proliferation of and reliance on publications from Moghaddam's 'first world'.

REFLECTIVE EXERCISE 13

Answer these five questions and then look for the answers in the text below.

1. Which country has the highest percentage of psychologists per million of population?

    Netherlands   Argentina   USA   Slovenia

2. Which correlation coefficient describes the relationship between GNP and number of psychologists per million of population?

    0.14   0.44   0.61   −0.14

3. Which country came bottom in a recent survey of national numbers of psychologists per million of population?

    China   Uganda   New Zealand   Romania

4. What percentage of psychological researchers operating worldwide is estimated to be from North America?

    40   52   64   99

5. Which city boasts the world's highest number of psychoanalysts?

    Buenos Aires   London   New York   Beijing

Textbooks

Relative representation of US/European/'other' research in typical psychology textbooks is estimated at 80%/18%/2% (Smith & Bond, 1998). The same authors reviewed the regional distribution of citations in several popular social psychology textbooks; in Baron and Byrne (1994) and Myers (1996) proportions of references to studies from outside the US were 6% and 8% respectively. For books published outside the US this regional over-representation was less pronounced but still present. Hewstone *et al.*'s (1996) European and Hogg and Vaughan's (1995) Australasian texts had 25% of non-US citations, with less than 3% from the developing world.

This situation is also seen in textbooks produced for a non-US readership. One Spanish textbook published in 1989 had 74% of its studies based in North America (Rodriguez & Seoane, 1989), and an edited volume entitled *Psychology and the Developing World* featured 3/21 contributions from that region (Carr & Schumaker, 1996). In the field of developmental psychology it has been suggested that research samples featured in mainstream texts are drawn from representatives of only 5% of the global population (Zukow, 1989a). Furthermore, a look through the references in Berry *et al.*'s *Cross-Cultural Psychology* (2002) textbook shows that (excluding those pertaining to the authors' own research) there are 94 books from North America; 24 from the UK; nine from France; seven from The Netherlands; four each from Canada and Switzerland; two each from South Africa and Hong Kong; and one each from the Czech Republic, Germany and Australia.

As an interesting point of comparison, it was found that textbooks on the natural sciences published in the US had a higher proportion of citations for 'foreign' research (44%) than was the norm for psychology books (Stevens & Gielen, 2007). A consequence of the over-proliferation of US texts and citations in global psychology books is that students in many nations find themselves using American texts which inevitably carry a culturally constructed outlook (Stevens & Gielen, 2007).

Journal articles

There are approximately 1500 peer-reviewed psychology-related academic journals and 17% of them are published in a language other than English (Pawlik & Rosenzweig, 2000). Only 5% of articles in PsycINFO (the most widely used online psychology database, set up by the American Psychiatric Association) appear in languages other than English. The trend towards the marginalisation of non-English-language journal publications is set to continue, with many, especially introductory and general, publications opting for an English-only format. The danger here is an alienation of a potentially large global readership (Pawlik & Rosenzweig, 2000).

Against this it has been suggested that while US authors remain overwhelmingly the highest contributors of articles, the extent of this dominance is in decline. Bauserman (1997) found a 16% drop in the proportion of US articles featured in PsychLIT (a CD-ROM database of research abstracts) between 1975 and 1997. Adair *et al.* (2002) found 55% of PsychLIT articles to be from the US, which supports the declining dominance suggested by Bauserman (Stevens & Gielen, 2007).

Figure 4.1 Is there culture bias in psychology books and articles?

The whereabouts of psychology's practitioners

It seems that your place of residence may influence your chances of becoming a professional psychologist. In 1985 the US had 23 times as many academic psychologists working in universities as Britain had, and 234 times as many as Nigeria (Moghaddam, 1987). But the global distribution of psychologists is in flux and not entirely predictable.

Before reading on, try the reflective exercise on p. 63. You may be surprised by some of the answers (all of which appear in the next few paragraphs).

It is estimated that around 40% of the world's 1 million or so psychologists practise in the US (Hogan, 1995; Pawlik & Rosenzweig, 2000) and that as many as 64% of psychological researchers operating worldwide are North American (Rozensweig, 1999). There are approximately 290,000 trained psychologists in Western Europe, compared with 277,000 employed in the US (Tikkanen, 2004). Yet the extent of the US hegemony may be in decline in relation to psychological personnel, and it is likely that this US dominance will recede in coming decades (Stevens & Gielen, 2007).

Psychology's own globalisation is under way. There has been a recent upsurge in the number of psychologists across Spain, Israel, South Africa, Brazil and Argentina (Stevens & Wedding, 2004). In terms of the number of licensed psychologists, Buenos Aires is actually psychology's world capital (Klappenbach, 2004), though the accent here and in much of the developing world is on psychoanalysis rather than experimental research. Interestingly though, the US still has around 25 times as many psychologists as China does, with just a quarter of its population (Stevens & Gielen, 2007).

We should be wise to note that the reliability of these figures suffers somewhat from regionally differing definitions of (and qualifications necessary to become) a 'psychologist'. A master's or PhD qualification is a requirement in some nations, though not others, for chartered psychologist status. Such vagaries notwithstanding, the International Union of Psychological Science (IUPsyS) (1998) surveyed the number of psychologists per million of population in 32 nations. League leaders in this respect were the Netherlands (1290 per million), Argentina (1069), Finland (843), Portugal (816) and Spain (758), while the US was eighth overall (664). Fewest psychologists per million were found in China (2.9) and Uganda (4.7), with several other nations outside Western Europe and North America also towards the foot of the table. A concentration of psychologists in nations with higher levels of economic wealth (measured by Gross National Product (GNP) per capita) and more affluent lifestyles (measured by the Human Development Index (HDI)) is also reflected in significant correlations between the number of psychologists per million of population and both GNP (0.44) and HDI (0.51) (Fu & Jing, 1994). These associations suggest that for less affluent nations, training in fields such as agriculture, medicine and commerce is a higher priority than the training of psychologists (Pawlik & Rosenzweig, 2000).

So what do all these figures about psychology publishing and practice across continents tell us about its regional concentration? Well, clearly the US remains the world leader in terms of publishing, resources and personnel. But it is emerging that the discipline is now a global phenomenon. True, you are still more likely to learn about psychology from textbooks and journals that draw heavily on US research. But in terms of where in the world you are likely to practise psychology, opportunity appears to be knocking across five continents for both researchers and applied work. Indeed, as we will learn later in this chapter, the research interests of psychologists are becoming increasingly international and sensitive to indigenous questions about behaviour and experience.

Etics, emics and ethnocentrism in psychological research

Questions about psychology's ethnocentrism cannot be reduced to a numbers game in which cultural bias is judged according to the concentration of publishers and researchers in a particular region. If ethnocentrism is present in psychology it will manifest itself in how researchers go about their business, not just in their whereabouts.

There are many ways to conduct global research. Some are more open to accusations of ethnocentrism than others are. The question of culture bias in global research has been considered with the aid of two concepts borrowed from the field of linguistics: phonetics and phonemics (shown here as a key concept). These concepts have long been seen as analogous to two alternative approaches to carrying out

KEY CONCEPT

Two concepts borrowed from linguistics

Phonetics	The approach to linguistics that investigates the universal properties of spoken sound
Phoneticists	Linguists who are interested in the sounds that all spoken languages share
Phonemics	The approach to linguistics that investigates spoken sounds that are particular to certain languages
Phonemicists	Linguists who are interested in unique qualities of particular languages

research across cultures; the so-called etic and emic approaches (Pike, 1967). Distinctions between the etic and emic approaches are summarised below as a key concept (Berry, 1989).

   Etic research aims to highlight universals of human behaviour and experience, just as phoneticists strive for linguistic universals. The emphasis is on uncovering what all humans have in common by looking for universals in behaviour across cultural circumstances. Comparisons between behaviour in different cultures are subsequently made (Pawlik & Rosenzweig, 2000). This approach is allied to the cross-cultural, replication research method (see Chapter 1). It generally involves taking existing theories out into the cross-cultural field of study for testing.

   Meanwhile **emic research** aims to highlight the distinctiveness of human behaviour and experience as it manifests itself in different cultural settings. Rather than searching for cultural universals, this approach is more 'grounded' in particular cultural locations. Emic

KEY TERMS

Etic research. Research that aims to highlight universals of human behaviour and experience.

Emic research. Research that aims to highlight distinctiveness of human behaviour and experience as it manifests itself in different cultural settings.

KEY CONCEPT

Etic and emic approaches to global research

Etic researchers . . .	Emic researchers . . .
• decide what to study and how to analyse it before arriving in the field	• select their subject matter and instruments for analysis once the research is in progress.
• apply and compare their research findings globally	• apply their findings to the field where they were gathered
• analyse behaviour using established theories and data collection methods brought in from outside	• use tools for analysis that are informed by 'local knowledge', often in collaboration with indigenous researchers
• begin gathering data as soon as they arrive in the field.	• begin to collect data only when they're familiar with the local culture.

For example
Ainsworth et al.'s (1978) Strange Situation experimental scenario investigates the incidence of secure/insecure parent–toddler attachments. The original experimental scenario (as well as the original criteria for designating secure/insecure attachment) was used to compare attachments in 32 nations (Van Ijzendoorn, 1995). This enabled researchers to ask Are secure parent–toddler attachments culturally universal?

For example
Collaborating with indigenous researchers, Manson et al. (1985) studied 'heartbrokenness' among North American Hopi Indians. Extended analysis of local meaning systems enabled Manson et al. to ask Do Hopis have their own unique illness categories to refer to depressive experiences? Can local knowledge be used to design a meaningful diagnostic instrument to identify these experiences?

Arguably the most enjoyable holidays are those where we allow ourselves to respond openly to unfamiliar places by participating fully in the ways and manners of diverse cultures (eating durian fruit in Malaysia, dancing the polka in Hungary). So the tourist who is likely to have the dullest time is the unresponsive one, who carries into the resort all the habits (marmalade for breakfast, bed at 10pm) and accoutrements (tea bags, knife and fork) of home.

But there is a dilemma here. The responsive tourist who surrenders to the novel setting may be playing a dangerous game by leaving his identity at the border. Is he the one who will find it most difficult to retain his sense of who he is, to maintain his integrity of judgement while on holiday, and to readjust to mundane reality when returning home?

Figure 4.2 The tourist's dilemma

researchers immerse themselves in the ways and manners of the cultural group they are studying, adopting the attitude of the 'responsive tourist' (see Figure 4.2). They strive to create research scenarios that are meaningful within the cultures being studied (Pawlik & Rosenzweig, 2000). So instead of asking whether a particular behaviour is universal across Belgium, Brazil and Bangladesh, emic research would look at an aspect of behaviour that is peculiar to Belgium, or Brazil, or Bangladesh. This would then be studied in detail, *in situ*. The need to replicate, generalise or compare behaviour across cultures is resisted by the emic researcher.

The etic–emic distinction highlights the tendency of etic research in global psychology to take questions and methods that were 'born in the US' and apply them in other parts of the world without taking account of indigenous meanings and methods. Differences between etic and emic orientations mimic those between an unresponsive and a responsive tourist (see Figure 4.2). The latter opts for immersion in the novel environment. But just like these two types of tourism, in reality the distinctions between etic and emic research are often not so clear-cut. Indeed, many research projects (and many holidays) begin with an etic (unresponsive) outlook, only to become more emic (responsive) in time. Behaviour in the field may initially be viewed through the eyes of an outsider, using an outsider's instruments and devices for analysis. Yet once a researcher is acquainted with a cultural setting s/he responds to novel circumstances by looking at phenomena 'through the eyes' of the indigenous culture (Berry *et al.*, 2002). This transition involves modifying concepts and methods in the light of local knowledge, gained from experience in the field, perhaps in collaboration with indigenous researchers. In effect, the research

REFLECTIVE EXERCISE 14

Imagine you are planning to conduct research into the nature and quality of healthy parent–toddler attachments in different cultures, using an *emic* approach. Outline how you might design your research.

adapts to the new cultural circumstance, arguably becoming less ethnocentric into the bargain. This strategy enables the researcher to dodge the ethnocentric trap of imposing concepts and methods from the researcher's own cultural setting into the cross-cultural field of study – an imposition known as the **imposed etic**.

Berry (1989) sets out three steps that guide the global researcher from an initial, imposed etic phase to a more responsive form of cross-cultural engagement, as shown in the key concept overleaf. He sets out a strategy that derives at least some of its impetus from the culture being studied.

A large-scale study by a team of Israeli researchers illustrates the shift towards a less ethnocentric, more derived etic approach.

Is power a guiding principle in your life?

Schwartz (1992) wanted to know if values such as 'power', 'hedonism' and 'conformity' are highly prized by people across a diversity of cultural backgrounds. He gave participants from 25 countries questionnaires featuring questions such as 'Is power a guiding principle in your life?' Instead of making up his own list of values and importing them into the research field, Schwartz culled the 56 values they tested from sources across the various cultural settings where the research took place. Also his sample, being drawn from students and secondary schoolteachers, was well used to the questionnaire method of collecting data. By using concepts that were drawn up after consulting with local knowledge, as well as methods that were familiar to the sample, this researcher was nicely placed to consider how many of these values were shared from culture to culture. For the record, he did find a high level of across-culture consistency in many of the values.

The etic–emic distinction highlights differing approaches to global research. More specifically, the journey from imposed to derived etic is designed to right an ethnocentric wrong that often sees concepts and methods shipped, wholesale, into the research field. Yet while adapting concepts and methods to new cultural settings is a useful strategy for reducing ethnocentrism, the etic–emic model does have its limitations.

> **KEY TERM**
>
> **Imposed etic.** Imposing concepts and methods from the researcher's own cultural setting into the cross-cultural field of study.

KEY CONCEPT

Three steps from imposed etic to derived etic

STEP 1. The imposed etic

The global researcher adopts a 'transport and test' approach to investigating behaviour across cultures. Theories, concepts and methods used for investigation are imported from Culture A into Culture B. For example, in researching 'intelligence', definitions of what this is and how it is measured are imported from Culture A and used, unchanged, to test participants in Culture B.

STEP 2. From the etic to the emic

Knowledge and experience gained in the field are used to adapt imported theories, concepts and methods to cultural circumstances. Efforts are made to ensure that the concepts being studied have equivalent meaning and function in Cultures A and B. Also, the researcher tries to ensure that the methods used in the study make sense in both cultural settings. For example, it is noted that definitions of 'intelligent behaviour' vary from one place to another. In Culture A it may refer to cognitive agility while in Culture B it may also include interpersonal awareness. An extended stay in the field helps to produce an understanding of local definitions and the development of intelligence tests that are familiar and user-friendly for local participants.

STEP 3. The derived etic

The researcher selects 'shared concepts' from Cultures A and B with the intention of drawing conclusions about universal human behaviour and experience. These can then be applied more globally. For example, aspects of intelligence that are shared or comparable in Cultures A and B are identified. This might aid the development of a universal concept of intelligence, derived from the influence of both cultures, rather than simply being imposed by one culture onto another. This concept of intelligence might then be used and further adapted elsewhere.

Limitations of the etic–emic model

1 *Derived etics are hard to establish*. Finding concepts and methods with equivalent meaning and function across cultural settings is not

always a realistic option. Unearthing concepts (such as *intelligence* or *schizophrenia*) that are robust enough to translate across diverse meaning systems often proves elusive.

2 *Even derived etics are too standardised.* While deriving concepts and methods in part from the cultural groups being studied does show a desire to reduce ethnocentrism, ultimately the aim of the 'derived etic' is to produce a standardised concept or test that is then applicable across various cultures. For example, a definition of intelligence might be derived, following research in various locations, which can then be tested elsewhere. Arguably though, the establishment of standardised, quantifiable phenomena, however 'culture-fair', should not be the aim of global research. Instead, more interpretive, qualitative, non-standardised methods for analysing behaviour in unique cultural contexts should take precedence (Berry *et al.*, 2002).

3 *Derived etics still begin life as imposed etics.* Modifying original concepts and methods to the nuances of different cultures may be admirable, yet the process still originates with research questions that began life elsewhere. Rather than trying to make an originally imposed research question equally meaningful for different cultural groups, perhaps the best way to rid global psychology of culture bias would be to begin the research process by formulating research questions from diverse cultural settings. Such an approach prompts an examination of the indigenous psychology movement, where ideas for research and the methods for exploring them originate in diverse worlds.

Beyond ethnocentrism: Indigenous psychologies

Arguably global psychology's strongest defence against accusations of ethnocentrism is that psychologists from all over the world are engaged in the research process. This global network reveals diverse regional traditions in psychological research, reflecting differing cultural concerns, which are often referred to as **indigenous psychologies**. The indigenous psychology movement illustrates the idea that psychology should reflect the realities and preoccupations of diverse cultures. Indeed, it has been argued that indigenous psychologies in India, Japan, Latin America and other regions represent an explicit revolt against North American dominance of the field (Pawlik & Rosenzweig, 2000; Allwood, 2005). Practitioners in developing countries have lamented mainstream psychology's apparent indifference to the psychological consequences of phenomena that are especially pertinent to

KEY TERM

Indigenous
psychologies.
Diverse regional
traditions in
psychological
research, reflecting
differing cultural
concerns.

less affluent countries (poverty, illiteracy, civil war), and their ignorance of non-western philosophical traditions (Confucianism, Buddhism). Markus and Kitayama's (2003, p. 280) sentiments illustrate this critique:

> Psychology as we knew it . . . appeared to be the indigenous psychology of America or perhaps, more specifically, the psychology of middle-class Anglo-America.

According to this view US research reflects US concerns, just as Ugandan research reflects Ugandan concerns, Australian Australian and so on. The problem with this scenario is that while each of these indigenous psychologies may represent distinct traditions, they don't all have equal influence worldwide. We have already seen that a disproportionate amount of resources and research emanates from the US, whose citizens' behaviour and experiences are therefore more widely documented than are those of others. This imbalance exacerbates the need for us to explore a wider range of indigenous traditions in psychology.

Indigenous psychology in the developing world

Indigenous researchers provide pictures from around the globe, painted by practitioners who have variously chosen to study human development in Cameroon (Nsamenang, 1992), psychopathology in New Guinea (Schieffelin, 1985), self-esteem in Brazil (Lane & Sawaia, 1991). Indigenous psychology is more established and autonomous in some nations than in others. India is acknowledged to have the longest established research tradition among all developing nations, its first psychology laboratory having opened at the University of Calcutta in 1915. Sub-Saharan Africa was a later starter. The University of Nigeria opened the doors of the region's first psychology department in 1963.

In many countries psychology was initially introduced by outsiders, though indigenous interests and specialisations later emerged. Pakistan and Bangladesh are examples of this. Though psychology arrived in the region with British colonialists in the first half of the twentieth century, 'home-grown' research interests have since followed distinctive paths. Bangladeshi researchers have investigated motivational issues surrounding agricultural development. Psychology in Pakistan has developed an interest in gender studies (Shouksmith, 1996). In the Middle East, though the overall impact of psychology isn't extensive, it has spurned an interest in special education. India meantime has seen a growth in applied clinical psychology in its urban centres, as a corollary of increasing numbers of professional psychologists across the country (Shouksmith, 1996). Within the indigenous psychology movement, adopted research questions tend to relate closely to cultural circumstances and political realities. So in Bangladesh in the 1960s, since rural development was a pressing concern, no wonder psychologists were involved in studying motivational aspects of agricultural practice. In Thailand in the 1950s, where the development of educational programmes was especially high on the agenda, it is hardly surprising that psychologists ploughed their energies into the applied researching of child development (Shouksmith, 1996). In Costa Rica in the 1980s, where neighbouring El Salvador and Nicaragua were living through revolutionary upheavals, war and its psychological effects were a high priority (Dobles Oropeza, 2000).

Psychology is a relatively young phenomenon in many developing countries, yet we can see a growth in indigenous research interests. Such indigenisation in response to local circumstances is a recurring theme in the indigenous psychology movement (Sinha, 1997). Enriquez (1993) argues that the indigenisation process can be instigated from either 'without' or 'within'. In the former, research questions and methods are imported into a region by outsider researchers before being modified in response to local concerns (a process reminiscent of the one described in the key concept on p. 70). Indigenisation from within involves the formulation of unique research questions in response to a cultural group's norms, priorities and everyday realities. Chinese research into behavioural aspects of Confucianism's teachings (perseverance, thrift) is an example of this (Chinese Culture Connection, 1987). Indigenisation from within follows guidelines set out by Yang (2000), which are designed for anyone who is thinking of practising indigenous psychology (see Figure 4.3). Table 4.1 outlines indigenous psychologies from India, New Zealand and El Salvador.

---

1 Be indigenous to the culture being studied.
2 Allow the research question to emerge gradually from the context in which the research takes place.
3 When selecting topics for investigation, prioritise culturally unique phenomena.
4 Reject research questions and methods that have been imported from outside.

Figure 4.3 Tips for budding indigenous psychologists

TABLE 4.1
Indigenous psychologies from around the world

Psychology in India (Jain, 2005)	Calcutta University established India's first psychology department in 1915. Before India's independence in 1947 research interests mirrored those of British universities, as indigenous concepts (ayurvedic medicine, yoga) were subsumed under western scientific paradigms. Post-1947 this situation was tempered, though psychology continued as a largely 'Anglo-American' enterprise (Sinha, 1997). More recently, though the scientific paradigm continues to thrive, variables selected for research are increasingly selected indigenously and reflect burning Indian issues, such as • inter-group tensions • caste • prejudice • stereotyping. There has been a growth of research into a range of internationally recognised and indigenous fields, from social and forensic psychology to traditional Indian and cross-cultural issues. Courtesy of indigenisation, western scientific techniques rub shoulders with yogic and Hindu systems of thought. For example, cognitive behavioural therapy and meditation are combined in the treatment of depression.
Psychology in New Zealand (Shouksmith, 2005)	The 1840 *Treaty of Waitangi* confirmed New Zealand as a British colony and the western scientific tradition held sway over indigenous (predominantly oral) Maori thought for many decades thereafter. Colonial administrations successively suppressed Maori culture until indigenous activism heralded increased recognition of the rights of their communities in the late twentieth century. In psychology these social changes now manifest themselves in an increasingly indigenised outlook. The *community psychology* movement encapsulates this. Its advocates reject the idea that a western paradigm can uncover objective truths with rigorous scientific research. Instead, community psychology *promotes a socially constructed and locally instigated research agenda that is shaped by unique histories and culturally endorsed beliefs.* Special research interests for community psychology include: • self-determination among minority groups • minority influence • multicultural integration • ethnocentrism in non-Maori psychometric tests. Community psychology is practised in numerous universities (beginning with the University of Waikato) alongside more globally mainstream, western approaches.
Psychology in El Salvador (Martin-Baró, 1994)	Throughout the twentieth century El Salvador was racked by revolt, authoritarianism and inequality. Continual mismanagement of elections prompted violent demonstrations from opposition groups, and the 1970s saw a descent into civil war. Prominent thinkers of the time eked out an indigenous tradition in psychology whose goal was consciousness-raising among the poor and oppressed, and their ultimate liberation (Freire, 1971). The so-called *Liberation Psychology* movement in El Salvador, pioneered by Ignacio Martin-Baró (1996), was a *movement that aimed to tie the the study of behaviour to the relief of oppression.* Martin-Baró argued that laboratory-based objectivity denied local practitioners the chance to take a partial stand against oppression and inequality – the pressing concerns of Latin Americans. Liberation psychologists were, he urged, duty-bound to alter and improve human experience, not just study it. Furthermore, psychology should strive to take the viewpoint of the oppressed. The research agenda for a Liberation Psychology therefore eschewed the 'inner workings of the mind' in favour of • urban overcrowding • domestic violence • social deprivation. Though outside the mainstream of Latin American psychology, Liberation Psychology has had a key influence on the continued indigenisation of the subject.

Of course, the questions that indigenous psychologists investigate are not necessarily only of interest within their own cultures. Increasingly, global psychology is recognising that questions that are first posed in diverse locations often turn out to be relevant and applicable more widely. For example, Chinese research findings about the beneficial effects of calligraphy have been applied in the treatment of children with attention deficit disorders elsewhere (Kao et al., 1997). It seems that psychology's 'first world' does not have a monopoly on the export of psychological concepts.

Indigenous methods

The distinctiveness of indigenous psychology goes beyond simply devising questions that have particular relevance. It extends to finding regionally relevant methods for investigating these questions. For example, a characteristically European methodological preference for naturalistic, qualitative data collection emerged out of the social representation approach to psychology (Moscovici, 1976). Though not used by all European psychologists, such methods are more common there than, say, in the US. The approach stresses the importance of communally shared aspects of identity, and often translates into research that asks how we define ourselves as members of some groups and not others (Catholics or Protestants, male or female). So there is less interest here in studying human beings as individual units. Instead, the relationships between people are high on the research agenda. This difference in emphasis has spawned a European indigenous methodological preference for contextualised (naturalistic), interview-based research, rather than quasi-experimental methods using artificial scenarios and high levels of control (Smith et al., 2006).

Indigenous psychology can complement the mainstream

While indigenous psychologies are often seen as a challenge to mainstream cross-cultural psychology (see Chapter 1), the two approaches may be more compatible than they appear at a glance. Diverse traditions from across the globe can complement the work of mainstream psychologists who try to uncover culturally universal phenomena (Allwood, 2005). True, research that is instigated by researchers who are indigenous to the cultural group under investigation is naturally sensitive to local values and preoccupations. But this approach may also benefit from the unique perspective of outsiders who are furnished with experience gained in the wider international research community.

Outsider contributions might include methodological expertise gained from working in different settings, as well as the ability to compare findings and variables with those gained elsewhere. Very often this kind of outsider knowledge is provided by so-called *bicultural* researchers: practitioners who are indigenous to the region, but who trained elsewhere before returning home to practise (Stevens & Gielen, 2007).

Indigenous and cross-cultural psychologists can form mutually beneficial partnerships that draw on the unique contributions of insiders and outsiders. Cross-cultural outsiders can offer a degree of objectivity that is encapsulated in their third-person accounts as they test their theories in 'other cultures'. Insiders provide local knowledge and first-person accounts that afford the people they study a degree of meaningful involvement and human agency. They literally become active participants (not subjects) in research, with influence over what is to be studied. This combination of third-person objectivity and first-person insight arguably adds scientific rigour to the enterprise of global psychology (Stevens & Gielen, 2007): rigour that would probably elude cross-cultural psychologists and indigenous psychologists who work exclusively of one another.

REFLECTIVE EXERCISE 15

1. Suggest a difference between a *cross-cultural* researcher and a *bicultural* researcher.

2. As a global psychologist you are developing topics for study that draw less on imported theories and methods and more on those that are relevant to your own cultural setting. Which of these words most accurately describes the process you are conducting?
   a. Reverse ethnocentrism
   b. Indigenisation
   c. Eticisation

Limitations of the indigenous psychology movement

1 *Global inequality.* Visions of a level global playing field on which psychological researchers in the developing world challenge the power imbalance between them and the west are destined to

be clouded by wider issues of economic inequality. Funding for worldwide research facilities and peer-reviewed journals is sparse in regions with weak economies (Adair, 1995). Consequently, researchers from these regions can find themselves working in unequal collaborations with western researchers who command greater influence over the project's direction (Allwood, 2005).

2 *Reverse ethnocentrism.* Sometimes what may appear to be an indigenous psychological concept (meaningful only in the value system of a particular cultural group) turns out to be universal after all. For example, Cheung *et al.*'s (2003) *interpersonal relatedness* personality dimension, originally posited as being indigenous to China, later showed a degree of validity with US participants (Smith *et al.*, 2006). Similarly, the characteristically Japanese concept of *amae* (Doi, 1973), which relates to social situations where someone agrees to perform a rather demanding favour for a close friend, has also been observed in US and Taiwanese samples (Yamaguchi, 2004). Arguably, 'pigeonholing' (seemingly) indigenous concepts in global psychology may lead to a kind of reverse ethnocentrism (Stevens & Gielen, 2007), where such concepts are wrongly seen as being exclusive to particular regions.

3 *The danger of fragmentation.* While indigenous psychologies are invaluable in the struggle against a one-dimensional, western-dominated psychology, a proliferation of uniquely formulated psychologies with separate, local concerns is also undesirable (Poortinga, 1989). A fragmented universe of indigenous traditions would transform global psychology into a multiplicity of incoherent searches for diversity and difference. Arguably then, the contributions of indigenous traditions should be used to complement the work of those who concentrate on a more objective search for cultural universals.

So, is psychology ethnocentric?

There is no short, snappy answer. We can, though, propose some informed conclusions in the light of what has emerged from these pages. Broadly speaking, in terms of the global disproportion of psychology's publishing and personnel, we do seem to have an ethnocentric science on our hands. If we consider 'etically' oriented research as representing the mainstream of cross-cultural psychology, a similar conclusion emerges. Yet if we toss emic research orientations and indigenous traditions into the mix, psychology doesn't seem too ethnocentric after all.

Figure 4.4 summarises the evidence from this chapter to help you arrive at a balanced judgement about the level of culture bias in psychology. Ultimately, if you really want to know the answer to the question, scan the evidence and decide for yourself.

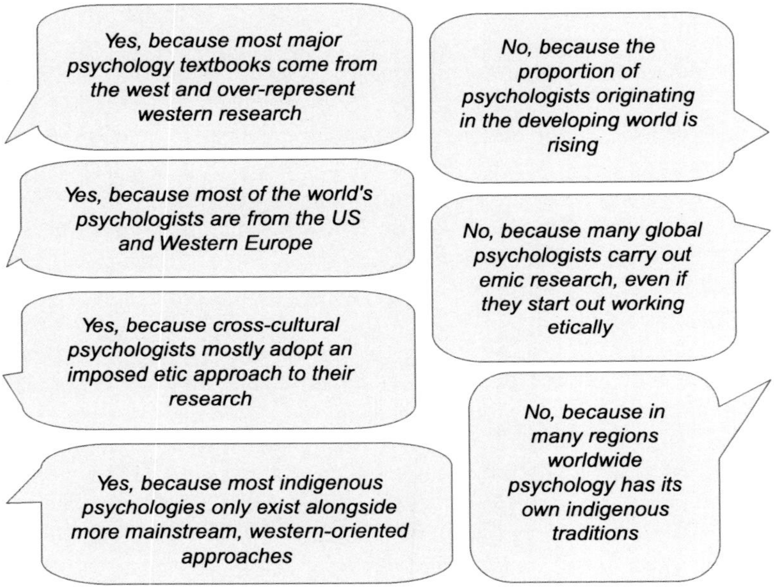

Yes, because most major psychology textbooks come from the west and over-represent western research

No, because the proportion of psychologists originating in the developing world is rising

Yes, because most of the world's psychologists are from the US and Western Europe

No, because many global psychologists carry out emic research, even if they start out working etically

Yes, because cross-cultural psychologists mostly adopt an imposed etic approach to their research

No, because in many regions worldwide psychology has its own indigenous traditions

Yes, because most indigenous psychologies only exist alongside more mainstream, western-oriented approaches

Figure 4.4 Is psychology ethnocentric? Yes and no

Summary

Chapter 4 tackles ethnocentrism – also known as 'culture bias' – in psychology. Claims that the science of human behaviour has long been restricted by a bias towards theories, research methods and publishing interests that are centred in Europe and North America are reviewed and debated. The proliferation of psychology publishing in selected global locations is examined. Global distribution of psychological practitioners is also examined. Are there really more psychiatrists in Argentina than anywhere else?

Perhaps more importantly, degrees of ethnocentrism in psychological research traditions also come in for scrutiny. Distinctions between 'etic' and 'emic' research are identified and explored; the latter is widely seen as an attempt to challenge alleged ethnocentric tendencies of the 'imposed etic', sometimes seen as characteristic of mainstream cross-cultural psychology.

We explore the seldom publicised (in mainstream European texts at least) development of indigenous psychology. Research traditions from Asia, Australasia and the Americas are reviewed as an alternative to the dominance of Euro-American global psychology. Having sifted the evidence, there is an attempt to arrive at an answer to our starting question – is psychology ethnocentric?

REFLECTIVE EXERCISE 16

Match up the definitions on the right with the terms on the left (see p. 224 for answers)

Taking results from a restricted sample of participants and mistakenly applying them to the population as a whole

Selected geographical and cultural locations, mostly concentrated in North America

Emic research

Imposing concepts and methods from the researcher's own cultural setting into the cross-cultural field of study

Sampling error

Ethnocentrism

Research which aims to highlight distinctiveness of human behaviour and experience as it manifests itself in different cultural settings

Etic research

Diverse regional traditions in psychological research, reflecting differing cultural concerns

Indigenisation

Seeing other cultural groups solely from the point of view of one's own culture

Psychology's first world

Growth in indigenous research interests

Imposed etic

Indigenous psychologies

Research which aims to highlight universals of human behaviour and experience

---

FURTHER READING

- Berry, J. (1989) Imposed etics-emics-derived etics: the operationalisation of a compelling idea, *International Journal of Psychology*, 24, 721–735.
- Moghaddam, F. (1987) Psychology in three worlds, *American Psychologist*, 42 (10), 919–920.
- Stevens, M. & Gielen, U. (eds.) (2007) *Towards a Global Psychology*, London: Lawrence Erlbaum Associates.

Challenging cross-culturalism

Alternative paradigms in global psychology

5

What this chapter will teach you

- What is **cultural psychology**?
- Are culture and mind really so distinct?
- What is ecological validity?
- What is situated research?
- What is **critical psychology**?
- Is psychological research a political act?
- Is psychology value-free?

Challenging cross-culturalism

Chapter 1 introduced the dominant approach in the field of global psychology – cross-cultural psychology. Since one aim of Part 1 of this book is to discuss controversies in global psychology, it seems fitting to conclude it by considering some ideas that challenge the received wisdom of cross-culturalism. In global psychology, as in the discipline as a

KEY TERM

Paradigm. View about the discipline's proper subject matter and the best method for studying it.

whole (where behaviourists, humanists and psychoanalysts disagree in perpetuity), not everyone subscribes to the same **paradigm**. In other words, there is more than one view about the discipline's proper subject matter and the best method for studying it. All of which spawns continual epistemological and methodological debates. True, cross-cultural psychology has a coherent position in these debates and many are in agreement with them (see Chapter 1). Yet there are those who dissent.

This chapter is devoted to the views of these dissenters. It provides a space for their critiques, and for some alternative, perhaps complementary, views about how global psychology should be conducted.

Cultural psychology: Global research in naturalistic settings

> Cross-cultural psychology and cultural psychology are elements of global psychology.
>
> (Stevens & Gielen, 2007, p. 9)

Imagine yourself in a room full of global psychologists. Let's say you ask them to form a line, with all those who prefer to carry out etically oriented research (see Chapter 4) to your left and all those who favour emically oriented research to your right. After some jockeying for positions you will soon see mostly cross-cultural psychologists gathering leftwards, while the right-hand end of the line will be populated by advocates of **cultural psychology**. Cultural psychology has been called the heretical alternative to the cross-cultural approach (Shweder, 1991). It is a paradigm in global psychology which challenges the consensus that research should focus on culturally universal behaviour and experience. Indeed, for cultural psychology, the existence of underlying psychic structures that all humans share (*psychic unity*, see Chapter 1) is rejected. Advocates of this approach assert that the human mind is inseparable from the cultural settings we inhabit, and is therefore not a discrete entity at all (see Figure 5.1). Rather, the mind is only brought into being by our involvement in external, cultural worlds (Geertz, 1973). It is inseparable from culture. It follows then that for the cultural psychologists who have congregated to your right, global psychology's subject matter is *how the human mind manifests itself differently in different cultures*.

KEY TERM

Cultural psychology. A paradigm in global psychology that challenges the consensus that research should focus on culturally universal behaviour and experience.

REFLECTIVE EXERCISE 17

1. Can you suggest one difference between a *cultural* and a *cross-cultural* psychology?

2. How do we distinguish between different *paradigms* in psychology?

A key idea in cultural psychology is its portrayal of the relationship between cultures and minds, which are seen as inseparable (Cole, 1998; Shweder, 1991). Culture and mind are regarded as a theoretical double act whose two elements give meaning and coherence to one another. In other words, they are mutually constitutive (Matsumoto & Juang, 2004). To grasp this inseparability, consider a definition of culture that dovetails with the cultural psychology paradigm:

> **Culture is a system of meanings (attached to objects, events and institutions) shared by a distinct social group**.

> (Rohner, 1984)

According to this definition, culture amounts to our shared beliefs and attitudes about whatever takes place around us – not the events themselves. Defined like this, aspects of culture (church, art, family, crime) are not objectively existing realities. They only exist courtesy of our interpretations of them, the meanings we attach to them. You could say that we *think them into being* (Shweder, 1991). According to this constructivist view, we don't simply observe events around us; we actively interpret them. Indeed, in cultural psychology there is no such thing as a neutral, objective observation of events. The external world is inseparable from our mind's representation of it (Shweder, 1991). The role of the cultural psychologist is to investigate how different cultural groups attach diverse meanings to events in their worlds. They aim to study the meanings attached to events, not the events themselves. To do so they attempt to enter the indigenous mindset of cultural groups to see how they make sense of what happens around them. This approach to global psychology requires psychologists to investigate not the human mind in isolation, nor human cultures in isolation, but *cultures in the mind* (Geertz, 1973).

Figure 5.1 Cultures in the mind: culture and mind are inseparable

The human mind in everyday life

The roots of cultural psychology lie in the work of those who, in the mid-twentieth century, urged psychology as a whole to abandon the controlled, artificial environment of the laboratory and instead study behaviour in everyday settings. Kurt Lewin (1936) and Egon Brunswik (1943) lobbied for a methodological shift from the controlled experiment towards more naturalistic research, as well as a theoretical shift in psychology's self-image. They urged the discipline to see itself as the study not of the human mind or internal psyche, but of the relationship between people and their multiple (physical and social) environments – their *ecologies* (Cole, 1998). This approach, known as **ecological psychology**, urged psychologists to concentrate on how people operate in the context of their everyday lives, rather than on their inner psychological processes. As Brunswik (1943, p. 263) himself put it, a truly ecological psychology should analyse situations that are

> carefully drawn from the universe of the requirements a person happens to face in his commerce with the physical and social environments.

Brunswik's dissatisfaction with mainstream psychology stemmed from what he saw as the narrow applicability of its experimental findings.

KEY TERM

Ecological psychology. The study of the relationship between people and their multiple (physical and social) environments.

KEY CONCEPT

Contexts for human behaviour (Brunswik, 1943)

For Brunswik the artificial *assessment context* in experimental psychology yields findings that lack *ecological validity*. This is because behaviours that are assessed experimentally represent only a fraction of the *ecological context* (behaviour as whole). Indeed, they may even lie outside the normal behavioural repertoire altogether.

Ecological context: the arena of everyday action. It originates from *experiential factors* (parenting and educational inputs that provide the basis for learning and the development of personality) and situational factors (cues in our immediate environment that influence our behaviour and decision-making)

Assessment context encompasses the testing scenarios designed by experimental psychologists to assess human behaviour

He argued that laboratory research places participants in a range of scenarios that are out of kilter with the states of affairs, persons, objects and behaviours that form everyday contexts – known as **life space** (Lewin, 1936). To illustrate this argument he distinguished between *ecological* and *assessment* contexts for human behaviour (see key concept above). Where assessment contexts are rather artificial, the degree to which research findings have relevance in the outside world is compromised. This critique suggests that psychological research as a whole often lacks **ecological validity** and should draw on behaviour from more culturally diverse, naturalistic contexts.

Naturalistic research in cultural psychology

Methodologically, cultural psychology pursues a naturalistic agenda. It is primarily concerned with studying humans *in situ* – as they operate

KEY TERMS

Life space. The states of affairs, persons, objects and behaviours that form everyday contexts.

Ecological validity. The degree to which research findings have relevance in the outside world.

naturally in diverse cultural settings. Remember, the aim is to see how the human mind reveals itself in everyday (ecologically valid) situations. It seems logical then that 'situating' research in a participant's life space is a defining methodological trait of cultural psychology. It reflects the will of the researcher to engage with participants' own representations of their worlds (Lave & Wenger, 1991). In practice this often means creating research scenarios in areas of occupational or domestic expertise (e.g. How do Liberian apprentice tailors develop arithmetical problem-solving during their 'on the job' training? (Lave, 1977)).

Besides being naturalistic, research with a cultural psychology orientation has several other defining characteristics. It tends to be qualitative, non-comparative and value-laden.

- It is *qualitative* because researchers strive for detailed understanding of how participants make sense of the persons, objects and behaviours that form their everyday contexts (life space). Participants' own meanings and interpretations are sought, so measured behavioural responses are much lower on the agenda. Large-scale quantitative testing is eschewed in favour of interview, case study and participant observational data collection methods.

- It is *non-comparative* since the meanings and value systems of those who inhabit single cultural groups are studied in depth (Stevens & Gielen, 2007). This is distinct from making cross-cultural comparisons of psychological phenomena across several cultures (Berry *et al.*, 2002). You could say that cultural psychology operates within, rather than across, cultures. This non-comparative tendency reflects the shared methodological roots of cultural psychology and cultural anthropology, wherein ethnographic methods are employed to study single cultural groups extensively and longitudinally (see key concept overleaf).

- It is *value-laden* since the beliefs and values of participants and researchers are not banished from the data. Instead, they are part and parcel of them. In short, research is interpretive rather than objective. This reflects cultural psychology's affiliation to the philosophy of **social constructivism,** which espouses the view that there is no such thing as a knowable objective truth or reality since all truth is generated in cultural contexts (Lincoln & Guba, 2000). In other words, all knowledge is seen as reflecting partial values and diverse meanings.

KEY TERM

Social constructivism. The view that there is no such thing as a knowable objective truth or reality since all truth is generated in cultural contexts.

KEY CONCEPT

Ethnography: research method and long-term commitment

Ethnography is *a method for collecting data for descriptive purposes, focusing on a particular culture or setting.* The term was coined by the linguist August Ludwig Schlözer (1777) and the method was subsequently adopted by cultural anthropologists. Global psychologists have adapted the ethnographic method and claim their own distinct fieldwork tradition (Munroe & Munroe, 1986). Yet whichever field the researcher comes from, doing ethnography effectively is a considerable personal commitment since it involves leaving behind the comfort and security of one's own cultural circumstances.

> The fieldworker as sojourner experiences acculturation, and may also experience acculturative stress in which self-doubt, loss of motivation, depression and other problems may become great enough to hinder the work.
>
> (Berry *et al.*, 2002, p. 234)

For the anthropologist Sir Raymond Firth, ethnographic research

> attempts to understand, by close and direct contact, how a living community works and what the beliefs, norms and values by which it lives are.
>
> (Firth, 1972, p. 10)

Yet often global psychologists are less concerned with understanding entire living communities. They tend to use fieldwork as a means of gathering data about how a selected issue or variable figures in the lives of a community. Psychological research questions posed by ethnographic work include the following.

- *Do distinct styles of remembering predominate among the Swazi of East Africa?* (Bartlett, 1932)
- *Do differences in cognitive style affect the problem-solving performance of Central African indigenous groups?* (van de Koppel, 1983)
- *How does communal childrearing among the Central African Efe reflect the norms of that cultural group?* (Tronick & Morelli, 1992)

Doing ethnography involves *actively observing and taking part in the behaviours and experiences that are being studied.* Fieldwork, in short, is *participant observation.* Ideally, behaviours and experiences that are studied by ethnographers barely depart from the way people routinely act and feel (Banister *et al.*, 1997). As participants in the social transactions acted out with and around them, ethnographers don't just observe life objectively. They interpret it with subjectivity. Indeed, *the ethnographic art of writing accounts of research that combine participation, reportage and interpretation* has been termed *thick description* (Geertz, 1973).

Researchers who opt for the ethnographic method face several practical questions. For example, the fieldworker must decide how embedded s/he wants (or is able) to become. Though involvement is central, over-involvement may lead to a situation in which the behaviours being studied 'become soon so familiar they escape notice' (Malinowski, cited in Stocking, 1983, p. 100). Here are a few more of the pressing questions faced by ethnographers in the field.

Questions of proximity
Unlike researchers who use other methods, ethnographers surrender the opportunity of retreating from the research scenario after a long day. Individual researchers must decide about their preferred degree of spatial segregation. Too little can be a personal strain; too much may yield superficial data.

Questions of collaboration
Ethnographers constantly re-examine their relationships with representatives from the groups they are studying. They need to ask themselves *who stands to benefit from this project*? For emically oriented cultural psychologists, indigenous groups are involved in advising ethnographers on data collection methods and in devising research questions.

Questions of ethics
- *Deception.* It has been known for fieldworkers to gain entry into cultural groups for study purposes without fully divulging their aims. In one notorious example, allegations of deception were levelled at Napoleon Chagnon's work with the Brazilian Yanomamo (Tierney, 2001). He is accused of covertly precipitating a measles epidemic in order to test his theory about the Yanomamo's unique genetic resistance to the disease.
- *Debriefing.* Doing ethnography may be conditional on host populations receiving reports on the findings. This may compromise the content of such reports. This again relates to the question of who the project is supposed to benefit in the first place, and is less of an issue for the truly emically oriented researcher.

- *Ethical codes*. All psychological researchers tend to follow a preset code of conduct, laid down by their professional body. Interestingly, though, in the case of ethnography, since the idea is to gain entry into the beliefs, norms and value systems of another cultural group, the researcher may question the desirability of sticking to moral codes brought in from outside.

Fieldwork is a combination of methods (observing, interviewing, experimenting, surveying) which yields *an ongoing record of observations, events and conversations*. The resulting *fieldnotes* typically include three broad varieties of recorded data (Munroe & Munroe, 1986).

- *Census data* involve building a demographic profile of the region or group being studied. They include details about the number of households, first languages spoken and occupations.
- *Context data* are more interpretive, less factual. They reveal the local meanings of a culture, its manners, norms, the characteristics of its key institutions. They may include insider knowledge about gender roles, kinship practices and social taboos.
- *Variable-related data* are the most focused of the data types. They relate directly to the variable that is the subject matter for the study.

There are, however, relatively few classic ethnographies to grace the archives of global psychology. This reminds us that the method itself remains more anthropological than psychological. Even so, for those who are keen to explore the terrain between the two disciplines, Banister *et al.* (1997) argue that the ethnographies can uniquely contribute to our understanding of living cultures, as seen through the eyes of an active participant.

The following quote from Denzin and Lincoln (2000, p. 8) illustrates the compatibility between cultural psychology and qualitative, value-laden research methods.

The word qualitative implies an emphasis on . . . processes and meanings that are not experimentally examined or measured in terms of quantity. Qualitative researchers stress the socially constructed nature of reality . . . and the situational constraints that shape inquiry. Such researchers emphasise the value-laden nature of inquiry. They seek answers to questions that stress how social experience is created and given meaning.

Research modelled on everyday practice

When collecting naturalistic, qualitative data, researchers are effectively 'out of control'. In other words, they relinquish overall control of their research. Studies arise from the everyday activities of participants, not the researcher's theoretical interests or data collection preferences (Cole, 1998). They are moulded to the immediate environment of the participants, very much in the emic tradition (Stevens & Gielen, 2007). For example, if you are investigating problem-solving among waitresses in a short-order restaurant, you aim to situate your research in the waitresses' life space (Stevens, 1990). In short, you take your research to the restaurant rather than lifting the participants out of context and into a laboratory. Here are some more research questions that have been tackled in the situated style of the cultural psychologist.

- Are traditional Papuan body-counting techniques threatened by technological developments in the local economy? (Saxe, 1982)
- Do the everyday mathematical abilities of Brazilian coconut vendors enhance school performance? (Carraher *et al.*, 1985)
- Can culture-bound syndromes only be understood within the meaning systems of host cultures? (Ritenbaugh, 1986)

Methodologically, situated research can take a variety of emically oriented forms. Methods enabling the researcher to embed themselves in the life space of the people being studied are the instruments of choice for the cultural psychologist. They favour qualitative methods that barely disturb the life space and tune in to participants' interpretations of their world. Favoured options include ethnographies (see key concept), open-ended interviews and longitudinal case studies.

Another innovative research method associated with cultural psychology is the **located experiment** (Cole, 1998; Lave, 1977). This is an experimental method in which research questions and testing procedures are modelled on participants' everyday practices. This is an emic manifestation of the mainstream psychology experiment. Located experiments feature psychological testing, analyses of performance on prescribed tasks – all the trappings of mainstream experimental research, yet with the key difference that they are derived following efforts to understand the everyday practice of the participants. They are designed with local knowledge about the attitudes, abilities and beliefs of participants about their own universe. As participants are studied *in situ*, the researcher can claim to be investigating the mind in its everyday context (a central philosophical tenet of cultural

KEY TERM

Located experiment. An experimental method in which research questions and testing procedures are modelled on participants' everyday practices.

psychology, remember). The following example displays the theoretical and methodological principles that typify located experiments.

Do we learn to communicate by writing letters?

> Scribner and Cole (1981) studied the acquisition of literacy among children from the Liberian Vai culture. They distinguished between school literacy and Vai literacy, which has its own written form and is largely acquired outside school. Combining experimental and ethnographic methods Scribner and Cole compared the role of these two systems of literacy in hastening cognitive development. They modelled their research on key aspects of everyday Vai life, such as letter writing, which is central to daily Vai communication. In one scenario a popular Vai board game was used to test the effectiveness of Vai literacy in aiding communication and problem-solving. Participants who were Vai-literate – and those who were not – had to learn the game's rules, then explain them to someone else, either face to face or by letter. Vai literates fared especially well on this task. Scribner and Cole ascribed this partly to the way the practice of letter writing had prepared them for communicating difficult ideas.

Research with a cultural psychology orientation demands to be seen in the contexts inhabited by participants. As an approach to research it is grounded in everyday practice, so no two research designs are the same. This is a far cry from the cross-cultural idea of replicating pre-designed studies to test established theories in numerous cultural settings. Yet it has been argued that cultural psychology and cross-cultural psychology can form a complementary axis for researching global psychology (Berry *et al.*, 2002). In this ideal case an emic, qualitative approach would coexist with an etic, quantitative orientation. Others have downplayed the contribution of cultural psychology, stressing instead its limitations.

Limitations of cultural psychology

1 *Unhelpful relativism.* Perhaps the most common criticism of cultural psychology highlights the relativism that forms its basis. Since this is a paradigm that strives towards a detailed understanding of the meanings of events within particular cultures, little hope is offered for establishing culturally universal knowledge about human behaviour and experience. Rather, a series of seemingly disparate

culturally relative findings will inevitably emerge. From a cross-cultural,
universalist viewpoint, all of this
undermines the gathering of data
that can be generalised or compared
across cultural groups (Berry *et al.*,
2002).

2 *Interpretive validity*. Cultural psychology's roots in ecological psychology bolster its claims to a level of
ecological validity that cannot
necessarily be matched by cross-
cultural research. However, questions remain about the paradigm's
interpretive validity (Greenfield,
1997). In other words, since the sub-
jective meanings of researchers are acknowledged as part and parcel of the data, assurances as to their verifiability cannot be given.
After all, a constructivist approach does not allow for the acknowledgement of data as verifiably true. Nevertheless, in such circumstances the cross-checking of researchers' interpretations (with
each other and with participants who have contributed to the study)
can improve interpretive validity (Lincoln & Guba, 2000).

3 *Gaining entry*. Research undertaken from the cultural psychology
orientation aspires to being devised in the light of local knowledge.
To become well-informed a researcher might consult secondary
sources (books and other resources that have already been written)
about a cultural group, carry out preliminary ethnographies, or consult with representatives of the participant group. Yet however
meticulous their groundwork, there is no guarantee that it will bear
fruit and provide reliable grounds for claiming entry into a community. After all, secondary sources may be unreliable and collabor-
ators may be unrepresentative of their group.

> **REFLECTIVE EXERCISE 18**
>
> 1. How do ethnographies differ from located experiments?
>
> 2. Cultural psychologists regard the values and beliefs of participants and researchers as part of the data that emerge from the studies they conduct. Which of these terms *cannot* be used to describe this approach?
>   a. Interpretive
>   b. Constructivist
>   c. Objective

Critical psychology: Global research for action

Besides cultural psychology, a second challenge to the cross-cultural
mainstream in global psychology comes from **critical psychology**. If
cultural psychology is distinct because of its ideas about the culture–
mind relationship, critical psychology distinguishes itself by its ideological stance regarding the aims and nature of psychological enquiry.
It can be defined as a paradigm in global psychology that conducts

KEY TERM

Critical psychology. Paradigm in global psychology that conducts goal-directed research with the aim of transforming situations of oppression.

goal-directed research with the aim of transforming situations of oppression.

For critical psychology, research is a political act, a stepping stone towards the transformation of oppressive situations. Critical psychology is applied rather than theoretical, since it is bent on developing evidence-based strategies for relieving suffering and liberating marginalised groups (Lincoln & Guba, 2000). Historically, critical psychology gained momentum in Latin America following the work of several pioneers (Freire, 1975; Fals Borda, 1988; Martin-Baró, 1994 (see Figure 5.2)) who conducted research amid military conflicts and economic crises that racked their countries during the 1970s and 1980s (Sanchez, 1996). Across several of the world's less affluent regions, critical psychologists have contributed to programmes for developing building projects for low-income groups, resettling victims of urban renewal and tackling violent crime (Sanchez, 1996). You could say that the paradigm of critical psychology is borne of adversity.

An abbreviated mission

Ignacio Martin-Baró (1942–1989), Jesuit priest and psychologist, was a founding figure of the critical '*liberation psychology*' movement in **El Salvador**. His mission was to create a psychology which would improve the conditions of El Salvador's poor. It ended prematurely. Along with a handful of colleagues, he was murdered on the campus of Universidad de Centroamerica in 1989 by agents of the Salvadorian military government. During his abbreviated career he was as critical of the state of Latin American psychology as he was of the military regimes which successively misruled his country.

The enslavement of Latin American psychology

Latin American psychology itself, he argued, had become enslaved and powerless on three counts. First, laboratory-based research, using artificial tasks and unrepresentative samples, revealed little about the real life problems facing ordinary people. Second, in seeking to become scientific and objective, psychology had become unethical and value-less, limiting its capacity to speak out against injustice. Third, reliance on theory and methods imported from the US had stifled the development of indigenous traditions which could tackle the problems of Latin America. To escape these restrictions Martin-Baró argued that psychology should seek to transform the reality suffered by most Latin Americans. In other words it should be *transformative (changing human experience and conditions)*, not just explanatory (theorising about them).

Towards a community-based liberation psychology

Martin-Baró's (albeit interrupted) project aimed to turn Latin American psychology into an independent discipline, indigenous to the region, founded on the interests of the region's poor. Practical research projects for a liberation psychology should be directed at the tangible social problems of Latin America, he argues. They should arise out of a community's needs and be designed in their interests, rather than in those of governments, academics, big business. This represents an alternative to the theory-testing approach that arguably prevails in mainstream psychology.

Figure 5.2 Ignacio Martin-Baró, pioneer of liberation psychology

KEY CONCEPT

Conceptual cornerstones of the critical paradigm (based on Prilleltensky & Nelson, 2002)

Power is inextricably linked with the practice of doing psychological research. Relationships between researchers and participants are power-laden because, far from being disinterested observers of behaviour, researchers interpret events around them and have views and opinions about socio-political realities in the world. They may even be (unwitting) representatives of interest groups (such as governments and multinational corporations) that might use their findings to pursue their own goals. In short, psychological knowledge is power.

Well-being is regarded as a collective goal, not just an individual one. The struggle for well-being is undertaken not just by individuals – alone in the world – but in the nested context of family, community and society. It is an ecological struggle, located in the external world, not just in the mind. Psychology can effectively promote well-being by studying their economic and socio-political contexts.

Oppression arises when individuals or groups dominate other individuals or groups socio-politically or psychologically. States, multinational companies and individuals can all be agents of oppression. Oppression prevails when power is unequally distributed between individuals or groups. Its effects can be felt individually as internal psychological problems, or externally in the form of economic or political powerlessness.

Liberation occurs when power asymmetries are eradicated. Throwing off the shackles of oppression involves confronting both individual and institutional misery. Critical psychologists regard socio-political liberation as a precondition for psychological well-being. In other words, the personal and the political are complementary and interconnected spheres.

Research as a political act

Like cultural psychology, the critical approach rejects the portrayal of researchers as objective observers (Nsamenang, 2000). Instead they are seen as active participants in (and interpreters of) their subject matter. Research is carried out by people with values and ideological standpoints (Lincoln & Guba, 2000). All humans are regarded as

effective agents who have intentions and capacities to change the circumstances in which they live (Eckensberger, 1996). This human
agency casts us all in the role of goal-directed beings, not mere products of our circumstances and surroundings.

One consequence of the view that all research is necessarily value-
laden is that all data are open to abuse by various interest groups
(governments, multinational companies) with agendas of their own:
agendas which may, in some cases, be discriminatory or oppressive.
Note the US government's funding of Project Camelot in the 1960s,
with the aim of using psychological knowledge to subdue worldwide
national liberation movements (Prilleltensky & Nelson, 2002).
Instances of scientific racism (see Chapter 2) provide more examples
of the political abuses of psychological knowledge.

Research for positive change

Critical psychology is founded on the principle that the political uses of
research can also be positive. The transformative potential of psychological knowledge is the sleeping giant that motivates critical research.
Advocates of this paradigm want to awaken the rest of the discipline to
the possibilities of research as an instrument of social change (Prilleltensky & Nelson, 2002). **Transformative research** is built on four
conceptual cornerstones of the critical paradigm (see key concept on
p. 93). Instead of dwelling on people's reactions to inequality and
oppression, transformative research investigates how disadvantaged
individuals or groups can achieve social justice by bringing about
change in their material and political circumstances. Examples of
transformative research questions are:

- How can underlying prejudice and discrimination in relations
  between white Western Australians and indigenous groups be
  reduced? (Contos, cited in Drew *et al.*, 2000)
- How can poverty reduction influence the educational performance
  of disadvantaged children in India? (Sinha, 1986)
- How can conflict reduction programmes among Aboriginal
  communities in Canada increase feelings of cultural identity and
  reinforce Aboriginal values? (Connors & Maidman, 2001)

Action research

Critical psychology urges a shift in the research methods of global
psychology. The proposed and, in many regions, already developing
critical method acknowledges that well-being can only be understood

KEY TERM

**Transformative
research.** Research
that investigates how
disadvantaged
individuals or groups
can achieve social
justice by bringing
about change in their
material and political
circumstances.

by researchers who are prepared to look beyond the responses of the individual participant, towards wider community and socio-political contexts (Sloan, 1996). The critical researcher thus rejects experimental, laboratory-based methods that portray the participant as an individual who is detached from the social and societal context. Favoured methods for investigating social justice and inequality have attracted the umbrella term **action research** (Fals Borda, 1988; Sanchez, 1996). Action researchers assume the role of political activist, ideologically interpreting situations being studied, not just observing them. They conduct studies that help develop an understanding of phenomena so that practical solutions can be found to local and global problems. Action research is not designed to yield neutral knowledge. It is formulated with the active involvement of participants, to raise the consciousness of communities and wider society about the liberating potential of psychological knowledge. The hallmarks of action research are outlined in Figure 5.3 and displayed in the Brazilian study outlined below.

KEY TERM

Action research. Studies that help develop an understanding of phenomena so that practical solutions can be found to local and global problems.

What did my grandmother's grandmother do for a living?

Lane and Sawaia's (1991) study of self-esteem was conducted in a Brazilian shanty town. Female migrants from rural areas in the north of the country formed the sample. Displaced from their homeland in search of work, these women were low in confidence and low in optimism about their chances of prospering amid the economic demands of their new urban landscape. Talking with the women, researchers saw them as having internalised the stereotypes of native urban dwellers – seeing themselves as lazy, passive, unable to make it in the big city. This study aimed to reverse the trend of self-deprecation and elevate self-esteem levels. Coaching sessions were set up in which the women were encouraged to reacquaint themselves with traditional handicrafts that were indigenous to their homeland. These skills, which included doll and tablecloth making, echoed traditions inherited from their mothers and grandmothers. One effect of this stimulation of collective memory was to instil the women with a sense of pride in their heritage. It also provided income. Overall, the research project helped transform the women's self-image and sense of identity.

Critical psychology remains outside the global mainstream and, as the comments below show, does have its critics. Yet its orientation towards finding solutions in areas characterised by poverty, inequality and discrimination may mean that from its regional base in the developing world it will someday export its ideas and methods elsewhere

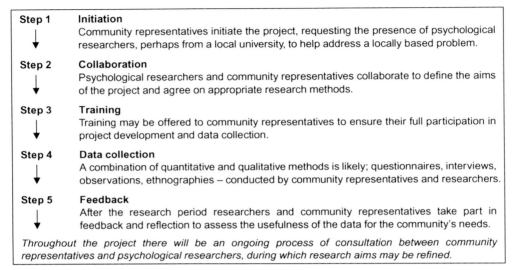

Step 1 ↓	Initiation
	Community representatives initiate the project, requesting the presence of psychological researchers, perhaps from a local university, to help address a locally based problem.
Step 2 ↓	Collaboration
	Psychological researchers and community representatives collaborate to define the aims of the project and agree on appropriate research methods.
Step 3 ↓	Training
	Training may be offered to community representatives to ensure their full participation in project development and data collection.
Step 4 ↓	Data collection
	A combination of quantitative and qualitative methods is likely; questionnaires, interviews, observations, ethnographies – conducted by community representatives and researchers.
Step 5 ↓	Feedback
	After the research period researchers and community representatives take part in feedback and reflection to assess the usefulness of the data for the community's needs.

Throughout the project there will be an ongoing process of consultation between community representatives and psychological researchers, during which research aims may be refined.

Figure 5.3 Critical global research in five steps

(Moghaddam, 1990). After all, oppression, inequality and discrimination are not exclusive to nations with undeveloped economies.

Limitations of critical psychology

1 *The cross-cultural critique.* Being essentially an applied approach, the critical paradigm is open to criticism from cross-cultural psychologists who like their psychology to be more theoretical. Indeed, a 'theory-testing' approach, wherein established theories are tested in different cultural settings under equivalent circumstances (see Chapter 1), is arguably not commensurable with the critical paradigm (Lincoln & Guba, 2000). Critical psychology, being primarily transformative, has indeed been criticised for being too practically based, too lacking in supporting theory (Dobles Oropeza, 2000). Projects are set up very much from the bottom up, as reactions to social injustice or oppression. Cross-cultural psychologists may criticise this on the grounds that established theory ought to set the agenda for research. In other words, studies should be devised at least in part in order to test theories, rather than deal with existing social problems.

2 *The global applicability problem.* Critical research gains its impetus from regions where poverty, inequality and discrimination are

endemic. It specialises in researching into power asymmetries in sites of oppression, predominantly in developing regions. This leaves it open to the accusation that it produces findings which are primarily gathered from – and applicable only to – the developing world. It is, in other words, in danger of limiting its wider applicability. Arguably then, it needs to broaden its appeal. Unless critical psychology can export its values and methods to areas such as North America (where, after all, poverty and inequality are also common) it may remain on psychology's periphery.

3 *A lack of objectivity*. Critical research is value-laden. Action researchers are unashamedly engaged with their subject matter, both politically and collaboratively. Findings cannot therefore be read as the neutral observations of researchers endeavouring to remain objective. Rather, they are ideologically charged interpretations of events. Any degree of political engagement obliges the researcher to relinquish all claims to objectivity in their work. Furthermore, collaborative engagement with community representatives obliges the critical researcher to relinquish ultimate control over the research project. All things considered, then, a high degree of ideological and collaborative engagement effectively limits the critical researcher's levels of objectivity. For those who do not empathise with the social constructivist viewpoint, this subjectivity arguably produces contaminated research data.

> ## REFLECTIVE EXERCISE 19
>
> In the context of research, 'validity' refers to the degree to which studies produce findings that convey the truth about behaviour and experience. Valid research effectively investigates what it sets out to investigate, yielding findings that are applicable to the outside world. Since the cultural and critical paradigms both regard knowledge as being open to the interpretation of researchers and participants, what strategies are available to them to increase levels of interpretive validity?

The challenge for cross-cultural psychology

The paradigms covered in this chapter offer alternatives to mainstream cross-cultural psychology. They remind us that etic-oriented research that aims to test established theories in diverse locations is not the only game in the town of global psychology.

Can these alternative paradigms be viewed complementary to cross-culturalism? This is debatable. Arguably, qualitative, ethnographic, case-specific data can usefully augment quantitative research findings from cross-cultural replications (Berry *et al.*, 2002). On the other hand,

TABLE 5.1
The paradigms of global psychology at a glance

Paradigm	Aim	Epistemology	Method
Cross-cultural psychology	To empirically test established theories about human behaviour and experience in different cultural settings	Objective knowledge is sought and approximately obtained by controlling extraneous variables and standardising research procedures across cultures	Replication research using data collection methods established according to universally applicable empirical principles
Cultural psychology	To study the human 'mind' as it manifests itself in everyday life. Since the 'mind' is a property of lived experiences, it emerges in diverse forms in diverse settings	Value-laden knowledge is sought according to locally constructed meaning systems of individual cultures	Situated experiments or ethnographies. Modelling data collection on existing practice
Critical psychology	To develop goal-oriented, locally initiated projects in different cultural settings in order to transform situations of inequality and discrimination	Knowledge is value-laden because interpretations of reality are subject to perceived inequalities and agendas of diverse interest groups	Community-instigated, goal-oriented action research
Indigenous psychology	To reflect regionally diverse traditions in psychological research, based on culturally distinct concerns	Knowledge reflects phenomena that highlight regional philosophical traditions, such as individualism, Confucianism or Buddhism	Regionally relevant methods, based on locally derived research questions

perhaps the constructivist view that all knowledge is subjective is ultimately incompatible with cross-cultural psychology's search for universal truths above and beyond interpretations of researchers (Lincoln & Guba, 2000). This debate is ongoing. For now, we can see cultural and critical psychology, as well as the indigenous psychology movement (see Chapter 4), as valuable challenges to the dominant cross-cultural paradigm in global psychology. Their presence reminds us that global psychology itself is as diverse as its subject matter. A recap of the defining characteristics of these four approaches can be found in Table 5.1.

Summary

Chapter 5 looks beyond the mainstream cross-cultural paradigm. Alternative approaches to cultural issues in psychology take centre stage here, unusually in a mainstream text. In particular, detailed descriptions and critical evaluations of both cultural psychology and critical psychology are given, with a number of research examples to illustrate these distinct approaches to the study of culture and human behaviour. For cultural psychology the emphasis is on studying mind and behaviour as inseparable from cultural context. In other words, the mind is portrayed as being fundamentally influenced – formed, even – by culture. Advocates of this perspective carry out research that emerges out of and reflects cultural diversity, rather than seeking cultural universals. Such research tends therefore to be high on ecological validity, often using the ethnographic method.

Another alternative to cross-culturalism is critical psychology. Here the emphasis is on using psychological research to help find material solutions to situations of inequality, poverty or conflict. Research is more political than theoretical. Studies on conflict resolution, child soldiers and the psychological effects of poverty typify the action research approach that is integral to critical psychology. Overall the aim of this chapter is to raise reader consciousness about varying approaches to global psychology.

REFLECTIVE EXERCISE 20

Match up the definitions on the right with the terms on the left (see p. 225 for answers)

Terms	Definitions
Action research	*Study of the relationship between people and their multiple (physical and social) environments*
Ethnography	*States of affairs, persons, objects and behaviours that form everyday contexts*
Located experiment	*Paradigm in global psychology that challenges the consensus that research should focus on culturally universal behaviour and experience*
Ecological psychology	*Experimental method in which research questions and testing procedures are modelled on participants' everyday practices*
Cultural psychology	*View about the discipline's proper subject matter and the best method for studying it*
Paradigm	*Method for collecting data for descriptive purposes, focusing on a particular culture or setting*
Life space	*Degree to which research findings have relevance in the outside world*
Ecological validity	*Ongoing record of observations, events and conversations*
Field notes	*Paradigm in global psychology that conducts goal-directed research with the aim of transforming situations of oppression*
Critical psychology	*Studies that help develop an understanding of phenomena so that practical solutions can be found to local and global problems*

FURTHER READING

- Cole, M. (2000) *Cultural Psychology*, London: Harvard University Press.
- Martin-Baró, I. (1994) *Writings for a Liberation Psychology*, Cambridge, MA: Harvard University Press.
- Prilleltensky, I. & Nelson, G. (2002) *Doing Psychology Critically*, Basingstoke, UK: Palgrave.
- Shweder, R. (1991) *Thinking through Cultures*, London: Harvard University Press.

Cultural issues

PART 2

Culture, cognition and intellect

Thinking through cultures

6

What this chapter will teach you

- How is **perception** different from **sensation**?
- How is **perceptual ability** related to cultural background?
- Are some cultural groups more susceptible to **visual illusions**?
- Do different cultural groups perceive visual art differently?
- Is **intelligence** defined differently in different parts of the world?
- Do intelligence tests measure different abilities worldwide?
- Can there be culture-fair intelligence tests?
- Is intelligence learned from cultural experience?
- Are there indigenous intelligences?
- Is there a link between culture and **cognitive style**?

KEY TERM

Perception. How we make sense of sensory information.

Does culture change the way we think?

If so, where we are from should influence our cognitive habits. The development of intellectual abilities, such as **perception** (how we make sense of sensory information) and problem-solving, should owe a great deal to the places, people and values that form our cultural backgrounds. This notion of cognition as a culturally relative phenomenon seems obvious and frankly fairly harmless at first glance. Obviously Germans think about the world differently from the way Papuans or Cubans do. But wait. Can we assume that if the German intellect is qualitatively different from, say, the Pacific intellect, it is quantitatively different too? Could it be that styles of thinking that are indigenous to Culture A are somehow better than those from Culture B? This sounds rather simplistic (even simple-minded), but a glance at Chapter 2 reminds us that psychologists have written many controversial pages down the years about the (now largely discredited) idea that quantitative intellectual differences separate people from different cultures, or with different-coloured skin.

These controversies notwithstanding, it seems reasonable to assume that while culture may affect how we think, it is equally likely that there are certain cognitive characteristics that are common to us all. In this chapter we will see that some authors emphasise cultural universals in cognition, while others stress cognitive cultural relativism. We will also learn that the knotty question of quantitative differences in intellect across cultures remains a contemporary concern. Questions about culture and cognition will be explored in the light of three cognitive domains that have attracted the attention of global psychologists: *visual perception*, *intelligence* and *cognitive style*. Research on these topics tells us much about culture's influence on thought – and about how our thought processes express themselves in the development of cultures.

Culture and visual perception

What is perception?

KEY TERM

Sensation. Stimulation of sensory receptors.

The hot–cold paradox (Figure 6.1) goes back nearly 300 years (Berkeley, 1713/1927). It neatly demonstrates the distinction between **sensation** and perception. Sensing involves the stimulation of sensory receptors. Perceiving involves making sense of sensory information. In other words, when we perceive the world around us we interpret information from our five senses, making it coherent. Unlike sensation,

1   Take three mugs of coffee; one hot, one cold, one tepid.
2   Lower one of your index fingers into each of the first two.
3   Leave them there for three minutes.
4   Lower both fingers into the tepid coffee.
5   The same coffee feels cold to one hand, hot to the other.

Figure 6.1 An ancient recipe for hot and cold coffee

perception is an interpretive process requiring active cognition. Thus, identical sensory information can be perceived (interpreted) differently by different people (even different fingers belonging to the same person), depending on previous experiences. By extension, we might legitimately expect perceptual habits across cultures to differ due to diverse cultural experiences (Hawaiians and Finns might perceive the same visual information differently because of their cultural backgrounds). And, of course, regarding the nature–nurture debate, global psychologists who highlight cultural relativity would align themselves with what is known as the empiricist (**empiricism** is the idea that all knowledge comes from our experiences) approach when trying to explain habits of visual perception (see key concept overleaf).

Culture, visual illusions and the Torres Straits expedition (again)

Cultural differences in perception have long been on global psychology's agenda. Ever since W.H.R. Rivers conducted pioneering field research on the 1889 Torres Straits expedition (see Chapter 2 and Figure 2.4), the influence of culture on perceptual habits has been a cornerstone of cross-cultural psychology. Rivers' assertion that island 'primitives' somehow possessed advanced visual acuity, yet lagged behind Europeans in higher cognitive abilities, went largely unsupported on the expedition. Nevertheless, he did uncover some other counterintuitive cultural differences in susceptibility to (likelihood of

KEY TERM

Empiricism. The idea that all knowledge comes from our experiences.

KEY CONCEPT

Nature, nurture, culture and visual perception

I, John Locke (1632–1704), see the world as I do because of my unique experiences.

NURTURE

English philosopher John Locke warned against those who peddled the existence of an objective, observably true world. Rather, he towed the empiricist line that each of us perceives the world through the prism of our own unique experiences. This doctrine of **perceptual relativism** dictates that **we interpret objects and events, and are occasionally misled by them, courtesy of these experiences**. Locke's early ideas are residual in the cultural relativism of the **carpentered world hypothesis** (Segall *et al.*, 1999), which suggests that **because of their distinct *ecologies*, people from different cultural backgrounds interpret identical visual illusions differently**.

NATURE

Nativist James Gibson (1966) argued that all the information necessary for processing retinal images is contained in the image itself. The nervous system, he argued, has an innate ability to perceive the world in three dimensions. We don't need to *learn* how to perceive three-dimensionally, we can do it at birth. Gibson also uses the word *ecological* to refer to perceptual ability, since it has evolved to help us operate in real, everyday environments (ecologies). Prior experience and guesswork, he argued, only distort perception where there is incomplete information, as in laboratory experiments, or when trying to decipher optical illusions. Gibson's brand of **direct realism** suggests that **our senses tell us all we need to know when perceiving real-world phenomena**. We engage in direct perception courtesy of our senses. Gibson's twentieth-century ideas about innate perception descend from those of Thomas Reid, another direct realist.

I, Thomas Reid (1710–1796), that famous Scottish philosopher, insist that there is an objective world out there that is knowable by my senses.

Which line is longer, A or B?

Participants who are susceptible to this illusion judge A to be longer, even though the lines are the same length.

Figure 6.2 Müller-Lyer illusion

being misled by) **optical illusions**. He compared islanders' and Europeans' reactions to selected pictures or objects that create false visual impressions, including the Müller-Lyer (Figure 6.2) and horizontal–vertical (Figure 6.3) illusions. Rivers (1901) found that susceptibility to the illusions varied with cultural background, but in unexpected ways. Torres Straits Islanders were on average more susceptible to the horizontal–vertical illusion, yet less susceptible to Müller-Lyer, than Europeans. These two-way differences between cultural groups (no group being more susceptible to both illusions) rendered implausible any idea that one group was somehow intellectually better equipped to deal with illusions. They railroaded any attempts to link illusion-susceptibility to schooling (Matsumoto & Juang, 2004), since Europeans were overwhelming more 'schooled' than their Pacific counterparts. Differences in susceptibility thus demanded an alternative explanation.

> **KEY TERM**
>
> **Optical illusions.** Pictures or objects that create false visual impressions.

> **REFLECTIVE EXERCISE 21**
>
> 1. What is the difference between *sensation* and *perception*?
>
> 2. Which of these two phenomena is most likely to be culturally relative?

Which line is longer, A or B?

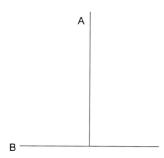

Participants who are susceptible to this illusion judge A to be longer, even though the lines are the same length.

Figure 6.3 Horizontal–vertical illusion

Optical illusions and carpentered worlds

Brunswik (1956) helped develop this alternative explanation. He suggested that people living in visually distinct environments (forests, cities, open plains) necessarily perceive the world (and therefore visual illusions) in different ways because the ecology and architecture (or lack of it) in their surroundings prime them differently for dealing with incoming sensory information. As in the hot–cold paradox, experience paves the way for diverse perceptions. For Brunswik the development of diverse perceptual habits in response to diverse physical surroundings is a matter of environmental adaptation. Developing differing ways of seeing the world in response to experience has considerable survival value. A drawback of such adaptations is that incoming information can sometimes be misinterpreted due to the inference habits we develop in response to our surroundings. Visual illusions are cunning devices for provoking such misinterpretations. Segall *et al.* (1990, p. 73) articulate this ecology-based view of the development of culturally relative perceptual habits:

> If human groups differ in their visual inference systems, it is because their environments differ.

They tested this maxim using the carpentered world hypothesis (Figure 6.4) and the front-horizontal foreshortening hypothesis (Figure 6.5). They also compared illusion-susceptibility in samples from different

The carpentered world hypothesis states that people who grow up in carpentered environments (with rectangular walls, floors, ceilings) perceive the world differently from those whose environments have alternative ecologies. Being surrounded by walls, floors and ceilings produces distinct perceptual habits. For example, it may lead to the habitual perception of the obtuse and acute angles in (2D) drawings of parallelograms as though they belonged to (3D, wall-like) rectangles extending into space. Carpentered-world dwellers are thus likely to be more susceptible to the Sander parallelogram illusion (below). Why? Because they would misjudge A to be longer than B, since they perceive the (2D) parallelogram's angles as though belonging to a (3D) rectangle extending into space.

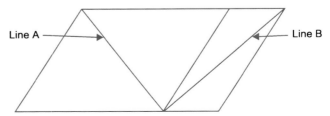

Figure 6.4 Carpentered world hypothesis

Vertical lines are often perceived as horizontal lines projected into the distance. Illustrators use vertical lines in this way, as in this representation of a football field.

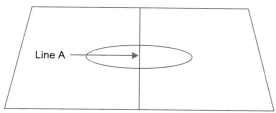

Line A

Vertical **line A** represents the field's halfway line – a horizontal line projected into the distance. Front-horizontal foreshortening hypothesis predicts that the physical environment we habitually experience affects how we perceive these indicators of distance. People who live in open spaces or flat planes will have different perceptions from those who live in restricted environments, such as forests. Open-space dwellers will habitually perceive vertical lines as representing horizontal lines projected into the distance. For forest dwellers, this will not be the case. These ecologically based differences in perception are likely to yield different responses to the horizontal-vertical illusion (Figure 6.4). According to front-horizontal foreshortening, open-space dwellers will be most susceptible.

Figure 6.5 Front-horizontal foreshortening hypothesis

cultural groups by using the Sander Parallelogram (see Figure 6.4), horizontal–vertical (see Figure 6.3) and Müller-Lyer illusions (see Figure 6.2). They wanted to know whether groups from different ecologies would vary in their susceptibility. Over 1800 participants were tested, predominantly from Africa, though North Americans and the Filipinos also participated. There were three westernised or European groups, including South Africans of European descent and North American undergraduates. Among the non-westernised Africans were Bayankole open country dwellers and Bete forest dwellers. Findings generally supported the link between perceptual habits and cultural–ecological differences.

- Cross-cultural differences in mean illusion-susceptibility showed up on all three illusions, so the likelihood of being misled seemed to be related to cultural background.
- On the Sander parallelogram and the Müller-Lyer illusion, westernised participants were most susceptible.
- On the horizontal–vertical illusion the Bayankole were more susceptible than westerners, while the Bete showed fewest illusion-supported responses.

Two aspects of the findings especially support the association between illusion-susceptibility and the shape of samples' surroundings. First, westerners' extra susceptibility to the Sander parallelogram supports the predictions of the *carpentered world hypothesis* (see Figure 6.4).

Second, on the horizontal–vertical illusion, open country dwelling Bay-ankole's extra susceptibility, coupled with the (forest dwelling) Bete's lesser susceptibility, supports the predictions of the *front-horizontal foreshortening hypothesis* (see Figure 6.5). Segall *et al.* (1990, p. 77) concluded:

> These findings accorded well with a theory that attributes perceptual tendencies to ecologically valid inference habits.

Segall *et al.*'s data offer an explanation for Rivers' finding that Europe-ans were most susceptible to Müller-Lyer, yet less susceptible to the horizontal–vertical illusion (Matsumoto & Juang, 2004). The *carpentered world* and *front-horizontal foreshortening* hypotheses can be used to shed retrospective light on Rivers' apparently unexpected find-ings. Subsequent research also supports an environmental theory of differential illusion-susceptibility. Brislin and Keating (1976) built enlarged, wooden, three-dimensional versions of Müller-Lyer and found inhabitants of uncarpentered environments (in Pacific Microne-sian, Melanesian and Polynesian islands) to be less susceptible than North Americans, as Segall *et al.* would predict.

Limitations of Segall's theory

1 *Age before ecology*
   Support for Segall *et al.*'s ideas is not universal. Stewart (1973) and Weaver (1974) both found susceptibility to the Sander parallelogram and Müller-Lyer illusions to decline with age. This is puzzling, since the carpentered world hypothesis would predict that increased exposure to carpentry (with age) would increase susceptibility (Segall *et al.*, 1999).

2 *Analytic sophistication*
   It has been suggested that as children grow older, the perceptual habit-forming effects of the environment are overridden by the acquisition of more sophisticated perceptual abilities. These matur-ational changes enable older children and young adults to overcome any effect that ecologies may have on illusion susceptibility (Berry, 1969; Dasen, 1972). This would lead to the decline of illusion susceptibility with age.

3 *Retinal pigmentation*
   Jahoda (1971) explored a biological explanation for cultural differ-ences in illusion-susceptibility, based on retinal pigmentation. Levels of retinal pigmentation affect the transmission of blue light, but not

red. Africans have higher pigmentation levels than do Northern Europeans. Jahoda found that when presented with blue and red versions of the Müller-Lyer illusion, Scots were equally susceptible to the two, yet Malawians' susceptibility varied with colour. This suggests that physiology, not ecology, may be at the root of variations in susceptibility.

All of this suggests that factors besides environment and ecology are influential in the development of perceptual habits. Yet Segall *et al.*'s ecological theory is still taken seriously and has partial support. Moreover, further evidence of cultural relativity in visual perception comes from research into our interpretation of pictures that are not optical illusions.

Pictorial perception and culture

Comic-book connoisseurs will know the cartoonist's convention of representing people turning their heads in shock or disbelief by showing the head in various stages of rotation. You could call this the cartoonist's take on a 'double-take'. Yet on seeing such an illustration one group of South African Bantu schoolchildren thought the boy pictured was a three-headed freak (Duncan *et al.*, 1973). Perhaps then, this artistic convention is not culturally universal. Cultural relativism in the portrayal of the (three-dimensional) world in (two-dimensional) pictures presumably reflects regional artistic conventions. Furthermore, artistic styles differ historically as well as culturally. For instance, the convention of drawing two lines in convergence (like tramlines) to convey distance only emerged in European art during the fifteenth- to seventeenth-century Renaissance period (Berry *et al.*, 2002). Arguably, then, habits of picture perception involve skills that are taught and learned differently in different places and at different times. Support for picture perception as a function of culturally learned codes comes from Winter (1963), who observed South African miners misinterpreting 'red for danger' warnings on safety posters. Conventions in colour coding and the use of depth cues (see key concept overleaf) in pictures are not, it seems, universally applied across cultures (Gombrich, 1977). Arguably, cultural differences in picture perception relate to more general differences in cognition. When shown photographs and asked to describe them, Japanese participants were more likely to convey an overall (holistic) impression of the contents, including background and contextual elements, as compared with North Americans, who focused on central, de-contextual elements (Nisbett, 2003).

KEY CONCEPT

Depth cues

Depth cues are **devices used by artists and illustrators to give their (2D) drawings the impression of representing (3D) objects and landscapes**. They include the following.

- **Familiar size:** objects that are far away are drawn smaller and those that are nearer are drawn larger.

- **Overlap:** objects that are farther away are drawn as though they are obscured by those that are closer.

- **Convergence:** two lines get closer together to convey distance.

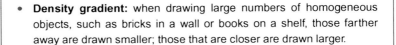

- **Density gradient:** when drawing large numbers of homogeneous objects, such as bricks in a wall or books on a shelf, those farther away are drawn smaller; those that are closer are drawn larger.

Another factor that has been linked to cultural differences in picture perception in general (and the use of depth cues in particular) is schooling. Correlations between levels of western-style schooling and the application of depth cues in picture perception have often been observed (Duncan *et al.*, 1973). Deregowski (1972) wanted to know more about cultural variations in picture perception. He reviewed several cross-cultural studies in which the same pictures were shown to people from different cultural groups and their interpretations recorded (see key study).

Pictorial perception and culture (Deregowski, 1972)

Study 1 *A test for 3D perception*
This test is designed to distinguish participants who use **depth cues** (see key concept opposite) for perceiving three dimensions (3D) in two-dimensional (2D) drawings. Hudson (1960) showed participants (black and white South African mine labourers, clerks, teachers, schoolchildren) pictures incorporating *familiar size, convergence* and *overlap*. Participants were asked:

What is the man doing?

Those who thought the man was spearing the buck (not the elephant) were classed as 3D perceivers and assumed to be conversant with the depth cues. Participants with a higher level of formal education were more frequently classed as 3D perceivers.

Study 2 *Deregowski's trident test*
Zambian primary schoolchildren were pre-tested, using a test similar to that in *Study 1*, to distinguish 2D/3D perceivers. They were then shown the trident illusion (below), plus a second, non-illusion picture of a three-pronged figure, and asked to copy the two pictures. To make things trickier they had to cover up the drawings while drawing.

Can you copy what is in the picture?

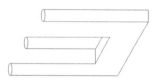

Those who had been classed as 2D perceivers spent the same amount of time copying each trident. 3D perceivers spent longer copying the illusion than the non-illusion. The illusion task was made more difficult by their 'ability' to perceive 3D. Once again, these findings suggest cultural differences in picture perception, evidently due to schooling.

Study 3 *The split-style drawing test*
This study deals with aesthetic (artistic) preference rather than 3D perceptual ability. Hudson (1960) wanted to know if some cultural groups prefer different styles of drawing. Southern African adults and children were asked:

Which elephant do you prefer?

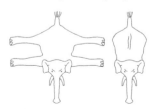

The first elephant is drawn in a *split-style*, typically showing more aspects of the object. The second view is more consistent with photographic representation. While the sample tested here was not representative of all Southern Africans, all but one of the participants preferred the one on the left. It appears from this study that aesthetic preferences may be culturally relative. Split-style preferences may appear unnatural to anyone accustomed to drawings that employ depth cues such as *overlap*. Yet they can be seen in the work of North-West American Indians, in Saharan cave art and in ancient aesthetic styles in New Zealand and Siberia – and in the drawing styles used by engineers in industrialised contexts.

Deregowski reveals several instances of cultural variation in the use of depth cues. He ascribes the label '2D perceiver' to some (usually less formally educated) groups, reserving the term '3D perceiver' to other (usually more formally educated) groups. These differences invite the conclusion that the perception of depth in pictures, which Deregowski regards as an ability, is regulated by cultural and environmental factors. Yet as the key study also shows, some group preferences for split-style drawings suggest that cultural diversity in picture perception is not simply a matter of understanding (or not understanding) depth cues. There are other aesthetic conventions to take into account. To achieve deeper insights into how people in different times and places view pictures, perhaps future researchers need to take greater account of diverse artistic styles. They may benefit from seeing picture production and perception through the eyes of diverse cultural groups.

Limitations of Deregowski's work

1 *Familiar materials*. Certain features of the design used in these studies are questionable, such as the way pictures were presented. Serpell (1976) points out that in *Study 1* (key study) only selected depth cues were used. Crucially, the cue of *density gradient* was omitted. In Serpell's (1976) Zambian replications of this test, with added depth cues of *density gradient* and *colour*, there were increases in 3D perceiving participants (from 54% to 64%, and 54% to 76% respectively). It seems that under optimal testing conditions, when more participant-friendly materials are used, 3D perception is more widespread. Indeed, Deregowski (1968) himself has tested depth perception by asking participants to construct and manipulate wooden, 3D objects – rather than using the often unfamiliar paper-based methods. In a series of experiments in Namibia (Deregowski & Bentley, 1986), the use of depth cues increased when 3D objects for manipulation were part of the research design.

2 *Are depth cues universally desirable?* Implicit in Deregowski's conclusions is the view that using depth cues illustrates an advanced ability to perceive pictures. He even suggests that while children in all societies may be naturally drawn to alternative aesthetic styles such as split-style drawing, the majority ultimately 'come around' to using depth cues. In most societies, he suggests,

> aesthetic preference is sacrificed on the altar of efficiency in communication.
>
> (cited in Gross, 1994, p. 20)

> Here the assumption is that split-style drawing is a retro-
> grade means of communication, even though those who
> use it have pointed out that split drawing reveals more
> features of an object than do other styles of
> representation.
>
> (Serpell, 1976)

There is little doubt that the perception of pictures in general (and of illusions in particular) is in part culturally constructed. It is demonstrably influenced by the learning of codes and conventions that owe some-thing to our ecologies. Yet the 'misinterpretation' of pictures by respondents from different cultures should by no means be overplayed. Common sense tells us that most of the time, most people worldwide interpret realistic, photographic representations of 3D worlds in fairly similar ways. Differing interpretations are perhaps most likely when 2D representations (pictures) are complex, unusual (in the case of visual illusions), lacking in certain depth cues, or perhaps simply presented on unusual materials.

Culture and intelligence

What is intelligence?

Your ideas of intelligent behaviour may differ from those of your friends and family. Likewise, the various definitions of intelligence within psychology and across different cultural contexts (see key concept) reveal the contested nature of the term. Many psychologists have squabbled over the meaning of intelligence and some notorious trans-atlantic disagreements typify these disputes. British author Charles Spearman (1904) espoused the idea of general intelligence ('g' factor) underlying all human intelligent thoughts and actions. In the US Louis Thurstone (1938) modelled intelligence as comprising seven *primary mental abilities* (PMAs), including perceptual speed, spatial ability and numeracy. For Thurstone, competence in one PMA didn't guarantee success in others. The idea of multiple intelligences, residing in sev-eral, uncorrelated factors (abilities where success in one does not pre-dict success in another), resurfaced in the work of Gardner (1983), who takes the idea a step further. He extends intelligence beyond purely cognitive competences to encompass interpersonal (knowing others) and intrapersonal (knowing oneself) capacities, all traceable to separ-ate neurological locations. Just as competence in any of these factors is not predictive of success in others, damage to part of the brain

KEY CONCEPT

Some definitions of intelligence from around the world

Obugezi	Buganda region, Uganda	Combined cognitive and social skills, reflecting steadiness and friendliness (Wober, 1974)
Ngware	Shona region, Zimbabwe	Caution, prudence, diplomacy (Sternberg, 2002)
Lakkal	Djerma-Songhai of Niger	Know-how and social skills (Bissilat *et al.*, 1967)
N'glouele	Côte d'Ivoire	Alertness and helpfulness (Dasen *et al.*, 1985)
Listura	Guatemala	Vitality, alertness, giftedness, independence, activeness (Klein *et al.*, 1976)
Kecerdasan	Malaysia	Speaking, reading, social and symbolic skills (Gill & Keats, 1980)

controlling, say, musical ability (Sacks, 2007) need not impair linguistic competence.

Transatlantic differences between (British) single-factor models and (American) multi-factor models are the tip of the iceberg of global disputes about what intelligence is and how it should be measured. Indeed, the field of **psychometrics** has yielded as many devices for measuring psychological abilities such as intelligence as there are definitions of it. All of which echoes Boring's (1923) famous remark that *intelligence is what is measured by intelligence tests*.

What is measured by intelligence tests?

Many assume intelligence tests to be neutral measures of intellect. Yet since the first tests were administered at the start of the twentieth century (Binet & Simon, 1905), certain cultural and social groups have repeatedly outperformed others. Average differences between group scores suggest that factors other than individual intellect are being recorded during testing. Chapter 2 showed us how differences in test scores have been interpreted as evidence for correlations between race and inherent intellectual capacities (see Figure 2.3). Yet these

KEY TERM

Psychometrics.
Measuring
psychological
abilities.

A nation of morons?

During the First World War Robert Yerkes tested 1.75 million US army recruits, using three separate intelligence tests. The 'Army Alpha' test was designed for literate recruits. 'Army Beta' was pictorial, and designed for those who failed the Alpha. Failures in Beta were given a spoken test. All of these were large-scale group tests, featuring analogies, filling in missing numbers and unscrambling sentences. Yet despite Yerkes' ambitions to test 'native intellectual ability' the tests were flawed because they featured questions that actually recorded cultural knowledge (as in questions about US presidents and baseball players; Banyard, 1999).

Apart from this inherent ethnocentrism, language and administration problems ensured that many whose first language was not English were still given the Alpha test and obtained a zero score. Others who scored poorly included recent immigrants to the US and those with little formal schooling. All this raises the question of whether intelligence, tested thus, amounts to any more than schooling and culturally acquired knowledge.

Army Alpha and Beta test results set the average white American IQ at a mental age of 13 (seen at the time as equivalent to a 'moron'). Scores correlated positively with length of stay in the US. In some quarters they also prompted the conclusion that blacks were less intelligent than whites. By 1924 a restrictive American immigration policy reflected this view, with several national groups barred from entry to the country (Gould, 1981).

Figure 6.6 Intelligence: native intellect or cultural knowledge?

conclusions have since been challenged by those who point out that group differences in intelligence test results also correlate with factors such as familiarity with the culture where the test was devised (see Figure 6.6) and familiarity with formal schooling/testing conditions. In other words, intelligence tests might partly be seen as tests of 'cultural know-how' or length of residence in a certain country (Gould, 1981), rather than merely of cognitive ability. Van de Vijver and Leung (1997) support the view that intelligence tests measure characteristics besides natural intellect. In a meta-analysis of 197 studies using tests of intellect there was a positive correlation between test success and experience of formal schooling. Income levels also correlated with intelligence test scores. Test scores were boosted by higher levels of shared cultural knowledge between the tests and the type of schooling the children has experienced, illustrated satirically by the intelligence test in Figure 6.7.

This is one of a handful of satirical attempts (see also Dove, 1971; Redden & Simons, 1986) to produce tests deliberately couched in the language and cultural knowledge systems of particular cultural groups – in this case, the Indigenous Australian Edward River Community in Far North Queensland. Unless you belong to the cultural group in question you should be disadvantaged by the ethnocentric questions, a feeling that may mimic those of non-Europeans who have been similarly disadvantaged by US or European tests in the past.

Questions
1 What number comes next in the sequence, one, two, three, _____?
2 How many lunar months are in a year?
3 As wallaby is to animal, so cigarette is to _____
4 Three of the following items may be classified with salt-water crocodile. Which are they?
   (a) marine turtle (b) brolga (c) frilled lizard (d) black snake
5 Which items may be classified with sugar?
   (a) honey (b) witchetty grub (c) flour (d) water-lilies
6 We eat food and we _____ water.

Answers
1 One, two, three, many . . . the kuuk thaayorre system of counting only goes to three. The word 'mong' is best translated as 'many' since it can mean any number between 4 and 9.
2 Those who say 'thirteen' are right in European terms but irrelevant in Edward River terms. Apart from having no word to designate thirteen, *yurr mong* or 'very many' is the right answer.
3 The right answer is 'tree'. This stems from the kuuk thaayorre speakers' early experience with tobacco which was 'stick' tobacco, hence it is classified with tree.
4 Crocodiles, turtles, birds and frill-necked lizards are all classified as *minh* (which broadly might be translated as 'animals'). Snakes along with eels are classified as *yak*, which may be broadly translated as snake-like creatures.
5 All the items are classified with sugar as belonging to the class of objects known as *may*. Broadly translated, *may* means vegetable food. Even witchetty grubs that are found in the roots of trees fall under this rubric – so does honey, which is also associated with trees and hence fruit.
6 'Eat' is the right word. Where some languages make a distinction between 'eating' and 'drinking', kuuk thaayorre does not.

Figure 6.7 The original Australian intelligence test

Yet the idea that intelligence tests fall short of measuring intellect is not universally supported. Herrnstein and Murray (1994) looked into whether intelligence test items requiring cultural knowledge were more difficult for African Americans or European Americans. They found that differences in performance across cultural groups were no greater on 'culturally loaded' items than on 'culturally neutral' items. It is clear from these exchanges that questions about whether intelligence can be measured as a discrete phenomenon, irrespective of cultural knowledge, remain pertinent. Indeed, they lie at the heart of the debate about how much of intellectual ability is inherited, and how much is nurtured through our interactions with culture.

The 'nature' of intelligence: the heritability hypothesis

Average differences in intelligence test scores between groups from different cultural backgrounds persist, with some minority groups lagging as much as 15% behind European descendants in the US (Matsumoto & Juang, 2004). How much of this variation is due to inheritance, or to a mix of social, cultural and economic factors? These questions have divided authors for most of psychology's history, and the publication of *The Bell Curve* (1994) by Harvard psychologist Richard Herrnstein and political scientist Charles Murray only stoked the quarrel (see Figure 6.8).

But hereditarian views on intelligence pre-date the *Bell Curve* dispute. Jensen (1981) has perhaps been the main protagonist on the nature side of the debate, arguing that group differences in intelligence test scores (for example, between African Americans and those of European descent) emerge because intelligence is predominantly (80%) biologically attributable. Others have set the proportion of variance attributable to genetic factors at 40% (Plomin, 1990). Reed and Jensen (1993) have also observed correlations between race and reaction time (a component of intelligence), adding further grist to the hereditarian mill.

Herrnstein and Murray (1994) argued that the best way to predict an individual's eventual position on the social ladder is by ascertaining their position on the normal distribution curve for intelligence testing – their IQ score. In short, if you want to get on, get a high IQ. Incorporated into this argument was their portrayal of intelligence itself as being **general** (an undifferentiated 'g', pervading all aspects of intellect), **immutable** (unalterable by education or training) and **culture-free** (unaffected by cultural knowledge or experience). Herrnstein and Murray thus saw comparatively low IQ scores among African Americans as reflecting unalterably low general mean intellect among that group, since intelligence itself was 'substantially heritable' (1994, pp.10, 23).

Critics of the *The Bell Curve* dismissed the book on the grounds that:
1 Intelligence cannot be reduced to a single measurable factor (Gould 1995).
2 IQ is not, as Herrnstein and Murray suggest, 'stable across much of a person's life' (1994, p. 23), since it can be manipulated by intervention programmes (Berry *et al.*, 2002).
3 The possibility that African Americans score relatively poorly in IQ tests due to their lack of schooling and testing experience receives only a brief mention (p. 285), despite the weight of evidence to suggest correlations between schooling and IQ scores (Greenfield, 1997).

Figure 6.8 The *Bell Curve* controversy: are intelligent people more successful?

Assumptions about a genetic component of intelligence have been supported by data from studies using twins. Identical (monozygotic (MZ), 100% genetically related) twins raised in different environments have shown greater intelligence test score similarity than have fraternal (dizygotic (DZ), 50% related) twins raised together (Bouchard & McGue, 1981). Positive correlations between genetic relatedness and test score similarity have been replicated on several occasions in twin studies (Newman *et al.*, 1937; Shields, 1962). Yet the hereditarian argument falters a little when we consider that MZ twins raised together also show greater test score similarity than MZ twins reared apart (Bouchard & McGue, 1981). Furthermore, studies using twins have been criticised on three counts.

1 Inconsistency: different intelligence tests have in some cases been used to provide scores for different participants in the same study.
2 Semantics: different definitions of 'apart' have been used in different studies (Birch & Hayward, 1994). Twins allegedly reared apart might in fact have had similar experiences.
3 We have seen that their mixed findings can be used to offer support for both the nature and the nurture arguments, to which we will now turn.

The 'nurture' of intelligence: the environmental–cultural hypothesis

Those who highlight cultural and environmental influences on intelligence have suggested that varying achievement between cultural groups illustrates how intelligence itself is made up of separate fluid and crystallised components (Cattell, 1971; Cavanaugh & Blanchard-Fields, 2006). **Fluid intelligence** involves forms of 'mental agility' that allow us to reason effectively irrespective of acquired knowledge, cultural background or experience. **Crystallised intelligence** involves the application of *knowledge and experience* in intellectual activity, and is therefore affected by upbringing and cultural background. Arguably, then, underachievement among certain cultural groups on tests of 'intelligence as a whole' (both fluid and crystallised) might be due to a number of environmental factors relating to knowledge, experience and their accumulation. Such factors include levels of unfamiliarity with cultural knowledge included in intelligence tests (see Figures 6.6 and 6.7), as well as to differing definitions of what counts as knowledge, or what constitutes intelligence (as shown in key concept above) in the first place.

KEY TERMS

Fluid intelligence. Forms of 'mental agility' that allow us to reason effectively irrespective of acquired knowledge.

Crystallised intelligence. The application of knowledge and experience in intellectual activity.

Affluence has been identified as another environmental influence on performance. Underachievement by people from low income groups has been attributed to economic deprivation and differences in parental influence, not inferior genetic heritage (Blau, 1981). Indeed, longitudinal research data from the UK suggest that less affluent children who score well on cognitive tests at three years fall behind their more affluent (though lower scoring at three years) counterparts by the time they are seven (Blanden *et al.*, 2007).

Yet another 'nurtured' factor implicated in differential achievement is low expectation of members of social groups who have traditionally done poorly on cognitive tests. Rosenthal and Jacobsen (1968) showed how school performance deteriorated for children who were labelled as under-achievers. Such 'labelling effects' can occur in children who are from social groups, or families, that traditionally score poorly on cognitive tests (Seaver, 1973). Cognitive scores can also be depressed when respondents are overtly reminded that they hail from groups whose members frequently fail. Black university students who were asked to fill in details of their race or ethnicity on an intelligence test questionnaire underperformed compared with others from similar groups who did not reveal their race or ethnicity (Steele & Aronson, 1995).

All of which suggests that a number of environmental factors can be used to explain why intellectual potential is regularly not converted into performance in certain cultural groups. Common sense (as well as the evidence) suggests that people score less well on intelligence tests when their own definition of intelligence is overlooked, or where others in their own cultural group have historically underachieved. Arguably, what is being tested in these situations is not intelligence as such (above and beyond cultural background and upbringing), but a version of intelligence that is inextricably wedded to the symbolic culture from which the test hails (Greenfield, 1997). Arguably these tests lack validity, since they are not tests of intellect but of cultural meanings, knowledge and language.

Can intelligence tests be culture-fair?

Attempts to measure intelligence *above and beyond culture* must wrestle with the influence of shared cultural concepts between those being tested and those writing the tests (Greenfield, 1997). History has shown that respondents whose intellectual heritage is similar to that of their assessors have a distinct advantage. Despite this, there have been attempts to devise **culture-fair tests** of intelligence. Culture-fair

KEY TERM

Culture-fair tests. Tests designed to assess intelligence without relying on cultural knowledge.

tests are designed to assess intelligence without relying on cultural knowledge, often using nonverbal questions. Cattell and Cattell's Culture Fair Series (1973) has paper-and-pencil questions involving the relationships between figures and shapes. Such tests are an attempt to rectify ethnocentrism in intelligence testing as it affects those who may be unfamiliar with the dominant symbolic culture of mainstream testing. Yet culture-fair tests show little external validity in relation to school performance. Furthermore, Nenty (1986) found that over half of the items in Cattell's test still contained cultural knowledge that alienated 'un-American' participants. Similarly, when Nisbett (2003) conducted research using test items modelled on ones from Cattell and Cattell's test, he found that Chinese and American participants who were matched on variables that correlate with IQ (such as memory speed) still scored very differently on the so-called culture-fair items. Difficulties in producing 'culture-less', all-weather assessments perhaps demonstrate the challenge of finding test questions that are equally meaningful in different locations.

Indigenous intelligence

The alternative to devising culture-fair tests is to investigate how intelligence manifests itself differently in different cultural settings.

Where we come from certainly affects our idea of what is clever or smart (see key concept above), as well as our beliefs about how we should assess such qualities. So much so, in fact, that the ideal of a culture-fair concept of intelligence has been abandoned by some authors, who search instead for indigenous conceptions of intelligence. This culturally relativist approach sets out to unearth intelligence as it is manifest differently in different cultural settings (Cole *et al.*, 1971). For example, members of Canadian Cree communities were interviewed to gain an understanding of their indigenous concept of 'smart' or 'intelligent' in the senses that English speakers use these words (Berry & Bennett, 1989). Qualities that emerged as nearest equivalents were Cree concepts of 'wise', 'respectful' and 'attentive'. Interestingly, a Cree quality that epitomised the opposite of intelligence was 'living like a white' (seen as 'cunning' or 'boorish'). This indicates that concepts of intelligence may never be universally agreed across all cultures.

Everyday intelligence and cognition

Global psychologists who investigate indigenous intelligence take a relativist approach, focusing on how knowledge and expertise are defined within diverse meaning systems (Segall *et al.*, 1999). Consequently they tend not to locate their enquiries in formal testing environments. Rather, aptitude and performance are sought in everyday contexts (where most of us would probably claim to carry out our most intelligent acts). Arch-relativist Cole (1992) suggests that we should identify intelligence not in the results of universally administered tests, but in its manifestation in culturally diverse practices. Unique cultural conditions, he argues, require unique intelligent adaptations.

Sternberg (2002) agrees that there is more to intelligence than *whatever it is IQ tests measure*. Studies by Lave and Wenger (1991, with US housewives), Lave (1977, with Liberian tailors), Stevens (1990, with US short-order waitresses) and Carraher *et al.* (1985, with Brazilian coconut vendors) all show that outside of formal testing, intellect flourishes in forms of expertise that have proved adaptive in specific cultural settings. Global psychology has thrown up numerous investigations into everyday cognition, largely from the cultural psychology perspective (see Chapter 5).

Scribner (1975) refers to research that is modelled on everyday intellectual practice as *located experiments*. In one study, Lave (1977) set Liberian tailors two sets of mathematical problems: formal, school-type and vocational, 'tailoring' problems (such as measuring and calculating quantities of fabric). Interesting patterns emerged in her results. Tailors with most 'on the job' experience performed well on the tailoring problems, while those with more formal educational experience did well on school-based tasks. Seemingly, intellectual abilities were compartmentalised rather than generalised, so vocational experience was no guarantee of effective problem-solving at school. Likewise, Carraher *et al.* (1985) showed that juvenile Brazilian coconut vendors excelled with problems that were embedded into their daily practice, yet underperformed at school.

These located experiments suggest that when testing scenarios make 'daily sense', the gap between aptitude (ability) and performance is narrowed. They also suggest that 'on the job' competence is no guarantee of proficiency in a formal testing scenario (and vice versa). Third, they illustrate a view of intelligence as being at least partly embedded in cultural practice, which suggests that we should fully expect conceptions of intelligence (of what is valued as intelligent) to differ across cultures.

Cultural and everyday aspects of intelligence were largely absent from the early models of Spearman (1904) and Thurstone (1938), though their stock has risen in later writing. We have seen how

For Sternberg (2002), successful intelligence has four key elements, enabling us to:

1 succeed in terms of our own personal standards, within our own cultural context
2 succeed by capitalising on our strengths and compensating for our weaknesses
3 succeed by achieving a balance of analytical, creative and practical abilities
4 use our abilities to help us adapt to and shape our environments.

Figure 6.9 Sternberg's theory of successful intelligence

crystallised intelligence is influenced by the accumulation of cultural experience (Cattell, 1971).

For Sternberg (2002, see Figure 6.9), intelligence is what enables us to make successful adaptations to diverse, everyday environments. Naturally, then, according to Sternberg the assessment of intellect should be carried out in contexts that have *mundane realism*. In short, it should be assessed in *contexts that are relevant to the real world where it is applied*. Testing everyday cognition would thus include social and practical problem-solving, often requiring a degree of creativity. Sternberg's idea of successful intelligence can boast a degree of face validity, since it arguably conforms closely to lay interpretations of what intelligence should look like (Sternberg, 2002).

It is interesting to note that research which acknowledges intelligence as belonging to everyday practice (waiting tables, cutting cloth, selling coconuts) has much in common with many indigenous definitions (see key concept above), which tend to incorporate adaptive, practical and creative qualities. Indeed, Sternberg also recognises intelligence as partly social, partly intellectual. Arguably, mainstream psychometrics has not always appreciated that intelligence in its broadest form amounts to more than what has often been included in traditional IQ tests. We should perhaps therefore be wary of attempts to produce universal models and tests of intelligence, since they naturally exclude content that relates to how we as humans adapt intelligently to the demands of different cultural settings.

Limitations of the relativist approach to intelligence

1 *What about general intelligence?* Viewing intellect as manifest in cultural diversity and therefore as culturally constructed may dovetail with an emic (see Chapter 4) viewpoint, but it is incompatible with the views of those who pursue the etic ideal of constructing standardised methods for assessing a globally recognised notion of intelligence. When intelligence is defined differently across cultures, the comparison of intelligence levels between cultural groups is no

longer viable. Arguably, this explains why many on the field have shifted their attention to investigating how intelligence is defined and expressed in different locations.

2 *Invalidity*. A valid definition (or test) of intelligence is one that refers to what it purports to refer to. We can assess the validity of conceptions of intelligence with reference to their external or predictive validity, in other words how well they predict performance on other measures of the same thing (such as school scores, or other IQ tests). However, where intelligence is regarded as specific to a certain cultural group, or where it is seen as an adaptive response to a set of environmental circumstances, there may be limited sources of external validity against which to measure its worth.

> ## REFLECTIVE EXERCISE 22
>
> 1. What is the difference between *culture-free* and *culture-fair* IQ tests?
>
> 2. At school you have learned that the Battle of Hastings took place in the year 1066 and that Italy won the football World Cup in 2006. Which of these three varieties of intelligence best describes what you have learned?
>   a. Fluid intelligence
>   b. Crystallised intelligence
>   c. Indigenous intelligence

Culture and cognitive style

What is cognitive style?

As we have seen, many researchers have tackled the vexed question of *how well* people from different cultural groups use their intelligence (however this is defined) to solve problems. Others have focused on *how* they solve these problems, using strategies that perhaps vary across cultures. Nisbett (2003) argues that our cultural background has an influence on how we approach and undertake problem-solving – known as **cognitive style**. This view stems from the idea that while underlying cognitive abilities exist worldwide, different cultural and ecological demands yield different patterns of cognitive performance (Berry *et al.*, 2002). One example of cross-cultural variations in cognitive style has been investigated by Peng and Nisbett (1999), who identify *dialectical* and *non-dialectical* thought as distinct cognitive strategies for making sense of the world. The first is rooted in Chinese philosophical traditions, the second in western logic (see Table 6.1). These two styles represent distinct ways of thinking about incompatibility and contradiction when one is solving problems.

KEY TERM

Cognitive style. How we approach and undertake problem-solving.

TABLE 6.1
Cross-cultural variations in cognitive style

Principles of Chinese dialectical thought	Principles of western logical thought
Change/Bian Yi Lu Reality is seen as constantly in flux and open to subjective interpretation. Nothing stays the same for very long.	*Identity* Anything that is true is irrefutably true and cannot be false. Any thing is irrefutably equal to itself and nothing else.
Contradiction/Mao Dun Lu Contrariness is a natural state. Good/bad, hot/cold, old/new happily coexist in all things.	*Non-contradiction* A statement cannot be both true and false, but must be one or the other.
Holism/Zheng He Lu Nothing and no one exists independently of others. All events and beings are connected. Phenomena cannot be studied out of context.	*The 'excluded middle' law* Only one of any two contradictory statements can be accepted. 'Middle way' compromise positions are unacceptable.

Differentiation (favoured, they argue, by North Americans) involves comparing two statements and ultimately selecting one of them as true, thus removing any contradiction. For example, either 'hawks' (warriors) or 'doves' (peacemakers) are seen as being right in a debate about world peace – but not both. Meanwhile *dialectical thinking* involves looking for a compromise position that tolerates inconsistencies and incompatibilities.

Peng and Nisbett (1999) compared North American and Chinese participants' preferences for dialectical solutions to various problems and contradictions. Their results support the view that there are culturally distinct strategies to addressing contradictions. American and Chinese participants seemingly apply differing heuristics (rules of thumb) when presented with contradictory statements, ambiguous proverbs, everyday quarrels and philosophical debates. The American way emphasises selecting a single true statement from a choice of two alternatives. The Chinese way seeks defensible positions in apparently (to some) incompatible statements. Links between culture and argumentative style have been made by a number of researchers. Leung (1987) found Chinese participants to prefer harmonious resolutions to conflict situations, with North Americans opting for a more adversarial approach. Nakamura (1985) noted that compared with Western Europeans and North Americans, Asians and Chinese are less likely to approach contradictions by engaging in formal debates that produce only one winner.

However, critics suggest that the art of compromise is something that develops with age, notwithstanding cultural background. Older people have been shown to be more likely to take dialectical stances in conflict situations (Kramer & Woodruff, 1986). Ho (2000, cited in Berry *et al.*, 2002, p. 142) suggests that some North American participants do prefer dialectical responses, and vice versa. Clearly, factors other than culture do influence cognitive style.

But how does culture manifest itself in diverse patterns of thinking? There is a suggested link between socialisation practices and cognitive style, especially in relation to visual perception tasks. In other words, the experience of living in different societies has been shown to encourage differential responses to certain perceptual tasks, such as the rod and frame test (see Figure 6.10). Cultures where conformity and subservience to authority are highly valued have been linked with a perceptual tendency towards rod and frame *field-dependence*.

The socialisation of assertiveness to authority correlated with *field-independence* on the same test (Witkin & Berry, 1975). Field-dependence has also been observed to correlate with overall structural differences between social groups. In rural India, nomadic hunter-gatherer communities have tended to score closer to the field-independence end of the continuum on perceptual tests. Agriculturalists tended towards field-dependency (Mishra *et al.*, 1996).

Further evidence suggests that in non-industrial societies, increased contact with western cultural norms (associated with an introduction to formal schooling) tends to correlate with increased levels of field-independence (Berry *et al.*, 2002). These data, which suggest a link between ecological–cultural factors and cognitive style, have been replicated in other cross-cultural studies (Sinha, 1979). In terms of problem-solving strategies, field-independent individuals have also been found to be more likely to make decisions without engagement

In the rod and frame test (RFT) (Witkin, 1959) you are asked to take *Figure 1* and rotate the rod until it appears to you to be vertical. The RFT is designed to reveal your level of 'field dependence'. How influenced is your perception of the upright by the potentially misleading frame around the rod? *Figure 2* shows the response of someone who would be described as 'field-independent'. *Figure 3* reveals a field-dependent respondent.

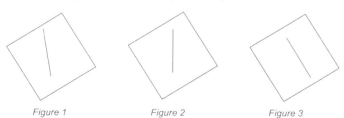

Figure 1   Figure 2   Figure 3

Figure 6.10 The rod and frame test

of or consultation with others, as compared with those who are more field-dependent. The former appear to function more autonomously (Witkin *et al.*, 1979). Interestingly, field-dependency is a construct that pervades both social and cognitive domains, echoing indigenous conceptions of intelligence (see key concept above) and those of Sternberg (2002).

REFLECTIVE EXERCISE 23

Imagine a meeting between two psychologists who are interested in the relationship between culture and cognitive ability. Psychologist A wants to devise a culturally universal means of assessing intellect. Psychologist B is a *cultural psychologist* who prefers to investigate *indigenous intelligence*. Outline how each of these psychologists is likely to assess intelligence differently.

So does culture change the way we think?

Having begun this chapter by posing this question, we might end by summarising some of the influences that cultural background can exert on our intellectual habits. There is, for example, a strong argument that the character of our environment or ecology has some bearing on our perception of certain visual stimuli, such as visual illusions and art. It is also likely that where we grow up – incorporating how affluent we are or how familiar we are with formal schooling and with aspects of cultural knowledge inherent in intelligence tests (including our definitions of intelligence) – is likely to influence how well we score in the formal testing scenario. Away from formal IQ, cognitive strategies for solving problems and disputes also vary from culture to culture. Intelligent behaviour is manifest in effective expertise, which expresses itself in various local, everyday and often quite specialised settings – where success is not necessarily predictive of educational achievement. Wherever we look, then, we can see that whatever cognitive character-istics we all share, our ecology, experience and environment have been shown to have some bearing on how we solve problems and make sense of the world.

Summary

Chapter 6 examines the study of cognition in varying cultural contexts. Cognitive psychology featured heavily in the early development of the cross-cultural perspective, with several early twentieth-century writers carrying out visual perception studies in order to examine the influence of ecology and environment on the way we perceive the world. A critical examination of these theories is our starting point here.

Another favoured topic for cross-cultural researchers of cognition is intelligence and IQ testing, which has spawned many debates and controversies over the years relating to inheritance, cultural bias in definitions and testing of IQ. These debates are covered here, along with some culturally diverse approaches to intelligence. These include indigenous approaches to intelligence from around the world, such as attempts to model intelligence on everyday behaviour rather than more traditional methods of IQ testing.

All of this leads into a broader discussion of culturally diverse styles of thinking, or cognitive style. In particular there is a review of some more recent research into the ways in which problem-solving strategies might be subject to cultural variation.

REFLECTIVE EXERCISE 24

Match up the definitions on the right with the terms on the left (see p. 226 for answers)

Terms	Definitions
Empiricism	*Assessments designed to assess intelligence without relying on cultural knowledge*
Depth cues	*The application of knowledge and experience in intellectual activity*
Culture-fair tests	*Idea that all knowledge comes from experience*
Fluid intelligence	*How we approach and undertake problem-solving*
Sensation	*Stimulation of sensory receptors*
Carpentered world hypothesis	*Idea that people who grow up in environments with rectangular walls, floors and ceilings, perceive the world differently from those whose environments have alternative ecologies*
Cognitive style	*Making sense of sensory information*
Crystallised intelligence	*Pictures or objects which create false visual impressions*
Optical illusions	*Forms of 'mental agility' that allow us to reason effectively irrespective of acquired knowledge*
Perception	*Devices used by artists and illustrators to give their (2D) drawings the impression of representing (3D) objects and landscapes*

FURTHER READING

- Herrnstein, R. & Murray, C. (1994) *The Bell Curve: Intelligence and Class Structure in American Life*, New York: Free Press.
- Nisbett, R. (2003) *The Geography of Thought: How Asians and Westerners Think Differently . . . and Why*, London: Nicholas Brealey.
- Segall, M., Campbell, D. & Herskovits, M. (1966) *The Influence of Culture on Visual Perception*, Indianapolis, IN: Bobbs-Merrill.

Culture, social cognition and social influence

Social psychology across cultures

7

What this chapter will teach you

- What is **social cognition**?

- What is **social identity theory**?

- Is self-serving **attribution bias** culturally universal?

- Is there global support for mainstream theories of **prejudice**?

- Is **romantic love** culturally universal?

- Do classic **obedience** and **conformity** studies replicate globally?

- Is **independent behaviour** spreading worldwide?

- Are **loafing** and **striving** global phenomena?

Does culture change the way we see ourselves – and others?

> I am a middle-aged Scottish newspaper vendor.
> I am an eight-year-old Icelandic schoolboy.
> I am a retired diplomat from Angola.

How would you describe yourself in a sentence, beginning with *I am* . . .? As with these anonymous quotes, you might mention the various groups you belong to (age, national or occupational). It is common for people to construe (perceive) themselves in this way, perhaps because much of our sense of identity derives from our perceptions about the in-groups (various groups such as the family, nation, age cohort with whom we share certain values) we belong to and the out-groups (groups whose values we don't share) we don't belong to. Furthermore, defining ourselves in terms of in-groups has implications for how we relate to the people around us.

Liu *et al.* (2003) point out that our interpersonal relationships are affected by whether or not we perceive others as belonging to our in-groups. Another way of putting this is to say that *our inter-group relations influence our interpersonal relations*. We're likely to treat someone differently after finding out they are 'one of us' (*Oh, you're a Quaker too, how nice to meet you*).

The idea that our perception of ourselves and others is affected by group affiliations has been around for a while in social psychology (Tajfel, 1970), especially in the field of **social cognition.** This blend of cognitive and social psychology, which looks at our attitudes and our perceptions of those around us, also suggests that these attitudes and perceptions are culturally influenced. In short, where we come from may affect how much influence group affiliation has on how we regard ourselves – and others.

Culture and self-construal

Am I me first, or am I one of us first?

KEY TERM

Social cognition. Blend of cognitive and social psychology that looks at our attitudes and our perceptions of those around us.

Answering a question like this requires me to consider whether I construe (define or regard) myself primarily as an *independent* person or as an *interdependent* affiliate of one or more social group (Markus & Kityama, 1991a), perhaps occupational, sporting, familial or religious (see Table 7.1). In some cultural settings personal identity may be

TABLE 7.1
Independent and interdependent self-construal styles: how do I see myself?

Independent self-construal	Interdependent self-construal
• Individual is seen as an autonomous free agent, relatively unaffected by social context • Behaviour likely to remain consistent across situations due to core personality traits • Associated with 'western' notions of self, common in US and Western Europe	• Self is perceived as interconnected with physical and social context • Person aims to preserve harmony with physical and social world • Behaviour seen as not necessarily consistent across situations, but affected by situational factors

construed more from individual traits, while elsewhere it arises from the social networks to which we belong (Rhee *et al.*, 1995). Research suggests that people from more individualistic cultural settings (US, Western Europe) are more likely to subscribe to an independent style of self-construal, with collectivist cultures fostering interdependent self-construal (see Chapter 1 for more on the *individualism–collectivism* dimension). Harrison *et al.* (1995) investigated this by comparing self-construal tendencies in Zimbabwean and US adolescents. Participants were asked to rate the contributions of their social relationships to their individual sense of worth. Zimbabweans showed firmer commitments to a wider social network than Americans did. They also relied more heavily on a wider group of social affiliates for intimacy and support than Americans did, and showed a greater tendency towards out-group denigration. The idea that we derive our sense of who we are from affiliation with social groups borrows heavily from Tajfel's (1981) **social identity theory**, which asserts that we categorise ourselves according to which social groups we find attractive, and seek out those who belong to the same group as ourselves. According to this theory it would make sense for someone with an interdependent style of self-construal not only to gain their identity from group affiliation, but also to habitually denigrate out-group members, as Harrison *et al.* (1995) found in their Zimbabwean condition.

Another self-construal study required participants from cultures normally regarded as individualist or collectivist to complete the phrase *I am . . .* twenty times (Bochner, 1994). Individualists mainly confined their answers to their own personality traits (*I am honest, I am laid-back*) while collectivists were more likely to invoke the roles they played in society (*I am a good parent, I am a conscientious student*). In similar vein Tafarodi *et al.* (2004) found Canadians to be more likely to judge their inner self as consistent across situations than were Chinese or Japanese participants, who saw contextual factors as influencing

KEY TERM

Social identity theory. Asserts that we categorise ourselves according to which social groups we find attractive, and seek out those who belong to the same group as ourselves.

their behaviour. Furthermore, when asked what made them angry, participants from collectivist cultures such as China and Japan were found to be more likely to cite incidents that happen to other people rather than themselves (Stipek *et al.*, 1989), compared with US respondents.

This selection of findings supports a link between independent–interdependent self-construal and individualism–collectivism (Triandis *et al.*, 1988). It suggests that collectivist cultures encourage in their members a deeper commitment to a few all-pervading (familial or religious) groups, requiring a greater level of commitment than do the more numerous (sports, church or music) social groups that make up more individualistic cultures (Matsumoto & Juang, 2004). Interdependent self-construal encourages a heightened sense of the self as part of a wider social network, rather than as an autonomous entity. Further consequences of interdependence may include a willingness to denigrate out-groups in collectivist culture and reluctance to break social taboos, such as discussing sexual fantasies (Goodwin & Lee, 1994).

Limitations of the independent–interdependent self-construal theory

1 Independence and individualism are not synonymous
   The link between individualism and independent self-construal is not universally supported. In some research, participants from the US employ more interdependent self-construal than do those from what might be regarded as less individualistic European nations (Gudykunst & Lee, 2003).
2 Self-construal varies within the same individual
   Independent–interdependent self-construal has been shown to vary within the same person according to whether they are at home or at work (Smith & Bond, 1998). Consequently, it seems questionable to assert that participants from certain cultures construe themselves according to a distinct, consistent style.

By and large, though, much of the evidence invites the conclusion that individualistic cultures are prone to more independent self-construal, while collectivist cultures foster more interdependence. So if our cultural background does influence how we see ourselves, we might logically ask how it affects our attitudes to others, especially those who lie beyond the limits of our in-groups.

Culture and attribution bias

We make attributions to explain the behaviour of ourselves and of those around us (*He did that because . . .*). **Attributions** are inferences we make to explain behaviour. Psychological research and everyday experience both suggest that we are not always entirely fair when making them. Indeed, the phrase *one rule for one, one for another* springs to mind. Our attributions often betray our most personal biases. These are never more obvious than when we make what are termed *internal* and *external* attributions. Internal attributions explain behaviours in terms of dispositions or personality traits (*He did it because he is kind*). External attributions invoke situational, contextual causes (*She did it because the weather was inclement*). Our self-centred, self-serving bias might dictate that our own negative or unsuccessful behaviours tend to be externally attributed (*I was unlucky*), while similar behaviours by others receive internal attributions (*He's just incompetent*). Such attribution bias is an example of what is known as the **fundamental attribution error** (Miller, 1984), which reflects our biased tendency to explain the actions of others using internal causes, so ignoring the effect that situational factors have on their behaviour.

KEY TERMS

Attributions.
Inferences we make to explain behaviour.

Fundamental attribution error.
Tendency to explain the actions of others using internal causes.

Is self-serving attribution bias culturally universal?

A popular method of investigating this question is to see how people from different cultures explain their successes and failures, for instance in school work. Some cultural differences have emerged, indicating that styles of attribution do depend on where you come from. Kashima and Triandis (1986) found that when asked to explain their own success Japanese participants were more likely to invoke external attributions (*I was lucky*). US participants favoured internal explanations (*I was skilful*). A so-called *self-effacing* bias, displayed here in the Japanese condition, has also been observed in China, where participants were more likely to put their own successes down to external causes than were US participants (Lee & Seligman, 1997). Crittenden (1991) supports this notion by reporting Taiwanese students' tendencies towards modestly attributing their own academic success to external factors, compared with US participants' preferences for internal attributions. Modest self-effacement is perhaps part and parcel of a style of social cognition that favours explaining behaviour in terms of contexts for action, also known as **allocentrism** (Smith & Bond, 1998). This contextual style of social cognition is consistent with

KEY TERM

Allocentrism. Style of social cognition that favours explaining behaviour in terms of contexts for action.

interdependent self-construal (discussed in the previous section). Arguably, allocentrism is a socialised characteristic of less individualistic cultures, rooted in parental practices that are particular to those regions (Bornstein *et al.*, 1998).

Another ingenious demonstration of cultural differences in attribution style involved a comparison of US and Chinese newspaper reports of homicides. Chinese journalists favoured situational explanations (*He did it because he comes from a rough district*). Americans tended to highlight dispositional factors (*He has a criminal personality*) (Morris & Peng, 1994).

All of this suggests that people from Asia are socialised towards seeing themselves as less separable from the social fabric into which they are embedded (interdependent), thus tending to attribute their own success to contextual factors. Comparatively, individualistic cultures foster a more autonomous view of the self, fostering a greater tendency towards invoking internal explanations. So, as to the cultural universality of attribution bias, it appears that the practice of praising oneself for success is not universally widespread, as in some cultures self-effacement is more the norm.

Limitations of attribution bias research

1 *Anyone can make any type of attribution*
   We should be wary of making a hard and fast link between collectivism, allocentrism and self-effacing attributions for fear of descending into the use of stereotypes (see key concept). After all, it has also been shown that the same person can display both self-serving and self-effacing biases in differing contexts (Kagitcibasi, 1996).

2 *Attributions are influenced by unique cultural contexts*
   The likelihood of making self-serving or self-effacing attributions can depend on cultural and contextual factors that override the individualism–collectivism dimension. For instance, within what are often represented as a collectivist cultures, self-serving and self-effacing attribution styles can coexist (Hewstone & Ward, 1985) and therefore have to be interpreted according to their unique social context. This is illustrated by the key study shown on p. 140.

> ### REFLECTIVE EXERCISE 25
>
> 1. What's the difference between *internal* and *external* attributions?
>
> 2. Cite one piece of evidence to suggest that culture influences attribution styles.

KEY CONCEPT

Stereotypes

What is a stereotype?

A set of fixed, simplistic views about a social group, which makes a *national stereotype* an *over-generalised set of attitudes towards a national group.*

Are there different types of national stereotypes?

Yes, there are *hetero-stereotypes* (stereotypes of out-groups) and *auto-stereotypes* (stereotypes of in-groups).

Is there consensus about different national stereotypes?

Yes, apparently so. Peabody (1985), Stephan *et al.* (1996) and McAndrew *et al.* (2001) all found a high level of agreement as to which traits are perceived as being 'typical' of a range of national groups. Germans, for example, are reputedly 'hard-working'.

Where do national stereotypes come from?

Simply perceiving the existence of an out-group with different values and beliefs can be enough for stereotypical attitudes to develop (Smith *et al.*, 2006). Linssen and Hagendoorn (1994) argue that the nature of stereo-types can be derived from a nation's characteristics, such as wealth (people from rich nations being seen as 'efficient') or its global influence (Americans may therefore be seen as 'dominant').

Does everyone hold stereotypes?

Certainly not to the same degree; their strength might depend on how much you feel threatened by another group or nation (Van Oudenhoven *et al.*, 2002). Small, politically unassuming nations are less likely to pro-voke negative stereotypes. Your likelihood of holding stereotypes may also depend on your perceptions of certain historical events (Smith *et al.*, 2006). For example, a negative view of Britain's colonial past might lead a British person not to identify with their own nation, rendering them less likely to develop negative hetero-stereotypes of other nations.

Are stereotypes accurate?

Just because a lot of people concur about what typical Italians are like, this doesn't make these views accurate. Lee and Ottati (1995) suggest a method for gauging the accuracy of national stereotypes, based on asking three questions about them:

1 Is there hetero-stereotype consensus? *(Does everyone tend to agree that Germans are hard-working?)*
2 Is there hetero-auto-stereotype consensus? *(Do German people agree with non-Germans about their typical traits?)*
3 Are there objective indicators to support stereotypes? *(If Germans are hard-working, is this reflected in their performance?)*

While research supports the first of these criteria on many national stereotypes, it is more equivocal in relation to national stereotyping on the basis of the other two criteria. Interestingly though, in one study Chinese and American participants concurred about certain Chinese stereotypical characteristics, yet the Chinese saw them as more positive traits than did the Americans (Lee & Ottati, 1995). Clearly, we are a long way from establishing agreed, reliable national stereotypes.

KEY STUDY

Historical case study: the influence of context on attributions

Research conducted in India, Malaysia and Singapore in the 1970s and 1980s shows how unique social contexts can affect attribution styles. It also shows how self-serving bias and self-effacing attributions can occur within a culture that is often labelled 'collectivist'.

Hewstone and Ward (1985)
This study was carried out among existing ethnic groups (Chinese and Malays), first in Malaysia and then in Singapore. Participants were given the following scenarios and asked to make attributions, which might be internal or external.

Scenario 1. A passer-by notices you have fallen off your bicycle. The passer-by is:
• Malay and helps you. Why?
• Chinese and helps you. Why?
• Malay and ignores you. Why?
• Chinese and ignores you. Why?

Scenario 2. It is raining and you seek refuge from a householder, who is:
• Malay and hospitable. Why?
• Chinese and hospitable. Why?

- Malay and inhospitable. Why?
- Chinese and inhospitable. Why?

A mixture of self-serving and self-effacing contextual attributions emerged. In Malaysia overall attributions, by both Malays and Chinese, seemed to favour Malays. Very often Chinese participants 'joined in' with attributions that were biased against them. Yet in Singapore, Malays denigrated Chinese less severely than they did in Malaysia, and the Chinese made attributions that reflected a more positive self-image. In all, trends towards unrestrained in-group bias were absent, as were across-the-board self-effacing attributions. Why?

Hewstone and Ward sought explanations in social contexts of their experiments. In Malaysia in 1985 ethnic Malays outnumbered Chinese by 53% to 36%. Yet the Chinese were an affluent minority. Government policy encouraged positive discrimination towards Malays to close the economic gap between the two groups. Inter-ethnic animosity was rife, as the data from the Malay respondents reflect. Another consequence of this scenario may have been a Chinese tendency to develop a 'second-class citizen' mentality, internalising the values of an out-numbered, marginalised minority. This may partly explain their negative auto-stereotypes (in a subsequent Australian study, Feather (1995) replicated Hewstone and Ward's discovery of out-group favouritism among arguably marginalised minority groups).

These contextual interpretations are consistent with the theoretical approach of *cultural psychology* (see Chapter 5).

Culture and prejudice

If culture affects the way we construe ourselves and attribute our successes and failures, we might also expect it to influence our attitudes towards those around us. In other words, our self-serving biases (me against you) may be echoed in our inter-group relations (us against them). In-group biases, along with out-group denigration that often accompanies them, are known as **prejudice.**

Social psychology has produced several explanations for the origins of attitudes (usually negative) towards particular social groups (see Table 7.2). These models have been researched in their cultures of origin but, as the following section indicates, there is some support for them across cultures.

KEY TERM

Prejudice. Attitudes (usually negative) towards particular social groups, based on their group membership.

TABLE 7.2
Social psychological theories on the origins of prejudice

Minimal groups theory (Tajfel, 1981)	Derived from Tajfel's (1981) *social identity theory* (see key study opposite), this theory argues that we are likely to compare in-groupers' attributes favourably with those of out-groupers simply because we perceive that the latter belong to a different social group. Prejudice against out-groups arises out of a perception of inter-group difference, however trivial the criteria are for those differences. For example: *Because your group supports a different football team I am prejudiced against you.*
Contact hypothesis (Allport, 1954)	Lack of contact between social groups is associated with the development of negative inter-group attitudes. Animosity will decrease as contact increases because of the resulting erosion in mutual ignorance. To be meaningful, though, contact must be *equal status* (where no group holds power over the other), *non-competitive*, with the existence of *superordinate goals* (shared by both sides) and *legitimised by authority*. For example: *Because I am ignorant of your group's lifestyle and values, I am prejudiced against you.*
Social dominance theory (Sidanius & Pratto, 1999)	Prejudice is related to differing status between social groups. High-status groups often adopt a *social dominance orientation (SDO)* to legitimise their dominance. SDO promotes in-group identification and prejudice against out-groups. Interestingly, SDO can be adopted by low-status groups, resulting in-group derogation. For example: *Because I want to protect our elevated status, I am prejudiced against your group.*
Realistic conflict theory (Sherif, 1966)	Knowing that someone belongs to a different group from us may be a basis for prejudice, but only where there is competition for scarce resources between those groups. Where group goals can be achieved only at the expense of another group's aspirations, conflict of interests will give rise to prejudice. For example: *Because there is only a limited amount of cake to be distributed between my group and yours, I am prejudiced against you.*
Historical representation theory (Liu *et al.*, 2003)	From the perspective of *cultural psychology* (see Chapter 5), Liu *et al.* see inter-group prejudice arising from conflicting interpretive representations of history. Past disputes over land claims or human rights abuses thus inform the development of present-day attitudes, perhaps precluding harmonious inter-group relations. For example: *Because of our ancient quarrels over land, I am prejudiced against your group.*

Global support for theories of prejudice

Minimal groups

Replications of Tajfel-like experiments (see key study) across seven industrialised nations revealed cultural differences in the minimal groups effect, with a pronounced in-group bias effect in the US, Germany and the Netherlands and smaller one in the UK, Ireland and Switzerland (Mullen *et al.*, 1992). Interestingly, though, in-group bias

KEY STUDY

Tajfel's minimal groups experiment

With English schoolboys as participants, Tajfel's (1970) experiments in inter-group discrimination yielded his *minimal groups* theory. Boys were allocated into groups on the trivial (to non-art critics) basis of whether they preferred the work of one European artist (Paul Klee) or another (Vassily Kandinsky). Unbeknown to the boys they were in fact randomly divided into two groups. When the opportunity arose to award points to 'in-group' or 'out-group' members, various strategies were open to participants.

- **Strategy 1: Maximum joint profit**. The in-group/out-group combined points allocation would be as high as possible, so no matter who comes out on top, the idea is to distribute as many points as possible.
- **Strategy 2 Maximum in-group reward**. The in-group is given as many points as possible, irrespective of what the out-group gets.
- **Strategy 3 Maximum difference**. The main concern is for there to be more points for the in-group than for the out-group, even if it means few point being allocated to in-groupers.

It transpired that S3 was the most popular, suggesting that the mere membership of a group – based on however trivial criteria – was justification enough for discrimination against out-groupers.

did not show up in groups that had been assigned low status. They often displayed out-group bias, which actually offers support for social dominance theory. Cultural differences in the minimal group effect have also emerged in a series of replications in Australasia, suggesting that the *maximum difference strategy* (see key study) is not universally preferred across cultures. Compared with a European condition which did adopt this strategy, Polynesian participants from Maori and Samoan communities were more likely to select the more egalitarian *maximum joint rewards* strategy (Wetherell, 1982).

Contact

Does presence make the heart grow fonder? Cross-cultural testing of Allport's hypothesis suggests that it might. Pettigrew and Tropp (2000) reviewed 2030 studies from various cultural settings, in workplaces, schools and experimental laboratories. There was general support for the contact effect, with the authors concluding that *optimal inter-group contact should be a critical component of any successful effort to reduce prejudice* (cited in Berry *et al.*, 2002, p. 375).

Building on such data, several worldwide policy initiatives have sought to improve relations by reducing inter-group segregation, notably among Northern Ireland's Catholic and Protestant communities. Yet despite such efforts in the domains of education, sport and residence, census data still suggest that most citizens of the province prefer to socialise with in-groupers (Niens *et al.*, 2003). Also, it seems that where inter-group friendships do exist they often do not translate into changes in attitudes towards the out-group (Trew, 1986).

Niens *et al.* (2003) investigated the potential positive effects of increased (quality and quantity of) contact between Catholics and Protestants. Their questionnaire data showed opportunities for inter-group contact to be frequent, yet inter-group friendships were infrequent. Nevertheless, statistical analyses revealed patterns that supported contact as a force for good. Quantity and quality of contact were both inversely related to inter-group anxiety. Also, increases in all types of contact were moderately associated with positive attitudes towards out-group members.

Social dominance

A social dominance orientation (SDO) involves high-status groups adopting a so-called 'just world' justification (*I am up here because I deserve it*) for their elevated social position. Indeed, this theory sees powerful and relatively powerless groups as both likely to identify with the upper echelons, for example by attributing the failures of low-status groups to internal dispositions (Smith *et al.*, 2006). Using locally devised measures of prejudice, Pratto *et al.* (2000) tested this hypothesis in Canada, Israel and Thailand. As predicted, high- and low-status groups did identify more with those in power. In the light of such findings, we might expect out-group identification by those in low-status groups to generate a desire to 'move into' those groups (Smith *et al.*, 2006).

In another telling example of 'just world' identification with powerful groups, Levin *et al.* (2003) asked Lebanese participants whether they supported the attacks on the World Trade Center in 2001. As social dominance theory might predict, the most fervent supporters of the attacks were those with the least pronounced social dominance (just world) orientation. This indicates that the less you identify with the powerful groups (the US), the more sympathy you might have for those who attack their power.

Realistic conflict

In line with Sherif's hypothesis, inter-group prejudice does seem to intensify where an out-group is seen as encroaching on one's material resources or symbolic values. For example, a perceived sense of threat among European Union citizens who felt their resources and values were being eroded correlated with high levels of prejudice against ethnic out-groups (Jackson *et al.*, 2001). A sense of threat also predicated a desire to clamp down on immigration, for example against Mexicans in the US (Stephan *et al.*, 2000). We should note, though, that within European or American samples, differing cultural contexts affect levels of out-group threat felt. For example, in Jackson *et al.*'s survey, French participants were significantly keener to reduce immigration than the Irish were.

Historical representations

Not satisfied that existing social psychological theories adequately explain inter-group prejudice in diverse cultures, Liu *et al.* (2003) urge us to view each site of conflict in relation to its inhabitants' unique cultural context and their particular representations of history. Liu and colleagues stress the influence of wars and land disputes on how we construe our identities in relation to other groups. For example, twelve cultural groups surveyed all identified the Second World War as the most important event in their history (Liu *et al.*, 2003). Furthermore, it is argued that where different groups share a polemical (disputed) interpretation of such historical conflicts (as for example in Northern Ireland), this is a recipe for inter-group conflict and prejudice.

Limitations of research on culture and prejudice

1 *Beware the imposed etic when applying imported theories*
   When assessing the replicability of theories of prejudice, we should remember that some of their key concepts – and the instruments used to assess them – were originally developed outside the replication context. Arguably, this gives rise to the setting up of experimental scenarios that, because they have not been devised with local knowledge, appear alien and meaningless to participants. For example, in the case of the minimal groups replications we might wonder whether Polynesian participants' responses to this unfamiliar experimental scenario could produce entirely valid findings (Smith & Bond, 1998).

2 *The theories may receive global support, they may not be mutually exclusive*

While models are presented here as discrete explanations for the origins of inter-group prejudice, applying them across cultures alerts us to the possibility that they perhaps should not be regarded as mutually exclusive or entirely in opposition to one another, since elements within them often overlap. For example, ascribing prejudice to conflict over scarce resources (Sherif, 1966) is not incompatible with seeing it as conflicting representations of historical events (Liu *et al.*, 2003).

Having reviewed the cultural applicability of social psychological theories of prejudice and found that, though cultural and historical contexts clearly influence the emergence of inter-group conflict, certain psychological elements of prejudice do appear across cultures, we will now ask whether friendship and intimacy take similar forms in different cultures.

REFLECTIVE EXERCISE 26

1. What is the difference between *minimal groups* and *realistic conflict* explanations of prejudice?

2. Which of these policies would Allport be most likely to recommend to reduce tension between Israelis and Palestinians?
   a. Integration
   b. Redistribution of wealth
   c. Segregation

Culture, love and intimate relationships

Is love culturally relative? Not a very romantic title for a song, perhaps, but an interesting question for global psychology nonetheless. The various marriage permutations worldwide (romantic, arranged, monogamous, polygamous) suggest that how we define, express and institutionalise love and intimacy is affected by culture. Researchers have explored issues of love and cultural variation in a number of ways, for instance by asking whether perceptions of attractiveness are the same the world over.

KEY TERM

Evolutionary psychology. A branch of psychology focusing on genetic and biological antecedents of behaviour.

Are we all looking for the same thing?

Evolutionary psychology (a branch of psychology focusing on genetic and biological antecedents of behaviour) predicts our taste in intimate partners to be dominated by the reproductive instinct, not by the vicissitudes of culture. Thus, the pursuit of physically and reproductively fit partners would supposedly be a culturally universal practice (Montepare & Zebrowitz, 1993). Males would seek females with most reproductive potential, with females seeking males who are most able to provide for their family.

Is there evidence to bear out this evolutionary stance? One large-scale international study of partner preferences certainly shows high levels of consensus in tastes in both genders. Surveying 10,000 participants in thirty-seven nations, Buss (1989) found that females rated partners with good financial prospects more highly than males did in thirty-six of those nations. Displaying similar levels of unanimity, males preferred younger (more fertile) female mates than females did in every nation. Youth and health were high on the desirability agenda for males. Industry and earning potential were both valued by females.

Buss *et al.* (2000) found that males expressing a preference for more children opted for younger partners. Schmitt *et al.* (2003) found that males wanted more sexual partners than females did, perhaps reflecting a biological need for multiple fathering. Such findings invite an evolutionary interpretation, indicating culturally universal tastes in potential partners, largely determined by biological heritage.

Yet critical voices have been raised against evolutionists. A re-examination of Buss's survey data revealed cultural variations that in some cases exceeded gender differences (Smith *et al.*, 2006). For example, national levels of affluence predicted differences in selection criteria for intimate partners. Specifically, participants from richer countries showed a greater preference for love (rather than status), for intelligence (rather than domesticity), for dependability (rather than good looks) and for sociability (rather than religion) (Chan, 2004). The influence of socio-economic factors on intimate partner choice is endorsed by Georgas *et al.* (2005). It seems then that the evolutionary proposition that all humans are biologically predisposed towards making similar partner choices should be treated with caution.

Is beauty more than culture-deep?

It is not the sole prerogative of evolutionary theory to identify cross-cultural agreement about intimate partner choice. Many researchers have produced data suggesting that the criteria for physical beauty are agreed worldwide. Cunningham *et al.* (1995) found consensus among Europeans, Asians and Hispanics about which facial features were attractive among participants rating photographs of female models (drawn from many cultures).

Elsewhere, when asked to rate physical characteristics for their attractiveness, Japanese and Koreans showed some overlap in their tastes. Koreans reported large eyes, high noses and thin faces to be typically attractive. Japanese participants agreed about the large eyes, yet were also aroused by small noses and small chins (Daibo *et al.*, 1994). Interestingly, there are also positive correlations between judgements about physical beauty and desirable personality traits (Feingold, 1992). In other words, beautiful people are often perceived as being good, even though our ideas about which traits are good may vary across cultures (Wheeler & Kim, 1997).

Against these findings there is evidence of differing perceptions of physical beauty across cultures and throughout history. For instance, slender figures have not always been regarded as normally desirable, even in Western Europe (Smith *et al.*, 2006). Contemporary data show UK residents from Caribbean and West African countries to rate larger female body size as most desirable (Hodes *et al.*, 1996; Cogan *et al.*, 1996). Indigenous Ugandan males and females endorse this preference for plumpness (Furnham *et al.*, 2002). This casts doubt on evolutionary or universalist approaches to mate selection. Yet we should perhaps allow for the possibility that as more cultural groups are exposed to western media images, a 'consensualisation' of opinion about what is attractive may develop (Matsumoto & Juang, 2004).

Is love necessarily romantic the world over?

Loving relationships may be a global phenomenon, but their nature and importance seemingly vary from culture to culture. **Romantic love**, characterised by passion and intimacy though not necessarily commitment (Matsumoto & Juang, 2004), is not necessarily the preferred form of intimacy everywhere. Simmons *et al.* (1986) found romantic love to be less valued in Japan than in Germany or the US, with close family ties more important in the Asian context. Furnham (1984) also found romantic love to be associated with a European, rather than an Asian or South African, outlook. French and US participants in intimate partner relationships reported more private disclosure (confiding) and greater feelings of belonging than did intimate Japanese partners. In line with these findings, Chinese and Asian participants equated intimacy more with friendship than did Europeans, with excitement being more of a priority for lovers in the US (Dion & Dion, 1993).

Love too, it seems, is more idealistic in some places than in others. Danes subscribed more to so-called idealistic intimacy (*no one else can love him like I do*) than did English and North American respondents (Landis & O'Shea, 2000). While selecting a partner because of being passionately attracted to their personal qualities may be a prerequisite for romantic love, one large-scale international survey

KEY TERM

Romantic love.
Passion and intimacy though not necessarily commitment.

found these criteria not to be universally applied (Levine *et al.*, 1995). Participants were asked how important love was to marriage, and those from countries associated with an individualist outlook (generally the more affluent ones) appeared to value love more than did those from collectivist and less affluent ones.

However, this association between so-called individualism and romantic love is not cut and dried. Anthropological evidence collected in over 180 societies suggests that in some more traditional societies, while attraction to personal characteristics was felt, cultural taboos such as arranged marriages (see key concept) can inhibit its expression (Jankowiak & Fischer, 1992). Furthermore, some participants in Levine *et al.*'s (1995) survey who were from collectivist contexts were reluctant to marry without love (Smith *et al.*, 2006).

KEY CONCEPT

Arranged Marriages

When did the practice begin?
They date back over 6000 years in some cultures.

What is an arranged marriage like?
Like all marriages they come in different varieties. Some involve parents selecting a potential spouse and exercising a high degree of authority. Other families act as a networking agency to help select an appropriate partner. Many arranged marriages are as much an expression of an alliance between families as between individuals (Dion & Dion, 1993). Love is seen as developing within an arranged marriage, rather than being a prerequisite.

Where do they take place?
They are indigenous to many cultures in the present day, including Egypt, India and China.

Are they in decline?
Yes and no. While still very common in some countries, among well-educated modern families as well as in more traditional contexts there is an increasing trend towards 'love marriage' in many societies where arranged alliances have traditionally been the norm, such as Japan, Egypt and Turkey (Arnett, 2002).

While a reliance on a single romantic partner for support, excitement and friendship may be more common in nations associated with individualism, the evidence suggests that we would be unwise to assume that intimate attachments necessarily take similar forms across cultures.

Limitations of research on culture, love and intimate relationships

1 *Beware the imposed etic when applying imported theories.* Conclusions about culture and intimacy are often drawn from data based on psychometric instruments and concepts such as 'romantic love' and 'secure attachments' which are imported from outside the cultures where they are used (Smith *et al.*, 2006). In short, western notions of love and intimacy have arguably been used as a yardstick against which to measure intimacy in diverse cultures. Arguably, a more *emic* approach might involve developing ways to explore culturally diverse conceptions of intimate attachment. This might for instance involve an acknowledgement of the diverse media used to express love, such as an analysis of the content of popular songs in different cultures (Rothbaum & Tsang, 1998).

2 *Romantic love can take various forms.* When considering whether romantic love is a global phenomenon, we should be aware that romantic attachment is not itself a homogeneous category. Intimate, loving relationships that may be considered romantic by the protagonists may assume different styles in different places. For example, an international sample of over 18,000 respondents (Schmitt *et al.*, 2003) showed that in most nations, if you are in an intimate relationship you typically hold positive feelings about yourself and others – known as a *stable* attachment type. The same survey also suggested that in nations such as Japan and India, loving relationships characterised by negative attitudes towards oneself in relation to others (a so-called preoccupied or *self-effacing* attachment style) are more common.

REFLECTIVE EXERCISE 27

A lovers' tiff

An argument between two partners in an intimate relationship develops, with the male partner insisting that their relationship is no different from any other the world over and they should simply accept this. She insists that there is no blueprint for love, and that it can blossom in multitudinous ways. Suggest two pieces of psychological research that each protagonist might cite to support their argument.

Our biological reproductive drives necessitate some degree of conformity in terms of mate selection, though cultural variations in behaviours relating to love and intimacy invite us to conclude that our love preferences owe something to upbringing.

Culture and social influence

To conclude this chapter we will look at how social psychology's classic **social influence** studies have fared cross-culturally. The term 'social influence' refers to processes by which people affect the actions and attitudes of others. This area of social psychology has traditionally focused on how much of our behaviour arises from the *instructions* of others (in the case of obedience), the *example* of others (in the case of conformity), or the mere *presence* of others (in the case of social facilitation). These three areas were famously studied in the mid-twentieth century in the US in what are regarded as classic experiments in social psychology. As we shall see, subsequent replications and modifications have explored the global applicability of these classics.

KEY TERM

Social influence. Processes by which people affect the actions and attitudes of others.

Culture and obedience

> If a system of death camps were set up in the US of the sort we had seen in Nazi Germany, one would be able to find sufficient personnel for those camps in any medium-sized American town.
>
> (Stanley Milgram, CBS news, 1973)

Milgram's gloomy reflections were based on over 1000 trials of his notorious **obedience** (defined as behaviour affected by instruction) experiments (see key study overleaf), which remain prominent on psychology reading lists today. He claimed that certain situational precursors can drive ordinary people to commit acts of torture and murder. A crucial feature of the obedience scenario is the agentic state, wherein a participant's responsibility for action is projected onto an authority figure (*I was just following orders*). But do Milgram's findings resonate beyond the American towns he spoke of? Would a 65% obedience level show up in research carried out elsewhere?

Milgramesque studies have taken place in numerous nations with comparable and often higher obedience rates (see Table 7.3). At first glance we might conclude that people from, say, The Netherlands are on average more obedient than those from Australia. But this would ignore variations in the testing scenarios across these studies. The samples used, the confederates and the instructions given to participants were not held constant from place to place.

KEY TERM

Obedience. Behaviour affected by instruction.

KEY STUDY

Behavioural study of obedience

Stanley Milgram (1963) wanted to find out if people would obey instructions even if it resulted in fatally injuring a colleague. Participants were drawn from a range of skilled and unskilled occupations. They responded to a newspaper advertisement requesting volunteers 'for a study of memory'. On the day of the experiment each participant reported to Yale University Psychology Department, where they were greeted by a lab-coated man in his thirties who then introduced them to 'Mr Wallace'. Mr Wallace was a confederate playing the role of another participant. The participant and Mr Wallace were informed that they would be working together on an investigation into 'punishment and learning' and that one of them would be assigned the role of 'learner' and the other the role of 'teacher'. Milgram ensured that the participant always got the role of 'teacher'.

Mr Wallace, by now strapped into a (fake) electric chair, was given a (fake) memory test in which he had to demonstrate to the 'teacher' that he had learned a sequence of words. The participant was instructed to give Mr Wallace progressively more intense (fake) electric shocks after each mistake he made. Each time a shock was administered the participant would hear (fake) screams of pain coming from the adjoining room, where Mr Wallace was sitting. Each time he complained of not wanting to continue, the lab-coated official, who was standing only a few feet away from him, would issue verbal prods such as 'please continue' or 'you must go on'.

Milgram wanted to find out how many of the 40 participants would follow the instructions up to the maximum reading on the (fake) voltage board, by which point Mr Wallace's screams had, rather ominously, faded to silence. The answer was 26, or 65%.

For example, one of the highest obedience levels was recorded in The Netherlands (Meeus & Raaijmakers, 1986), and a closer look at this study highlights its unique design. While Milgram's participants used physical violence (electric shocks) to punish their victim, Meeus and Raaijmaker saw psychological violence as more commonplace in the modern world in the form of verbal bullying. They wanted to know if words could be as hurtful as actions, so electric shocks were replaced

TABLE 7.3
Is obedience culturally universal? (based on Smith & Bond, 1998)

Who (and when)?	Where?	Sample	Participants obeying to maximum level
Milgram (1963)	USA	Males/females	65%
Ancona & Pareyson (1968)	Italy	Students	85%
Mantell (1971)	Germany	Males	85%
Kilham & Mann (1974)	Australia	Male students	40%
		Female students	16%
Burley & McGuinness (1977)	UK	Male students	50%
Shanab & Yahya (1978)	Jordan	Students	62%
Miranda et al. (1981)	Spain	Students	90%
Schurz (1985)	Austria	Males/females	80%
Meeus & Raaijmakers (1986)	The Netherlands	Males/females	92%

with verbal haranguing. Their 91.7% obedience level suggests that psychological violence may be easier to deliver than physical violence. Perhaps the consequences of psychological violence are less disconcerting for a perpetrator. This is interesting in itself, yet when making cross-cultural obedience comparisons we should bear in mind the lack of standardisation in the designs of these studies.

So, what can we learn from cross-cultural obedience research? Well, while conclusions about national obedience levels may be suspect, there are indications from these studies that some of the factors influencing levels of acquiescence in the original studies apply universally. For example, Milgram found that where participants were able to instruct a confederate to press the decisive 'shock' button instead of pressing it themselves, obedience rose significantly. This effect was endorsed in Australia (Kilham & Mann, 1974). Similarly, the presence of a dissenting peer, refusing to obey orders, depressed obedience levels in Germany and The Netherlands, as it did at Yale.

It seems, then, that doing as you're told is a global phenomenon. Furthermore, how far people will go may depend not just on culture but also on the prevailing testing conditions and on certain interpersonal properties of the prevailing obedience scenario.

Culture, conformity and independent behaviour

Just like everybody else, I tend to think of myself as unique. The reality, however, is that from time to time we all display behaviour affected by example, known as **conformity**. Perhaps more than any other research in social psychology, Asch's (1955) conformity experiments (see key study) alert us to this tendency to deny the evidence of our own eyes in the interests of not standing out from a crowd. But were

KEY TERM

Conformity.
Behaviour affected
by example.

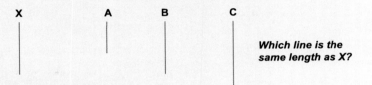

KEY STUDY

Asch's study of conformity

The classic conformity study was conducted by Solomon Asch (1955). Student participants were shown an array of lines (see below) and asked whether X was most similar in length to A, B or C. Prior to making an estimate each participant witnessed six confederates make obviously incorrect answers ('C'). Asch found that participants were induced to conform to the incorrect response on 37% of trials.

X   A   B   C

Which line is the same length as X?

Asch's findings a child of their time and place, or do they apply beyond 1950s America?

To investigate this question, Bond and Smith (1996) conducted a meta-analysis of Asch-style conformity studies from 17 nations. Table 7.4 ranks the resulting cross-cultural conformity effects from

TABLE 7.4
A meta-analysis of conformity studies (based on Bond & Smith, 1998)

Ranked size of average conformity effects, where rank '1' is the largest average conformity effect	Number of studies
1. Fiji	2
2. Hong Kong	1
3. Zimbabwe, Ghana, DR Congo	3
6. Brazil	3
7. Japan	5
8. Canada	1
9. Kuwait, Lebanon	2
11. Asch studies	18
12. Belgium	4
13. Germany	1
14. US (excluding Asch)	79
15. UK	10
16. Netherlands	1
17. Portugal	1
18. France	2

highest to lowest. In these samples at least, conformity was more pronounced outside Europe and North America. We might conclude from this that conformity is associated with life in technologically and economically less developed nations, those towards the collectivist end of the individualism–collectivism dimension (see Chapter 1). Indeed, Punetha *et al.* (1987) noted a greater endorsement of non-conformist values among British participants than among those from Asia.

However, conclusions from cross-cultural meta-analyses should be drawn cautiously. Several design factors were not held constant across studies, so variables other than culture probably affected the temptation to conform. Indeed, Bond and Smith found that when more confederate judges took part in the study, conformity increased. More face-to-face contact between judges and participants had a similar effect. Nevertheless, despite these variations in design there are grounds for arguing that societies that are organised in certain ways lend themselves to the socialisation of conformity. It seems reasonable to suggest that a society with a dense population and a more stratified organisation would engender more habitual conformity than would less stratified, less populous ones (Berry *et al.*, 2002). Berry and colleagues explored this link between conformity and societal organisation by focusing on how these effects were manifest in different types of subsistence economies.

When performances on Asch-like tasks were observed, participants from hunter-based societies (with looser forms of social organisation) produced fewer conforming responses than did farmers from societies with tighter levels of social organisation. Arguably, socialisation in more rigorously organised societies facilitates less assertive, more compliant attitudes (Stropes-Roe & Cochrane, 1990).

Are we becoming more independently minded, worldwide?

An interesting observation from Bond and Smith's meta-analytical data was that broadly (and globally) speaking, conformity effects fade with time. More recent studies (irrespective of culture) showed a smaller conformity effect size, which may indicate a historical rise in **independent behaviour**, or resistance to pressures to conform. It is often said that Asch's conformity effect was a child of its time (Perrin & Spencer, 1981), a waning phenomenon from a less assertive age. But we should perhaps point out that in some regions tolerance of resistance to social pressure to conform has long been observed experimentally. For example, during times of political unrest, research among Japanese students revealed a strong current of anti-conformity,

KEY TERM

Independent behaviour. Resistance to pressures to conform.

with a noticeable willingness to voice views against the consensus (Frager, 1970).

Is independent behaviour more socially acceptable in some places than in others? In cross-cultural comparisons of the treatment of those who stray from group influence, Schachter *et al.* (1954) observed attitudes towards eleven-year-old confederates who deliberately deviated from majority opinions about the attributes of a model aeroplane. He found that the tendency to criticise 'deviants' was stronger in some nations (US, France, Norway) than in others (Germany, UK, The Netherlands, Belgium). Once again, these results come with a health warning: the procedures were not standardised across cultures.

Research into culture and independent behaviour is inspired by Moscovici's (1976) work on social influence resulting from exposure to the opinions of a minority, known as minority influence. The influence exerted by minorities may be more gradual than compliance to a majority view, though its effect has been shown to be tangible and durable in various cultural settings. An experimental minority-influence scenario typically involves the altering of group opinions in response to an independently minded dissenter expressing confident, consistent views. In one study the 'deviant' labelled a blue-green slide 'green' and a tendency for the majority to follow suit was observed (Moscovici & Personnaz, 1980). The minority-influence effect is recorded first by participants making their judgements in the presence of the deviant confederate, and subsequently when asked privately what after-image they saw. Red-purple is green's after-image, so would be considered a response made under minority influence. A 'red-purple' response also demonstrates the durability of the effect.

Most cross-cultural minority influence replications have taken place in Europe, though they do reveal regional variations in the influence of the dissenting minority (Smith & Bond, 1998). In the after-image trial, respondents in France, Greece, Switzerland and Italy showed a significantly greater effect than did those in the US, the UK and The Netherlands. There appears to be a regional divide of sorts, with Southern Europeans more influenced by minority opinion.

The effect of a confident, consistent minority has also been demonstrated experimentally in Japanese research, using a variety of experimental designs (Koseki, 1989; Atsumi & Sugiman, 1990). Here too, minority influence shows signs of durability. In the Japanese context a deviant minority has been shown to have a greater effect where the deviant has higher social status and, predictably, in the event of close decisions that are difficult to call. While this may reflect a tendency to reduce collective anxiety during incidents of disharmony, it could be argued that the European trials using the blue-green colour estimations also demonstrate that the influence of a confident minority is likely to be greatest when issues at stake amount to relatively ambiguous, grey (or green) areas. Overall, evidence from research into independent behaviour shows that, under favourable conditions, a consistent, confident deviate can exert influence in a variety of cultural settings.

Culture and social loafing

The more cooks, the worse potage

(anonymous proverb)

The mere presence of others can affect how we behave, whether they are doing the same thing as us or simply watching. This effect, known as *social facilitation*, takes many forms and can either improve performance on a task or fluster us and force blunders. For example, it has been found that on familiar, relatively straightforward tasks, being watched can inspire us to do better than we would alone (Zajonc, 1966). But the social facilitation effect that has most occupied cross-cultural psychologists is **social loafing**, which occurs when an individual's performance on a task deteriorates when working with others. Anyone who's participated in a group tug o' war will recognise the opportunity to slack a little and let others take the strain. Latané *et al.* (1979) demonstrated this effect by asking participants to make as much noise as possible either alone or in a group. When measured individually, participants' noise levels far exceeded that which they made when in groups.

Social loafing studies from across cultures suggest some interesting cultural differences. Earley (1993) compared managerial trainees in the US with their nearest equivalents in China on tasks for which they were either individually accountable or working alongside colleagues to achieve a group goal. Loafing was significantly more common in the US than in the Chinese sample. Indeed, among Chinese schoolchildren enhanced performance when working alongside others (known as social striving) (Matsumoto & Juang, 2004), has even been observed (Gabrenya *et al.*, 1985).

It has been demonstrated that cultural differences in these effects are more common with more difficult tasks. Karau and Williams (1993) found few cultural differences between US and Pacific Asian participants in social loafing on simple tasks such as hand-clapping

KEY TERM

Social loafing. When an individual's performance on a task deteriorates when working together with others.

and generally being noisy. Yet when the same groups were challenged with more difficult tasks, Pacific Asian groups showed social striving when working in groups. In another study Israeli and Chinese managers were motivated to greater things when they thought they were part of a group, while US participants were inspired by the thought of working alone (Earley, 1993). Earley went on to correlate loafing scores with a measure of individualism–collectivism (see Chapter 1), and a tendency towards loafing was significantly predicted by positions on this dimension; more individualistic responses correlated positively with loafing, irrespective of a respondent's nationality. This suggests that individualism–collectivism is a reliable index of social loafing, which actually indicates that we can reliably predict behaviour to some degree without resorting to discussions of nationality (Smith *et al.*, 2006).

The differences in social loafing that we have discussed here, between participants in Asia and America, reflect historically acknowledged cultural norms of collectivism and individualism in these two regions. Yet such differences should not be taken for granted. The global rise of (individualistic) capitalism may erode collectivist attitudes in Asian regions and this may have a knock-on effect on social striving tendencies. By the same token, some US companies are embracing collectivist, team-based management styles from Asia (Matsumoto & Juang, 2004). This may conceivably have some effect on social loafing in the US. These cultural exchanges of ideas may explain why Westaby (1995) found no real differences between American and Japanese participants on social loafing tasks. On the contrary, the presence of others improved performance in both cultural groups in this study. It would, in summary, be no surprise if future research were to show cultural differences in social loafing becoming less polarised.

Limitations of research culture and social influence

1 *Experiments on social influence underplay human agency.* Some social psychologists have argued that classic laboratory research into obedience and other aspects of social influence has underestimated the way humans carry out independent behaviour under their own agency in more natural contexts. Haslam and Reicher (2003) argue that despite what has been found in the laboratory, harmful action is often initiated from lower down the social hierarchy, not necessarily by an authority figure. Equally, in everyday exchanges instructions are often given and obeyed between people

of equal rank. We might therefore suggest that occupants of lower rungs of the social ladder (prisoners, children, military personnel) are not simply passive respondents to social pressure (Mandel, 1998). They can instigate destructive, harmful, or pro-social acts from the bottom up. When analysing research findings from the world's laboratories, it may be worth remembering that they do not successfully mimic everyday conduct.

2 *It's easy to get hooked on the classics.* Critics of cross-cultural replications of social psychology's classic studies might legitimately argue that dwelling on this research as a means of exploring the relationship between culture and social influence shows a reluctance to decentre from psychology's American mainstream. In other words, to cling to global replications of the admittedly very influential work of Milgram and Asch may be to ignore the development of indigenous questions about social behaviour that arise from around the world. Arguably, too much reliance on research questions that were originally devised at American universities fuels the view that mainstream psychology is really only the indigenous psychology of Americans (Markus & Kitayama, 2003).

So does culture change the way we see ourselves – and others?

This chapter has shown us that self-construal, attribution, love, obedience and a variety of other social behaviours are mediated by culture, or at least our personal endorsement of values such as individualism and collectivism. Interestingly, these are two separate phenomena since actually, while individualist values may be more predominant in some regions of the world, all nations are likely to have individuals who vary along these scales. We cannot therefore glibly use 'nation' as a predictor of social behaviour. Arguably though, cultural variations in social behaviour may owe much to differential childrearing practices across cultures. These will be reviewed in the next chapter.

Summary

Chapter 7 reviews social psychology's forays into global research. Several classic studies of obedience, conformity, social loafing and other aspects of social facilitation have been widely replicated across cultures. Descriptions and evaluations of these replications are covered here, as are more contemporary studies of non-conformity, minority influence and independent behaviour. You will also find an overview of the global applicability of established theories of prejudice.

Besides these 'classics' of social psychology, Chapter 7 examines the global application of psychological research on social cognition. In particular, researchers have sought to establish whether the way we perceive ourselves and attribute causes to behaviour varies from culture to culture. Self-construal (how we see ourselves) and attribution bias (how we explain actions) appear to manifest themselves differently the world over.

Another area of social behaviour that appears culturally relative is love and relationships. Institutions such as monogamy, polygamy and arranged marriages are evidence for this. Several studies into cultural differences in relationships are described and evaluated here. All in all, this chapter reflects a wide diversity of social behaviour from the annals of global psychology.

REFLECTIVE EXERCISE 28

Match up the definitions on the right with the terms on the left (see p. 227 for answers)

Terms	Definitions
	Enhanced performance when working alongside others
	An individual's performance on a task deteriorates when working together with others
Social striving	Tendency to explain the actions of others using internal causes
Social loafing	Blend of cognitive and social psychology that looks at our attitudes to and perceptions of those around us
Minority influence	Social influence resulting from exposure to the opinions of a minority
Fundamental attribution error	Resistance to pressures to conform
Social cognition	We categorise ourselves according to which social groups we find attractive, and seek out those who belong to the same group as ourselves
Prejudice	Passion and intimacy, though not necessarily commitment
Allocentrism	Behaviour affected by example
Social identity theory	Attitudes (usually negative) towards particular social groups, based on their group membership
Conformity	Processes by which people affect the actions and attitudes of others
Social influence	Behaviour affected by instruction
Obedience	A style of social cognition that favours explaining behaviour in terms of social contexts
Independent behaviour	
Romantic love	

FURTHER READING

- Moscovici, S. (1976) *Social Influence and Social Change*, London: Academic Press.
- Smith, P. & Bond, M. (1998) *Social Psychology across Cultures*, London: Prentice Hall.
- Smith, P., Bond, M. & Kagitcibasi (2006) *Understanding Social Psychology across Cultures*, London: Sage.

Culture and child development

Childhood across cultures

8

What this chapter will teach you

- What is the relationship between childhood and culture?
- Does parenting differ across cultures?
- Is attachment theory applicable across cultures?
- What are **parental ethnotheories**?
- Does **temperament** differ across cultures?
- What are **sex** and **gender**?
- Are **gender expectations** culturally universal?

Does culture change our experience of childhood?

A lot of people around the world are children. In the developing world every third person is under the age of 15. Globally, the figure is 29% (World Population Bureau, 2007). Childhood, though, is not just a matter of being relatively young. The way in which it is experienced depends partly on its cultural and historical context. For example, being young in medieval Europe was, it has been argued, incomparable with contemporary notions of childhood since it lacked the emotional kinship ties that so characterise it today (Cunningham, 2006). It is also suggested that in the modern era childhood in certain cultural settings has unique characteristics. A typically American childhood, for example, may be characterised by a social desire for obedience to parental authority which may not be stressed so much elsewhere (Kessen, 1979).

Arguably, then, where you are brought up has an enormous bearing on the kind of childhood you are in for. Contextual factors such as family size, poverty and access to schooling are all likely to influence a child's 'career', and of course all these factors vary across cultures. We can infer from this that childhood is to some extent a culturally relative phenomenon. How relative, though, is a moot point.

The extent of cultural variation – and of any commonalities in childhood experience across cultures – will be explored in the light of psychological research in the following pages.

Culture and childhood in micro and macro

The relationship between culture and childhood can be viewed up close (at a micro level), or from a distance (at a macro level). At close quarters it is commonly portrayed as involving the transmission of values and beliefs between caregivers (usually parents) and children, via *socialisation* and *enculturation* (see Chapter 3). However, as the following key concept indicates, this may be an oversimplification. Socialisation is not a one-way street down which elders' beliefs pass to a younger generation. Rather, it involves the exchange and formation of ideas between adults, children and peers.

Typically, parents and children engage in socialisation by participating in ongoing transactions that lead to the movement and propagation of ideas in more than one direction (Matsumoto & Juang, 2004). Thanks to this bidirectional exchange, new cultural phenomena (beliefs, behaviours, artefacts) emerge. This bi-directional model of socialisation should strike a chord with any adult who spends time with children, who would surely have to concede that they learn as many things as they teach.

At the macro level the child's socialisation into its culture is part of a broader process involving biological, environmental and cultural factors. Cole (1998) explores the relative contributions of these factors in the wider context to human development. His *cultural mediation* model (Figure 8.1) stresses the pivotal part played by culture in the

---

KEY CONCEPT

Socialisation

Defined as . . .   . . . The process whereby an individual acquires the knowledge, values, facility with language, social skills and social sensitivity that enables him or her to become integrated into and behave adaptively within a society (Reber, 1997, p. 732).

In other words . . .   . . . it is a process by which children (and adults) learn to adapt to society, to conform to its expectations. It is also a two-way process since the individual influences the society of which he/she is a small part (Westen, 1999).

Agents of socialisation are . . .   . . . institutions with which the individual negotiates in order to adapt to society's norms and values. They include the family, schools, religion and the mass media.

Socialisation involves . . .   . . . the child actively making sense of the world by attaching meanings to new experiences at home, in the playground, in the classroom. In short, new ideas and skills (schemas) are accumulated through experience. The child makes sense of the world by the twin processes of assimilation and accommodation (Piaget, 1952). Assimilation involves dealing with new experiences by using existing, unaltered schemas. Accommodation involves altering and adding to existing schemas in order to adapt to new experiences; for example, learning a new word to label a newly encountered object.

---

developmental process. Borrowing from Tylor (1874), Cole views cultures as complex entities incorporating beliefs, morals, customs and artefacts (such as tools and language systems). Cultures are shaped by (and shape) external environments. They are also shaped by (and shape) human evolution. Thus, ideas emanating from previous generations influence the way future generations evolve culturally and biologically.

Cultural mediation theory (which is central to the *cultural psychology* approach (see Chapter 5) casts culture in the role of a filter through which other biological and environmental forces are mediated. The mediating role of culture in the development of humans urges us to understand childhood, adolescence and adulthood as phenomena that should be viewed in their unique cultural and historical contexts.

Micro and macro approaches to human development come together in Bronfenbrenner's (1979) ecological, layered model, wherein socialisation and its relationship with culture are portrayed in the form of a series of ever-increasing, concentric circles (see Figure 8.2). Here, the developing child is seen as simultaneously transacting with the

Cole (1998) proposes several alternative models for portraying the way in which human development fits into the grander scheme of environmental and biological influence. The first three models outlined here award varying importance to *biological* and *environmental* factors in human development. The fourth, *cultural mediation*, model offers an alternative explanation in which biology and environment do not directly interact with each other. Instead their influence is mediated by culture.

Biological maturation theory
Development proceeds through a sequence of invariant biological stages. Environmental influences affect the rate of development, though not the order or universal quality of maturation (Gesell, 1940).

Environmental learning theory
Like a lump of clay, the individual is sculpted by environmental influences (role models, reinforcements), while the genetic blueprint barely exerts an influence (Skinner, 1953).

Interactional theory
Biological maturation and environmental learning have equal weighting in development. As well as biologically determined maturation, individuals play an active role in adapting to their environment (Piaget, 1973).

Cultural mediation theory
Rather than biological and environmental factors vying *directly* for control over human development, their influence is mediated through a 'third force' – culture. Culture is seen as a distinct constituent of development, a medium through which biological and environmental factors are expressed. For developmental psychologists this means that an appreciation of the cultural context of behaviour is necessary for a full understanding of developmental processes.

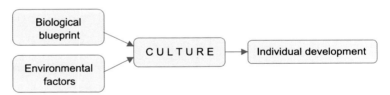

Figure 8.1 Macro-models of human development

world as a *micro-system*, an *exo-system* and a *macro-system*. In the micro-system the main agents of socialisation are the immediate, significant others such as families, schools and peers. More distant protagonists (local government agencies, friends of friends, mass media) engage with the developing individual at the level of the exo-system. Finally, larger cultural institutions and historic values constitute the macro-system: these are perhaps the most deeply rooted ideas to distinguish one culture from another. These three systems are distinct yet intertwined. They provide a context for the development of the individual and for the evolution of the culture itself through meaningful exchanges with its constituents.

However we portray the David and Goliath-like relationship between the individual and his/her developmental context, it seems fair to argue

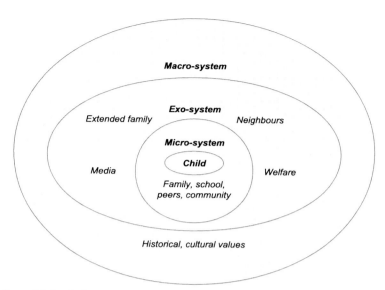

Figure 8.2 Bronfenbrenner's model of human development

that the elements involved will vary from culture to culture. For example, ideas about how children should be guided through childhood by those who are closest to them (most often parents) are likely to vary from one region to another. Indeed, you may have noticed your own neighbours disagreeing about how to raise their children, so we should certainly expect these differences of opinion to multiply across cultures. Yet as we shall see in the next section, there is also a high degree of agreement about what constitutes effective childrearing.

> ## REFLECTIVE EXERCISE 29
>
> 1. What is the difference between *micro* and *macro* socialisation?
>
> 2. What do we mean when we say that the socialisation process is *bidirectional*?

Culture and parenting practices

There's an old saying that while some people are brought up, others are dragged up. Not dissimilarly, one author has written that while in some cultures children grow up, in others they are brought up (Kagitcibasi, 1996). This reminds us that parental input takes various forms both within and across cultures. Arguably, some cultures traditionally sanction a more interventionist parenting style than others. Such cultural differences in socialisation have a profound effect on how youngsters 'turn out'.

Cultural variations in parenting: bedtime, playtime, doing as you're told

Culturally diverse parenting practices manifest themselves in many ways, from domestic discipline regimes to divisions of labour around the home, to the more general goals that parents set for their children. There are indications that the ways in which parents socialise their children vary considerably cross-culturally. Levine *et al.* (1996) compared household routines among the agricultural Gusii of Kenya with those observed in a sample of (US) Bostonian suburb-dwellers, and noticed a greater expectation for children to help with chores in the former, coupled with more parental emphasis on intellectual stimulation in the latter.

Domestic sleeping habits also reflect culturally diverse parenting. Anecdotally it is suggested that Spanish children stay up relatively late into the night, that rural African children fall asleep amid a hubbub of outdoor activity and that Japanese children rise relatively early for school. Is there any evidence to support these observations? Cross-cultural studies do reveal cultural differences in 'bedtime habits'. For example, US parents encourage their children to sleep alone more often than their rural European and (Central American) Mayan counterparts do (Morelli *et al.*, 1992). Such differences may of course reflect material differences in income and space, as well as differences in the desire to allow children more independence. Another comparison found Dutch parents to be particularly insistent on an 'early to bed and plenty of sleep' regime, with under-fives getting up to two hours' more sleep than a US comparison group (Super *et al.*, 1996). Interestingly, these findings correlate with what was perceived to be calmer waking behaviour in Dutch infants.

Sleeping patterns aside, divisions of parental responsibilities between genders also show cultural variation. Fathers in Mexico, France and Italy indulged in a greater proportion of playtime activities than did those from other national groups, with German fathers most likely to eschew playtime or leave it to mum (Best & Ruther, 1994). Elsewhere, differences have also been observed in parental discipline regimes. As you may remember from your own childhood, several strategies are open to parents seeking to get children to do as they're told. Compliant behaviour may be requested in the name of authority (*because I'm in charge*), feelings (*because so and so will be upset*), consequences (*because 'x' will happen if you don't behave*), rules (*because that's not allowed*), or modelling (*because good boys don't do that*). Comparing the use of these strategies across cultures, Conroy *et al.* (1980) found authority strategies to be common in a US sample, while stressing interpersonal relationships (such as feelings) was significantly more common in Japanese families. In a comparison of disciplinary techniques among cultural groups within the US, European American mothers preferred to use consistency, sensitivity and rule-setting, while Chinese Americans were more likely to yell and administer minor physical punishments, typical of an authority strategy.

It seems evident that from playtime to bedtime, parenting plays by different rules in different places. Arguably, cultural differences in parenting correspond with the transmission of norms, beliefs and behaviours that have an optimum survival value for those who operate in these cultures and for the cultures a whole. However, as we are about to discover, cross-cultural research into parenting has also revealed many common practices.

Cultural commonalities in parenting

Despite their differences, parents the world over operate in many similar ways. Certain common practices, such as baby-carrying to allow hands free access to other activities, may go back over a million years (Konner, 1972). This may partly explain why the human infant has evolved into a relatively immobile creature, unable to do much for itself in the first months, compared with the young of some other species.

Another global parenting practice with a long history is weaning (the gradual process of accustoming mammalian offspring to do without their mother's milk). Most non-industrial human societies share a pre-weaning phase of three to four years, which corresponds proportionally to pre-weaning in other primates as it represents one-third to a quarter of the age until female sexual maturity (Berry *et al.*, 2002). There are, however, limits to the cultural universality of this practice, with parents in many industrialised societies typically weaning earlier.

Language development in children reveals another parenting habit that has been identified as a global phenomenon: **motherese**. It appears that many of the world's parents are fluent in this strange language. This seemingly ubiquitous dialect involves vocal intonation patterns directed towards infants that are characterised by raising the pitch of the voice, exaggerated variations in sound (doing funny voices) and generally talking in nonsense syllables. Papousek and Papousek (1997) listened to motherese worldwide and pronounced it a truly inter-

KEY TERM

Motherese. Vocal intonation patterns directed towards infants that are characterised by raising the pitch of the voice, exaggerated variations in sound.

national language, though they found parents throwing themselves into it in some regions more than in others. Japanese mothers, for example, were found to use more 'singing and nonsense' than comparison groups.

It appears, then, that while we can identify aspects of parenting that seem to be culturally widespread, the influence of culture is detectible even in these behaviours.

Culturally diverse parental styles and ethnotheories

So far we have presented evidence to suggest that while parents in different cultures may all nurture, protect and feed their offspring, they approach the role of the parent in diverse ways. Could it thus be argued that parenting in different cultures assumes differing styles – some authoritarian, others *laissez-faire* or easy-going, for example? Baumrind (1971) distinguishes between three parenting styles:

- *Authoritarian:* requires high levels of obedience; displays little warmth.
- *Permissive:* allows autonomy; displays warmth.
- *Authoritative:* firm but fair; displays warmth.

The last of these is widely thought to be most associated with the development of healthy, stable, sociable children (Denham *et al.*, 1997). But how does this model fare when applied cross-culturally? Chen *et al.* (1997) found a correlation between authoritative parenting and good levels of social adjustment among Chinese children, thus supporting Baumrind's hypothesis. However, we should be aware that Baumrind's typology arises from a Euro-American context, so it may not translate to Asia. We cannot, for instance, assume the connotations of authoritarianism, which may be negative in certain cultural settings, to be similarly negative elsewhere.

Rather than using imported typologies to rate parenting across cultures, it may be more useful to identify theories and styles of parenting that originate in diverse locations, known as **parental ethnotheories** (Harkness & Super, 1995). These indigenous ethnotheories underwrite the diverse ideas held by parents on matters relating to learning, sleeping, discipline and play. For example, in a study by Tobin *et al.* (1989), Japanese parents' valuing of social interdependency (high levels of reciprocal interactions) was reflected in their approval of pre-school groups of over 30 pupils (*more social interaction is a good thing for my child and for our society as a whole*). Such a positive view would

KEY TERM

Parental
ethnotheories.
Theories and styles
of parenting that
originate in diverse
locations.

not gel with a stereotypically European outlook, emerging from a more individualistic ethnotheory (*too many children playing together may hold back my child*).

Parental ethnotheories also manifest themselves in the expectations parents hold for their children about how old they should be when they acquire various skills. For example, the mastery of various perceptual, cognitive and interpersonal skills has been anticipated at an earlier age by parents from more industrialised, more affluent regions (Harkness & Super, 1995).

KEY TERM

Temperament.
Biological
predisposition to
behave in certain
ways.

Parenting is a two-way street: the role of temperament

So far we have focused on variations and similarities in parenting practices across cultures. However, it should be obvious from our experiences as parents and children that the development of children is not just a question of how parents treat them. Rather, development is a two-way street along which parental influence and the **temperament** of the child interact. How a child turns out is due to its own biological predisposition to behave in certain ways, its parents' and caregivers' responses, as well as sundry other environmental factors (Berry *et al.*, 2002). Having already discussed various parenting styles, let us now consider the role of an infant's temperament in this ongoing interaction.

You often hear parents say of a child, *Oh she has a lovely temperament*. For psychologists, this term refers to a *biologically based style of interacting with the world* (Matsumoto & Juang, 2004) which, in turn, affects the parental response. Earlier we considered differing styles of parenting. Distinctions have also been made between various temperamental styles (Thomas & Chess, 1977):

- *Easy:* adaptable, consistent in responses and emotions.
- *Difficult:* inconsistent, moody, intense.
- *Cool:* withdrawn at first, becoming responsive with familiarity.

Together with the parental response, these styles yield a developmental outcome. But do these styles vary cross-culturally? In one cross-cultural study (which you might not want to try at home), a cloth was laid over an infant's head and face and the reaction described (Freedman, 1974). Chinese infants were more likely to simply let it happen, breathing through the cloth and lying still. A typically more agitated reaction was observed in an American sample. Other researchers have found temperamental differences in similar demonstrations, with Chinese and Navajo infants seemingly less irritable than those from the US and Ireland (Kagan, 1994).

What might precipitate differences in biologically predisposed temperament? The answer to this is not immediately obvious, although correlations have been found between average levels of blood pressure in mothers from certain cultural settings and infant irritability (Garcia Coll, 1990). Besides the mother's health, ecological factors also correlate with temperamental responses in the first 30 days after birth. For example, Peruvian infants born at high altitude were more agitated during these early weeks than were those born around sea level (Saco-Pollit, 1989). Although this suggests that newborns from some cultures may be predisposed towards certain responses, these behavioural differences may equally be explained by identifying very early parental practices such as body contact, massaging and vocalisation in the first thirty days. Clearly, parental responses and temperament are an influential double act whose mutual influence cannot easily be separated.

Temperamental differences, it should be remembered, are no more than a biological predisposition towards certain responses. They may be expressed or inhibited by the parental and environmental influence. Furthermore, we cannot rely on labels such as *easy*, *difficult* and *cool* to be equally meaningful, or indeed equally adaptive, across cultures. A child who is labelled as having a difficult temperament may actually have a positive survival advantage in some situations. Certain environments may require an infant to be fussy, demanding or challenging in order to survive large families or scarce food supplies (DeVries, 1989). Once again this reminds us of the dangers of applying generalised typologies across cultures.

Parenting styles and temperamental predispositions are ingredients that interact to yield a developmental outcome, the growing human being. The cultural manifestations of these ingredients are manifold, but those that have been observed worldwide are the ones that represent the best survival prospects of the cultures themselves, as well as the families who make them up.

Limitations of research on culture and parenting

1 *What do we mean by cultural differences in parenting?* When drawing conclusions regarding the proposed relation between culture and childhood experience and parenting practices, we should be wary of what is actually meant by the term 'culture' in this equation. On closer inspection it may be that cultural influences mask material

or economic differences between groups. For example, it has been noted that certain cognitive skills develop at different ages in different cultural settings. Closer inspection of this conclusion reveals that some skills are expected to develop later in less affluent nations, as well as in those where larger family size is the norm, or where mothers are educated to a lower average level (Willemsen, 1996). Findings like these suggest that what appear to be cultural differences in parenting often have a strong educational or economic element. Therefore, rather than labelling these differences as cultural, we may do well to recognise their socio-economic origin.

2 *Parenting is only part of the socialisation picture.* Although research into the effects of diverse parenting practices on the development of children is informative, over-concentration thereon runs the risk of not recognising the role of the agents of socialisation that form Bronfenbrenner's *exo-system* (see Figure 8.2). The effects of these exo-system values on the development of the child should not be ignored, especially when we consider that around three-quarters of non-European families in the US see themselves as extended organisations (Fields, 2001). Examples of research into attachments that are formed between children and extended family members will be considered in the next section.

> ## REFLECTIVE EXERCISE 30
>
> 1. What is the difference between *interdependent* and *individualistic* parental ethnotheories?
>
> 2. Which of these three concepts is not thought to be biologically based?
>   a. Socialisation
>   b. Temperament
>   c. Maturation

Attachment and strange situations

Developmental psychologists have long recognised that **attachment patterns** (emotional ties between people, such as parents and infants) formed in early childhood have lasting effects on our sense of who we are (self) and on how we interact (sociability). An influential view of early attachment is the so-called *epigenetic* model (from *epigenesis*, meaning to multiply gradually). The emotionally healthy infant is seen as moving from a single caregiver (usually the mother) in the first year towards numerous secondary attachments with extended family and peers (Smith, 1980). Variations on this epigenetic pattern are seen by proponents of this model as detrimental to the child's development (Bowlby, 1969). Proponents of the classic epigenetic view claim that the infant's bond with the mother is (biologically) qualitatively different

KEY TERM

Attachment patterns. Emotional ties between people.

KEY TERM

Monotropy. The infant's bond with the mother is (biologically) qualitatively different from any other, so any interruption to this bond is necessarily maladaptive.

from any other, so any interruption to this bond is necessarily maladaptive. This is also known as **monotropy** theory (Bowlby, 1951).

Several writers have disputed the unconditional primacy of the maternal bond as an essential building block for healthy development. For example, after extensive naturalistic observations of infant–caregiver interactions, Schaffer and Emerson (1964) concluded that a maternal bond must be of high quality to be primarily beneficial for the infant. Arguably, then, a maternal bond *per se* is not a prerequisite for healthy attachment.

Mary Ainsworth's *et al.*'s (1978) *strange situation* experiments sought to investigate further the primary nature of the attachment between mother and infant, and have been used to validate the epigenetic approach. In the original experimental scenario a twelve-month-old infant was observed interacting with its mother, then without her, then in variations on this theme (see key study). Infants were rated according to the security of their maternal bond as an index of their

KEY STUDY

Ainsworth *et al.*'s 'strange situation' experiment (1978)

Twelve-month-old infants are observed in various situations:

1 with their mother
2 as mother leaves the room
3 alone
4 with a stranger
5 as mother returns.

On the basis of their reactions to each situation, infants are assigned to one of three categories, reflecting the security of their attachment with their mother.

(a) **Securely attached child**: the infant returns to the mother when she appears and is easily consoled.
(b) **Anxious-avoidant child**: on the caregiver's return the infant turns away, avoiding comfort.
(c) **Anxious-resistant child**: the infant is often upset in the caregiver's presence and on separation; and on reunion, closeness is sporadically resisted.

reactions in each situation. Those with the most secure maternal attachments preferred mother to other carers, though they were not overly upset in the company of strangers. Ainsworth's research bolstered the epigenetic view of the primacy of the maternal bond as a foundation stone for healthy development.

Culture and strange situations

Various cross-cultural versions of Ainsworth's research have precipitated a debate about whether the securely attached child should be recognised as a global ideal. Indeed, even before Ainsworth's studies were conducted, cross-cultural support for the epigenetic model of attachment came from Konner's (1981) fieldwork with !Kung hunter-gatherers in the Kalahari region of southern Africa ('!' represents the linguistic clicking sound used by the group). During their first year, !Kung infants were with their mother for 70–80% of the time. This percentage subsequently fell as the social network expanded to include father and mixed-age peers.

Following Ainsworth's original studies, versions of the strange situation experiment were conducted in many cultural settings in order to investigate the cultural universality of attachment patterns. The classic experimental format was used as a standardised design and then replicated in accordance with a *cross-cultural* research paradigm (see Chapter 1).

So, are Ainsworth's findings replicated across cultures? Well, attachment patterns corresponding to 'secure' in Ainsworth's scenario have shown up to be ideal arrangements in many cultural settings. When Posada *et al.* (1995) asked mothers from China, Germany, Israel, Colombia and Japan to rate the characteristics of an ideal child, their profiles tallied closely with Ainsworth's securely attached model. Furthermore, more children invited the 'secure' classification than any other classification in a review of fourteen attachment studies across four continents (van Ijzendoorn & Sagi, 1999). In another meta-analysis, van Ijzenddoorn (1996) also found the securely attached pattern to be the most common across eight nations, inviting the portrayal of the securely attached child as the global ideal or norm.

Yet there is also counter-evidence. Grossman and Grossman (1990), Takahashi (1986) and others have revealed cultural variations in the degree to which infants in different cultures are assigned to Ainsworth's three categories (see Table 8.1). In short, infants in some countries appeared to be typically more securely attached, or anxious-resistant, than they were in others.

TABLE 8.1
Cross-cultural categorisations in the 'strange situation' (%)

Country	Secure	Anx-avoidant	Anx-resistant	Researchers
USA	67	21	12	Ainsworth et al. (1978)
Germany	35	52	13	Grossman & Grossman (1990)
Israel	57	7	34	Sagi et al. (1985)
Japan	68	0	32	Takahashi (1990)

Such regional variations have since invited two alternative explanations:

- *Explanation 1: Some cultures yield more secure infants than others do.* The strange situation scenario is a measure of emotional attachment that is equally valid (meaning it measures what it sets out to measure) in all cultures. Variable patterns show secure attachments to be more common in some places (North America) than in others (Germany). Furthermore, the anxious-resistant response seems to be more a feature of Japanese and Israeli society than it does elsewhere.
- *Explanation 2: The strange situation scenario is not meaningful in all cultures.* The strange situation scenario is not equally valid across cultures. It has different meanings for participants in different contexts. We cannot assume that categories used in Ainsworth's original study mean the same thing in all places. This standard scenario cannot provide us with 'like-for-like' cross-cultural comparisons of attachment patterns.

Defenders of the first of these explanations may conclude that North American infants are typically more securely attached than their German counterparts, with Japanese culture being associated with more anxious infants. Arguing for the second explanation, Grossman and Grossman (1990) suggest that Ainsworth's notion of 'anxious-avoidance' has a different meaning in Germany, where it is reinterpreted as 'autonomy' and considered a virtue. Takahashi (1990) too stresses the special cultural meaning of the strange situation scenario for Japanese one-year-olds, who traditionally rarely stray from their mothers. The strange situation experiment is therefore especially stressful for them, leading to their over-categorisation as 'anxious-resistant'.

Such diverse cultural interpretations reflect a methodological dilemma for Ainsworth's paradigm. *Explanation 1* invites the replication of her experiment in a standard form across cultures. Yet Cole (1992), writing from the viewpoint of *cultural psychology* (see Chapter 5), expresses concern that this rides roughshod over the diverse cultural meanings attached to these experiments. The way forward, he argues, is to develop research methods that take account of (and are partly modelled on) diverse local meanings and parenting practices. This may involve the use of less standardised, more qualitative or ethnographic methods. For example, Tronick and Morelli (1992) have shown that in certain cultural settings, meaningful attachments with multiple care-givers might serve as a normal prerequisite for a positive sense of self (see key study).

The debate about the universal desirability of the 'securely attached' child is not going to go away. The secure attachment pattern is evident globally, though we would be foolish to presume that the pre-ponderance of alternative or multiple attachments in some cultures somehow reflects defective childrearing. Instead, it may be helpful to see attachments, however they manifest themselves, as neutral

KEY STUDY

Multiple attachments in the Congolese Ituri forest

Ethnographic research by Tronick and Morelli (1992) with the Efe com-munity from the Ituri forest in the Democratic Republic of Congo (Zaire at the time of the research) exemplifies multiple attachment patterns. Efe infants of up to four months of age were observed interacting with carers other than their mothers for most of the time. Indeed, they interacted with at least five people per hour. Patterns of multiple caregiving emerged as the norm from these observations.

Tronick and Morelli cite *socio-ecological* explanations for the emergence of these multiple attachment patterns. In other words, elements in the social and physical environment of the Efe were seen as conducive to shared parenting. Efe values of co-operation and sharing, their com-munal living and community-based work practices, plus the dangers of the Ituri forest, were all conducive to bringing up children communally.

A socio-ecological approach to attachment, unlike a more biological, epi-genetic view (monotropy), leads us to view parenting as a culturally diverse practice. Healthy development, for Tronick and Morelli, stems from childrearing practices that are influenced by diverse cultural settings.

responses to diverse circumstances, without investing certain patterns (secure) with positive values and others (anxious) with negative ones.

Crittenden (2000) urges us to interpret attachment patterns – multiple, epigenetic or otherwise – as adaptive responses to diverse environments. Granted, the secure attachment pattern as Ainsworth defines it is a globally widespread, effective adaptation. In the Ituri forest, however, multiple attachments work pretty well too. Elsewhere, where cultural values or material circumstance are conducive, alternative attachment patterns represent other effective survival strategies.

Limitations of research on attachment

1 *Most attachment research comes from individualist contexts.* It has already been suggested here that the ideal of the securely attached child may have been used as a yardstick to assess alternative styles of attachment. This over-reliance on the secure attachment pattern may be due to a corresponding over-representation of research from regions that are seen as *individualist* (see Chapter 1 for more on the individualism–collectivism dimension) in that they value independence rather than interdependence (Cardwell, 2004). Children who are relatively independent may thus be seen as the norm in the context of research from the US, an individualist culture. Conversely, since research from more collectivist contexts is less common in the literature, there is less documentation of other emotional responses to being separated from the mother, such as feeling comfortable in the presence of multiple caretakers, as do infants raised in Israeli kibbutzim, for example.

2 *Does attachment theory exclude the atypical?* While the reaction of the infant to being separated from her mother is informative in the study of attachment, this research scenario does dominate the attachment literature, which thus does not fully represent the many forms of attachment that occur worldwide. Day-care, extended families, kibbutzim, single and multiple parenting all make up a global mosaic of childrearing that has not been adequately served by the

---

REFLECTIVE EXERCISE 31

A parental disagreement

Two parents are discussing the best familial arrangement for their son's upbringing. Mum claims that she should stay at home and look after the little lad for as many years as possible since he needs his mum around him in his early formative years. Dad is keen to send his son to nursery as soon as possible so mum can go out to work and the boy can feel comfortable with more caregivers from an early age. Cite a piece of evidence to support each of the parents' views.

preponderance of cross-cultural replications of mother–infant attachment. Indeed, even van Ijzendoorn and Kroonenberg's (1988) thorough meta-analysis of strange situation studies in eight countries excluded so-called 'special groups', like twins. Arguably, then, there is a tendency across the literature on this topic to leave out parenting arrangements which are seen as atypical.

Culture and the development of gender identity

The variable treatment of boys and girls worldwide reminds us that the socialisation of infants into gendered children and adolescents is influenced by culture. The use of children as sex slaves in some regions, and as soldiers in others, as well as controversial issues such as female genital mutilation (see key concept), all demonstrate that the expectations and demands placed on children by their maleness or femaleness differ from place to place.

KEY CONCEPT

Female genital mutilation: a controversy in cultural psychology

What does FGM involve?
Known by its advocates as female circumcision, at its least invasive it may involve the wetting of the clitoris with water. More invasive types of surgery include clitoral incision, the removal of the labia, or the smoothing out of the entire genital area. While all are controversial, the most controversial technique is infibulation; the partial stitching together of the labia, arguably practised to increase male enjoyment of sexual intercourse.

Who undergoes FGM?
Mainly African females under 18 years, some living outside Africa. Many participants are non-consenting. National proportions include 90% for Egypt, Sudan, Ethiopia, Sierra Leone, Gambia, Mali; 50% for Kenya; 43% for Côte d'Ivoire; 30% for Ghana (Shell-Duncan & Hernlund, 2000). FGM is practised in diverse religious and ethnic groups and is common among affluent and well-educated groups (Ahmadu, 2000).

What are the health risks?
This depends on the expertise of the surgeon and on the equipment used, but infections, obstructed labour, inhibited fertility, damaged reproductive organs and reduced sexual pleasure are frequently reported (Gruenbaum, 1996).

Why is it practised?
Explanations include

- *aesthetics*: removal of protrusions is seen as enhancing genital beauty (Lane & Rubenstein, 1996)
- *sexual identity*: the clitoris is seen as sexually ambiguous, so its removal enhances female identity (Boddy, 1996)
- *ethnic identity*: scars left by surgery are interpreted by some as evidence of ethnic belonging
- *initiation*: genital alteration can be a rite of passage into adulthood (Gwako, 1995).

Critics say
(all cited in
Shweder,
2003,
pp. 168–169)

Early societies in Africa established strong controls over the sexual behaviour of their women and devised the brutal means of circumcision to curb sexual desire and response – Olayinki Koso-Thomas

Female genital mutilation's disastrous health effects, combined with the social injustices it perpetuates, constitute a serious barrier to overall African development – Susan Rich and Stephanie Joyce

The dream is that the US could bring about the end of a system of torture that has crippled 100 million people now living upon this earth and every year takes at least two million more into an existence of suffering, deprivation and disease . . . That torture is female genital mutilation – A. Rosenthal

A minority view from cultural psychology

Critics call for a ban of FGM on the grounds of women's rights and health, citing pain, infection and fertility problems. Others though adopt a more conciliatory, if controversial, stance. Shweder (2003), an advocate of cultural psychology (see Chapter 5), sees some critics of FGM as ethnocentric outsiders who fail to grasp the culturally situated meaning of the practice. Before condemning it outright he asks us to consider the findings of some research in areas where circumcision is practised.

In a review of 435 research projects into female circumcision, Obermeyer (1999) found that in the studies that highlighted the negative health consequences of circumcision, little supporting evidence was presented. In another study in Egypt one field-worker met with revulsion and disbelief on revealing to her informants that she herself was not circumcised (Lane & Rubenstein, 1996).

Shweder argues that non-African-based critiques should be reconsidered in the light of evidence gathered in the indigenous context. He suggests that some of the arguments against circumcision are either flawed or ethnocentric since they underestimate the meaning of the practice in its own cultural context.

Research into the relationship between culture and the development of gender identity has a long history in psychology. The pioneering field-notes of Margaret Mead (1901–1978) were perhaps the first argument for the culturally constructed nature of gender. We will begin this section with a discussion of her work. First though, some important definitions to take note of.

- *Sex:* Biological functions differentiating males from females – for example, reproductive and hormonal.
- *Gender:* Socially sanctioned behavioural 'scripts' for males and females, such as the expectation in some cultures for females to adopt caring or nurturing roles.
- *Gender identity:* An individual's awareness of the degree to which s/he conforms behaviourally of attitudinally to his/her prescribed gender role.
- *Gender stereotype*: A prescribed set of expectations about how males or females behave.

A formative historical episode in gender identity research

The twentieth century saw many changes in our understanding of gender and culture and Margaret Mead, then a young trainee researcher, was at their vanguard. *Sex and Temperament* (1935), her ethnographic account of three years spent with the Arapesh, Mundugumor and Tchambuli communities of New Guinea, was inspired by Franz Boas (1858–1942), her teacher at Columbia University. Boas rejected the idea, prevalent at the time, that so-called 'primitive' societies aspired towards the status of allegedly more civilised Europeans and North Americans. Rather, Boas sought to investigate culturally diverse, unique practices in order to assess the effect of culture on human development. Furnished with such notions of cultural relativism, Mead embarked on her three-year investigation into gender roles. She wanted to find out whether gender identity manifested itself differently from one cultural setting to another – specifically, in three Pacific communities.

Mead's fieldwork took place in three sites on the north-eastern coast of the Pacific island of New Guinea, and yielded a detailed, qualitative account of her observations. She focused on aspects of life that related to how gender roles were socialised. She later wrote (1972, p. 196) that her goal was:

> to study the different ways in which cultures patterned the expected behaviours of males and females.

What emerged was three societies that apparently socialised gender roles in distinct ways (see key study). For the Arapesh, Mundugumor and Tchambuli, experiences of *maleness* and *femaleness* seemed qualitatively different. The diverse gender roles apparent in the three communities emphasised the importance of cultural factors on the formation of gender roles.

Subsequent critics have offered Mead a mixed reception. Errington and Gewertz (1987) revisited the Tchambuli region to try to verify the original data (Kuper, 1994). While the more contemporary community showed some of the characteristics Mead observed (women were assertive and practical, men vain and decorative), there was no neat reversal of North American gender roles as Mead reported. More complex dynamics were at play. Neither gender neatly fitted the temperamental template of North American men or women. Arguably, Mead had glossed Tchambuli gender differences through ethnocentric North American eyes.

KEY STUDY

Gender identity in three Pacific communities

Arapesh males and females were peaceful, parental, nurturing and cherishing. As a cultural norm, aggressiveness was considered unacceptable. According to North American stereotypes, males and females were somewhat 'feminised'. Arapesh men habitually took a passive role (even taking to their beds) during the birth of their children. Both men and women were keen and capable parents.

Mundugumor were a fierce, war-like community with a cannibalistic reputation. They often feuded with their neighbours. Their men often carried off females from neighbouring communities as trophies. Like the Arapesh, Mundugumor males and females behaved similarly to one another. They were both aggressive. Warm, cherishing behaviour was culturally disallowed. Sleeping infants were routinely hung in coarse fabric blankets and left against walls. Neither males nor females cared for childrearing.

Tchambuli males and females were typically different from each other, unlike in the Arapesh and Mundugumor. There was a reversal of typical North American gender roles. Females tended to be more businesslike, in charge of trade and community affairs. They were sexually assertive and tended to look after valuables. Men were discouraged from getting involved in the economy. They had long abandoned warfare, preferring instead to spend their time carving, painting and gossiping. Similar role reversals were evident in the neighbouring Iatmul, whose men experimented with transvestism and homosexuality.

Yet other reports of culturally diverse gender roles do support Mead's view of culturally relative gender identities. In some Madagascan and Alaskan communities males are raised in ways conforming to North American feminine ideals (Gross, 1992). Elsewhere, some American Indian groups incorporate a third gender type of 'man-woman' (or *berdache*; Barfield, 1997), who rejects warrior status to adopt feminine norms and behaviours. The term *berdache* can be traced to the Arabic 'bardash' (male prostitute) and has also been used to describe men dressed as women among North American indigenous Haudenosaunee (Iroquois) communities (Medicine, 2002). Further evidence of culturally constructed gender roles comes from differential manifestations of psychological androgyny, further illustrating the influence of culture on gender identity (see key study).

We can reflect that Mead's albeit simplistic view of culturally constructed gender roles remains a useful point of reference and is supported in principle by other field-workers. Arguably, the development of gender roles in diverse settings may reflect differing

KEY STUDY

Androgyny and sex-role transcendence across cultures

Psychological androgyny refers to **the coexistence in some individuals of stereotypically masculine and feminine traits.** Bem's (1974) *Sex Role Inventory* (BSRI) is a psychometric tool used to find out whether stereotypically masculine and feminine traits coexist in individuals, irrespective of their sex. Bem found that some participants had high femininity and masculinity scores, revealing themselves to be psychologically androgynous. BSRI has been used to assess psychological androgyny across cultures. In one study Maloney *et al.* (1981) found fewer Israeli males to be psychologically androgynous compared with a US sample. Elsewhere Marecek (1979) linked cultural variations in psychological androgyny to gender equality. In some societies, increased equality of opportunity in the labour market might be associated with a more permissible sense of psychological androgyny.

Yet Ravinder (1987) has criticised Bem's scale for failing to take account of the notion of *sex-role transcendence* (SRT): *the idea that self-concept is derived independently of gender identity.* In support of this criticism, an alternative psychometric tool, the *Ravinder Sex Role Salience Test* (SRST), measures not only androgyny but also the degree to which gender identity matters to that person's definition of self (identified by an SRT score). This recognises that some people derive little of their overall self-concept from their gender identity.

Do SRT tendencies differ across cultures? Ravinder investigated this by comparing SRT scores of Australian and Indian samples. This research rationale partly grew from the suggestion that more secular, industrialised societies may tolerate greater gender flexibility, with India arguably having more stringent roles for men and women (Hate, 1969; Williams and Best, 1982; Singh *et al.*, 1962). Ravinder found that:

- Indian males had higher *masculinity* scores than Indian females
- Australian males had higher *masculinity* scores than Australian females
- Indian females had higher *femininity* scores than Indian males
- Australian females had higher *femininity* scores than Australian males
- *SRT* was more prevalent in Australia than in India

- *Androgyny* was more prevalent in India than in Australia
- More individuals were classed as *sex-typed* in India than in Australia.

High Australian SRT scores support the view that in western societies, self-concept may be growing more independent of gender identity. However, SRT scores in Indian females were also quite high. Conversely, high Indian androgyny scores were predominantly confined to males. Arguably, this suggests that norms of duty and conformity to (Indian) society tend to override individualism among Indian males (Dasgupta, 1977). In other words, maybe Indian males' expressions of masculinity have been suppressed in favour of feelings of duty to Indian society.

However we interpret Ravinder's findings, there is some degree of cultural difference in gender identity between these two samples. In particular, the data tentatively suggest that *sex-role transcendence* (though not necessarily *androgyny*) is associated with a more westernised lifestyle.

expectations as to what it means to be male and female in different parts of the world. In other words, it may well be that gender stereotypes vary across cultures. Two researchers, Williams and Best (1982, 1990, 1994), have done much to reveal how much this is the case.

Gender expectations and stereotypes across cultures

Ideas about appropriate behaviours for males and females (or **gender schemas**) can be present in children at an early age (Westen, 1996). Even five-year-olds can have a good idea about the kinds of activities their culture sanctions for men and women. Global research into gender schemas suggests that there is plenty of agreement across cultures about the nature of these gender-appropriate behaviours. Williams and Best (1982) investigated this by giving a checklist of 300 adjectives (such as *caring*, *dominant*, *submissive*) to students from 30 nations and asking them to rate them as to whether they most typically described female or male behaviour. In most nations *active*, *dominant* and *aggressive* were deemed male-appropriate, while *passive*, *weak* and *nurturing* were seen as female behaviours. Furthermore, relatively stable gender-stereotypical behavioural expectations have been endorsed elsewhere (Trommsdorff & Iwawaki, 1989; Rao & Rao, 1985).

KEY TERM

Gender schemas.
Ideas about appropriate behaviours for males and females.

Yet Williams and Best also showed how some ideas about gendered behaviour can vary across cultures. When asked to identify favourable behaviours, Japanese and South African respondents were more likely to select typically 'masculine' behaviours, with Italians and Peruvians preferring 'feminine' behaviours. Despite these variations it seems that some degree of global consensus prevails regarding gender-stereotypical behaviour patterns, with males and females across many cultures being expected to fulfil prescribed behavioural characteristics.

Widely accepted ideas about which behaviours are appropriate or desirable for boys and girls are likely to be communicated and generated via socialisation. Gender-appropriate ideals are thus likely to survive through cultural transmission. The development and reinforcement of these gender schemas may be media-generated, with the mass media in the latter half of the twentieth century being especially awash with stereotypically gender-appropriate portrayals of men and women (Fejes, 1992).

Yet we cannot simply blame the media for the existence of gender stereotyping. Indeed, media outlets themselves are becoming more diverse and imaginative in their portrayal of gender, with an increasingly globally diverse media arguably contributing to the generation of ideal gender roles that differ from culture to culture, thus challenging the idea of consensual gender schemas.

What's your ideal male and female? Gender-role aspirations

In another study, Williams and Best (1990) asked participants what they thought males and females ought ideally to be like, rather than what they are like, as in their previous research. Interestingly, these gender-role aspirations varied across cultural groups. Participants from more affluent, traditionally Christian regions (Netherlands, Germany, Finland) were more likely to endorse *egalitarian* gender aspirations, wherein males and females ideally displayed less behavioural differentiation (both genders actively participating in the work economy, for example). Participants from less affluent, traditionally Muslim regions (of Nigeria, Pakistan, India) were more likely to endorse *traditional* gender aspirations, consistent with segregated roles and prescribed gender-specific behaviours.

How we idealise male and female gender roles appears to reflect less of a consensus than does a straightforward identification of how males and females are. Moreover, these gender-role aspirations may be undergoing some change worldwide. Research in a number of settings not generally associated with a westernised outlook has found many young women firm in the belief that the woman's role lies outside the home, in the economy (Gibbons *et al.*, 1991 (Sri Lanka), Mule & Barthel, 1992 (Egypt)). Arguably, then, some of the old predictable east–west differences in gender-role expectations are being challenged in a world where access to global media is becoming more widespread.

Limitations of research on culture and gender identity research

1 *The problem of the imposed etic, again.* When assessing gender stereotypes and expectations cross-culturally, some researchers have assessed the responses of participants from diverse cultural backgrounds against concepts of femininity and masculinity that were originally drawn from North America. For example, both Mead's pioneering research and other studies that used Bem's (1984) Sex Role Inventory cross-culturally employed this 'how similar to Americans are they?' model. Arguably, a less etic approach would involve exploring indigenous notions of masculinity and femininity as a starting point for investigating global gender identity.
2 *A call for methodological diversity.* The ongoing research of Williams and Best has had an enormous impact on our understanding of the evident cross-cultural consensus in gender stereotypes, as well as variations in gender ideals. Yet most data on this topic have emerged via psychometric, questionnaire-based methods. These might usefully be complemented in future by a more qualitative approach, offering greater detail and insights into the cultural meanings associated with often delicate topics such as the use of child soldiers, or female genital mutilation. Such research might use indigenously generated issues as its starting point.

So, does culture change our experience of childhood?

The research suggests that the short answer to this question is 'yes, to an extent'. For example, parenting practices and temperament appear to be susceptible to ecological and cultural influences, revealing diverse methods of adaptation. Furthermore, gender roles too, as well as our understanding of the idea that maleness and femaleness are influenced by culture, have undergone a series of changes in the past century. Margaret Mead alerted us to cultural variations in gender identity, with more recent evidence suggesting a high degree of consensus across cultures about stereotypical gender behaviours.

Tellingly, though, aspirations about how males and females ought to behave do seemingly differ from place to place. The fulfilment (or otherwise) of these gender ideals will undoubtedly provide fertile subject matter for future research into the link between culture and gender.

Summary

Chapter 8 centres on child development across cultures. The discussion begins by asking how culture, child development and parenting fit into the bigger picture of socialisation. After all, parental influence is only part of the wider context of socialisation. The importance of other agents of socialisation (extended families, for example) may vary from culture to culture. Likewise, parenting styles and attitudes towards parenting practice are culturally relative.

Cultural variations in rule-setting, bedtime routines and assertion of control have all been well researched by global psychologists, whose findings are discussed here. Besides differences and similarities in parenting, we consider the possibility that the child's temperament (biological pre-disposition to behave in certain ways) might be influenced by properties of its environment. Research into the formation of secure, insecure and multiple attachments is covered extensively, with particular attention given to the methodological difficulties of applying established attachment theories in diverse contexts. A review of global research on the development of gender identity, gender expectations and psychological androgyny concludes the chapter.

REFLECTIVE EXERCISE 32

Match up the definitions on the right with the terms on the left (see p. 228 for answers)

Socially sanctioned behavioural 'scripts' for males and females, such as the expectation in some cultures for females to adopt caring or nurturing behaviour

Monotropy

Biological functions differentiating males from females – for example reproductive and hormonal

Gender

The coexistence in some individuals of stereotypically masculine and feminine traits

Gender identity

A prescribed set of expectations about how males or females behave

Parental ethnotheories

Theories and styles of parenting that originate in diverse locations

Sex

An individual's awareness of the degree to which s/he conforms behaviourally or attitudinally to his/her prescribed gender role

Temperament

Biologically based style of interacting with the world

Gender stereotype

The idea that self-concept is derived independently of gender identity

Psychological androgyny

Sex role transcendence

The infant's bond with the mother is (biologically) qualitatively different from any other, so any interruption to this bond is necessarily maladaptive

---

FURTHER READING

- Mead, M. (1935) *Sex and Temperament in Three Primitive Societies*, London: Routledge.
- Shweder, R. (2003) *Why Do Men Barbecue? Recipes for Cultural Psychology*, London: Harvard University Press.
- Williams, J. & Best, D. (1990) *Sex and Psyche: Gender and Self Viewed Cross-culturally*, Beverly Hills, CA: Sage.

Culture and abnormality

Definitions, diagnoses and treatment across cultures

9

What this chapter will teach you

- What is the relationship between normality and culture?

- Does psychopathology differ across cultures?

- Is schizophrenia diagnosed consistently across cultures?

- Is there such a thing as a **culture-bound syndrome**?

- Are eating disorders culture-bound?

- Are all disorders culture-bound?

- Is psychotherapy universally effective?

- What therapies are used in Asia and Africa?

Culture, abnormality and psychopathology

In everyday discourse it is common (normal, even) to point out someone's behaviour and declare it unusual, weird, abnormal. This usually happens when someone steps out of line or does something that is considered extreme or socially unacceptable, eccentric or even courageous. However, psychologists are rather more cautious about labelling behaviour 'abnormal'. Traditionally they have struggled to establish workable criteria against which to judge behaviour as normal, abnormal or pathological (requiring medical treatment). Yet several criteria are open for consideration.

Abnormality might for instance be equated with deviation from the statistical norm. This would mean defining abnormal behaviour as that which only a minority practise (*being nocturnal is abnormal because hardly anyone does it*). Another yardstick against which to assess normality might be the ability to function occupationally or socially (*he's abnormal because he can't hold down a job and hasn't got any friends*). A third (and most relevant for our discussion here) criterion might be cultural. Thus, abnormal behaviour would be anything which transgresses the moral or behavioural codes of a particular social group (*your behaviour may be normal in some places, but not here*).

While all these criteria are useful, they don't offer an altogether reliable guide for identifying **psychopathology** (a psychological state without normal functioning, requiring treatment). After all, it is perfectly feasible to behave in a way that is statistically unusual (a vegetarian in Germany), occupationally dysfunctional (out of work during an economic boom) or culturally inappropriate (wearing shorts in Saudi Arabia) without requiring medical treatment. Nevertheless it does seem reasonable to assume that any attempt to outline the characteristics of acceptable, 'sane' or normal behaviour requires an acknowledgement of the cultural context in which it takes place.

The history of abnormal psychology teaches us that what is deemed abnormal in one cultural or temporal context may be perfectly acceptable elsewhere. For example, while homosexuality ceased to be regarded as pathological in the US in 1973, it remains legally questionable in China (Matsumoto & Juang, 2004). Elsewhere, the influence of cultural context allows such phenomena as auditory hallucinations, possession trance and glossolalia (speaking in tongues) to be considered pathological in one circumstance yet part of religious experience or therapeutic practice in another.

Going back even further, the case of *drapetomania* illustrates the historical relativity of psychopathology. This curious clinical phenom-

KEY TERM

Psychopathology.
Psychological state
without normal
functioning, requiring
treatment.

enon was described by the American physician Samuel Cartwright (1851), who argued that many slaves suffered from a form of mental illness that infected them with *the uncontrollable urge to escape* (Fernando, 2002). It seems that at certain points in history, diagnostic labels have served as convenient and temporary means of exerting control over vulnerable groups. Again this illustrates the variability in the yardsticks that have been used from time to time, and place to place, to establish behavioural norms.

The debate between universalists and relativists

While culture and abnormality may be intertwined concepts, arguably there are certain patterns of behaviour – perhaps dangerous, threatening or deviant – that might be considered atypical across all times and places. Are there culturally universally agreed psychopathologies? Attempts to answer this question form the crux of the debate between universalists and relativists in the field of global abnormal psychology. Proponents of cultural relativism urge us to see all pathologies as inextricably linked to the cultural meanings prevailing in particular contexts. For them, there is no such thing as a universal psychopathology. Advocates of universalism meanwhile veer towards the existence of underlying psychological mechanisms that are common to psychopathology across cultures (Murphy, 1976). Each of these viewpoints will be explored in turn in the light of disorders that have been explored in the global context.

> **REFLECTIVE EXERCISE 33**
>
> 1. What is the difference between *abnormality and psychopathology*?
>
> 2. What do we mean when we say that a definition of abnormality is *culturally relative*?

Universalism, relativism and schizophrenia

Schizophrenia: a pattern of psychotic features including thought disturbances, bizarre delusions, hallucinations (usually auditory), disturbed sense of self and loss of reality testing.

(Reber, 1995, p. 690)

Approximately 1% of people in industrialised nations are prone to a syndrome that, since it was first diagnosed in 1911, has become known as schizophrenia (Keith *et al.*, 1991). But how globally applicable is this figure – or indeed this syndrome? Would presentation of similar symptoms in Bermuda, Britain and Bangladesh prompt similar

KEY TERM

Schizophrenia. A pattern of psychotic features including thought disturbances, bizarre delusions, hallucinations (usually auditory), disturbed sense of self and loss of reality testing.

diagnoses? Well, despite the apparently authoritative dictionary definition (above), doubts have been voiced about whether the label 'schizophrenia' is consistently applied across cultures.

Prompted by such doubts, one large-scale cross-cultural study investigated the international reliability of diagnoses of schizophrenia (Leff, 1977a, World Health Organization (WHO), 1979). The aim of the *International Pilot Study of Schizophrenia* (IPSS) was to test the culturally universal credentials of schizophrenia as a diagnostic label. The study was prompted by growing concerns about the objectivity (Figure 9.1) and reliability (dependability, or *relating to comparable sets of symptoms across different situations*) of diagnoses, which some argued were routinely being made on the basis of the first five minutes of clinical interviews (Kendell, 1973). Further doubts about the trustworthiness of diagnoses had been raised by evidence of the culturally variable use of the label 'schizophrenic' (Jablensky *et al.*, 1992). In one study, case notes from 30 UK patients were distributed to psychiatrists in the US, Denmark, Norway and Sweden. European psychiatrists were less likely to apply the term 'schizophrenia', preferring 'depression' or 'obsessional disorder' (Rawnsley, 1968). Arguably, cultural variations in communication styles were among the factors preventing psychiatrists from arriving at reliable, culturally consistent diagnoses of psychological disorders (Leff, 1977a; Paniagua, 1998).

So how did the IPSS investigate the proposed cultural universality of

Leff (1977a) highlights factors that can influence the objectivity of clinical interviews.

Theoretical orientation
Psychiatrists from different traditions are oriented differently towards diagnosis. For example, humanistic psychiatry tends to be more client-centred, while psychoanalysis is more prescriptive.

Established syndromes
Where a symptom fits into an established set of symptoms (syndrome), it is less likely to be ignored. Conversely, sets of symptoms that straddle two or more established syndromes may be ignored since they threaten a syndrome's validity.

Cultural background
After seeing the same filmed clinical interviews, US psychiatrists identified twice as many pathological symptoms as did UK psychiatrists (Sandifer *et al.*, 1969). This suggests that the latter have a higher threshold of diagnosis. Seemingly, where psychiatrists come from affects their diagnostic habits.

Cultural knowledge
When dealing with patients from different backgrounds, a lack of knowledge about a patient's culture can leave a psychiatrist floundering when trying to diagnose. For example, the term *delusions* (symptomatic of schizophrenia) refers to *beliefs that are at odds with the patient's culture*. Psychiatrists lacking cultural knowledge cannot reliably identify delusions.

Figure 9.1 Are psychiatric diagnoses objective?

schizophrenia? The design of the research followed that of Cooper *et al.* (1972), who compared diagnoses of schizophrenia in hospitals in London and New York. In this initial study between 300 and 400 patients (half recently admitted to nine hospitals in New York, half to nine in London) were randomly selected and interviewed by the research psychiatrists, using a standard interview method for assessing psychiatric symptoms. The use of this method, the Present State Examination (PSE; Wing *et al.*, 1974), ensured that all the research psychiatrists were applying identical diagnostic criteria.

These research (PSE) diagnoses were compared with the hospitals' own diagnoses for the same patients, which revealed that 'schizophrenic' labels were applied more commonly in New York than they were in London. So it appeared that US psychiatrists used a definition of schizophrenia that encompassed more symptoms. It also emerged that the subsequent use of a standardised a diagnostic instrument reduced differences between US and UK practitioners. In other words, a more widely recognised model for the diagnosis of schizophrenia did seem to follow the use of more standardised procedures and guidelines.

In the light of these findings, the IPSS (WHO, 1974, 1979) broadened the scope of Cooper's transatlantic comparison. Diagnoses of schizophrenia across nine countries (Colombia, Czechoslovakia, Denmark, England, India, Nigeria, Soviet Union, Taiwan, US) were incorporated in order to find out whether international samples of psychiatrists applied the label 'schizophrenia' to patients with comparable groups of symptoms.

The PSE was translated into the first languages of the nine countries. Psychiatrists from each country were trained to use the instrument, ensuring that symptoms were being assessed using standard criteria. In all, 1202 patients were interviewed in their respective countries and symptom profiles for the patients were compiled. These profiles were compared with standard diagnostic classifications (also based on PSE data) provided by WHO psychiatrists. To what extent would the diagnostic habits of psychiatrists in each country deviate from WHO diagnoses for schizophrenia?

The overall finding was that there were close clinical similarities between patients being diagnosed as schizophrenic across the nine countries. In seven of the participating countries (excluding US and USSR) the overwhelming majority of patients diagnosed schizophrenic *in situ* were similarly diagnosed by the WHO procedure (there was an agreement level of 96% between WHO diagnoses and seven centres, excluding US and USSR). Notably, though, the incidence of US and USSR diagnoses for schizophrenia was marginally greater than elsewhere (the agreement level between US/USSR and WHO on schizophrenia diagnoses was 71%).

Overall, the IPSS showed that, especially with the use of standardised training with a single diagnostic instrument, there existed a common core of schizoid symptoms in most countries. Social and emotional withdrawal, delusions and emotional flatness were commonplace in those diagnosed as schizophrenic virtually across the board. However, there were local variations in symptoms. For example, Nigerian and Danish schizophrenics scored higher on auditory hallucinations than did US patients.

Another cultural discrepancy shows recovery from schizoid conditions to be better in developing nations than in more affluent nations (WHO, 1979). Recovery rates for patients in developing nations were higher: 36% of Nigerians showed full remission after an initial one-month period of schizoid illness, compared with India (27%), Denmark (2%), Moscow (1%). Perhaps these differences were due to stronger community and extended family support networks in some regions (Matsumoto & Juang, 2004).

Despite these local variations, the IPSS tentatively supports the proposal for schizophrenia as a culturally widespread syndrome with a common core of symptoms that are recognised by psychiatrists practising across diverse settings.

Limitations of schizophrenia research

1 *Cultural insensitivity of standardised instruments.* The IPSS research used the PSE to standardise criteria for diagnosing schizophrenia. This helped to ensure that all the psychiatrists involved followed similar guidelines. However, the use of the PSE, an instrument developed in the UK, in diverse cultural settings meant that these projects were unable to take account of local meanings attached to this psychosis. Patients from Nigeria, Colombia and India were being diagnosed according to a procedure that was insensitive to local notions of illness and health. Such a procedure carries the assumption that schizophrenia is a universal concept, defined and diagnosed in the west and then applied cross-culturally (Fernando, 2002). This approach arguably undervalues the view that psychological abnormality can be understood according to diverse systems of meaning.

2 *Further evidence of differential application of the 'schizoid' label.* Arguments about the cultural universality of schizophrenia as a syndrome are somewhat undermined by research showing that practi-

tioners in some regions are more likely to diagnose people from certain racial groups as schizophrenic. Loring and Powell (1988) showed that psychiatrists sometimes apply diagnostic labels differently when treating different racial groups. They presented 290 US psychiatrists with identical case notes for black and white patients, only to find that blacks were over-diagnosed schizophrenic. Interestingly, the effect showed up for black and white psychiatrists. There are other examples of over-diagnosis of schizophrenia for black patients (Steinberg, 1977; Mukherjee *et al.*, 1983; Harrison *et al.*, 1997; Bhugra *et al.*, 1997). Evidently, the term 'schizophrenia' can be applied differently by clinicians from different cultures and to patients from different groups.

> **REFLECTIVE EXERCISE 34**
>
> 1. What was the aim of the *IPSS*?
>
> 2. According to this research, in which of these nations are you least likely to be diagnosed with schizophrenia?
>   a. Belarus
>   b. US
>   c. UK

It remains debatable whether disorders such as schizophrenia, or other conditions such as depression or mania, can be understood as global phenomena that are defined and diagnosed against comparable criteria in different places. Those who doubt the cultural universality of psychopathology point to the incidence of conditions that seemingly are observable only in particular cultural contexts. It is to these that we now turn.

Universalism, relativism and culture-bound syndromes

In his book *The English Malady* (1733), George Cheyne suggested that a specific combination of nervous symptoms (hypochondriasis, low spirits, vapours) constituted a peculiarly English disease. Justified or not, Cheyne was one of the first to suggest that particular illnesses might be associated with particular cultural groups. As time went by, this idea became rather contagious. In 1893, Gilmore Ellis, a colonial official in Malaya (now part of Malaysia), identified two nervous conditions – *latah* and *amok* (Figures 9.2 and 9.3) – as being present among Malays but unknown elsewhere. Later still, in 1967, Pow Meng Yap, a Chinese psychiatrist working in Hong Kong, coined the term **culture-bound syndrome (CBS)** to denote a culture-specific disorder that tends to be undiagnosed or misunderstood elsewhere.

KEY TERM

Culture-bound syndrome. A culture-specific disorder that tends to be undiagnosed or misunderstood elsewhere.

First described in	Nineteenth-century Maine, US, then in Malaya (Yap, 1967)
Often glossed as	'Jumping', as in the case of the so-called 'jumpers of Maine'
Most likely to be diagnosed are	Males, including some boys, in the literature on Maine, although in other populations, such as Malay, it is not so restricted. Most cases are not diagnosed as illness. Rather, *latah* is often treated as an eccentricity
Symptoms include	Jumpiness, tics, echolalia (copying speech), echopraxia (copying actions), automatic obedience

Figure 9.2 *Latah*

First described in	Fifteenth-century Malay epics as an understandable reaction to frustration. By the nineteenth century *amok* was associated with illness and thought to require treatment
Often glossed as	Running amuck
Most likely to be diagnosed are	Malay males, although there have been cases elsewhere in South-East Asia (Laos, Philippines, Thailand) and Africa
Most commonly diagnosed during	Late nineteenth and early twentieth centuries, although still occurring thereafter
Symptoms include	An initial period of solitary depressive brooding, usually prompted by some form of personal frustration. This is typically followed by furious, violent (often homicidal) outbursts using bladed weapons, guns or grenades, then a period of amnesia regarding these attacks

Figure 9.3 *Amok*

Historically, much of the CBS literature focused on what have been rather dismissively referred to as 'exotic' diseases, meaning syndromes that are exclusively observed in regions outside North America and Europe (Fernando, 2002). More recently some writers have identified disorders from within western settings that might also qualify for CBS status on the grounds that they are associated with affluent lifestyles. For example, the widely recognised *Type A* behaviour pattern (incorporating competitiveness, work-related stress, pressurised deadline-chasing) has been linked with lifestyles prevalent in consumerist and capitalist economies (Littlewood, 1996). Another example of a 'western malady' is the eating disorder *anorexia nervosa* (Figure 9.4), though the worldwide dissemination of affluence and consumerism may be implicated in its increasing incidence in China, Hong Kong and Korea (Gordon, 2001).

Psychology has tended to approach the culture-bound syndromes from two theoretical directions, reflecting broader orientations in global abnormal psychology. The *universalist* approach regards these syndromes through the eyes of North American and European based (western) psychiatry, often reserving the term 'exotic' to refer to them.

First described in	Nineteenth-century Europe, but became more prevalent after 1960
Often glossed as	Slimmer's disease
Often abbreviated to	Anorexia, which is misleading since this term refers to a loss of appetite, which often occurs only in the late stages of the illness
Most likely to be diagnosed are	Young (under 30), middle-class females (over 90% of cases) in industrialised nations, especially dancers, athletes and models
Less likely to be diagnosed are	Inhabitants of cultures where attention is not drawn to the body or where physicality is not accentuated in public, such as in Saudi Arabia
Symptoms include	Weight loss, self-induced vomiting, binge eating, appetite loss, a false perception of being overweight, equating beauty with slimness

Figure 9.4 Anorexia nervosa

Symptoms are compared with those of disorders that are traditionally diagnosed by western clinicians. One might therefore look at *latah* and ask – *how similar is this syndrome to schizophrenia?* Strictly speaking, since universalists try to assimilate exotic syndromes into established diagnostic frameworks, they only marginally recognise the notion of culture-bound syndromes. Consequently these tend to figure only peripherally in the appendices of mainstream western classifications of psychiatric disorders.

A second, *relativist* approach has a more *emic* (see Chapter 4) agenda. The focus here is on the emergence of culture-specific, indigenous categories of pathology, occupying a space beyond the stronghold of western psychiatry. Here, syndromes are examined within the meaning systems of their host cultures, prompting questions such as – *what do Malaysians understand by the term 'latah'?* Ritenbaugh (1982) exemplifies this view, suggesting that according to certain criteria *all* disorders might be considered culture-bound. In other words, since all the world's illnesses can only genuinely be understood from within their local contexts and their own indigenous meaning systems, every disease is actually a unique product of its specific culture. In effect, all psychopathologies fit Yap's definition of *culture-specific disorders, which tend to be undiagnosed or misunderstood elsewhere*. Ritenbaugh argues that for an illness to qualify for culture-bound status it simply has to meet one or more of three criteria (Figure 9.5). And as only one criterion needs to be met, these parameters for culture-boundness are (she herself admits) pretty loose. Yet her aim is not to divide disorders into those that are culture-bound and those that are not. Rather, Ritenbaugh (1982, p. 350) aims to offer a:

> definition of culture-bound syndrome which in effect subsumes all diseases in all cultures to varying degrees.

For an illness to be deemed *culture-bound*, Ritenbaugh argues that one or more of the following must apply.

1   It is exclusively understood in its own indigenous culture.
2   It has causes that symbolise the core values/norms/beliefs of its own indigenous culture.
3   It is treated successfully only by healers from its own indigenous culture.

Figure 9.5 Ritenbaugh's (1982) criteria for CBS status

This relativist approach to mental health assumes that all syndromes (not just 'exotic' ones) can be best comprehended using detailed knowledge about the cultures from which they emerge (Fernando, 2002). This would be as true if we were talking about disorders from Malaysia (such as *latah* and *amok*), or from more western, industrialised contexts (such as *stress* or *obesity*).

Prince and Tcheng-Laroche (1987) reject such cultural relativism, asserting that it hampers any attempt to integrate diseases from different cultures into a culturally universal, internationally recognised system for classifying psychiatric disorders (like the American Psychiatric Association's *Diagnostic and Statistical Manual of Psychiatric Disorders (DSM)* – first published in 1952 and frequently updated). If we grant all diseases CBS status, they argue, we fail to pick up on overarching similarities between exotic diseases and disorders diagnosed by western psychiatrists. We thus lose the chance to compare syndromes cross-culturally using a worldwide diagnostic tool such as DSM. Attempting to bring order to what they term a relativistic 'trend toward meaninglessness', they offer a definition of CBS that is tighter than Ritenbaugh's (see Figure 9.6). They define CBS (1987, p. 4) as:

> a collection of signs and symptoms (excluding notions of cause) which is restricted to a limited number of cultures, primarily by reason of their psychosocial features.

Prince and Tcheng-Laroche's formulation is tighter chiefly because it stipulates that CBS status should be awarded to disorders based not on their causes (aetiologies), but on their signs and symptoms. The consequence of this is that a syndrome is deemed culture-bound according to how it looks and feels, not what causes it. The main reason for this stipulation is that while doctors in different cultures can usually agree on the signs and symptoms of an illness, proposed aetiologies are more contentious. For example, different causes might be attached to the same symptom sets by healers from different regions (as in the case of *bebainen* in Figure 9.6).

Clearly there are tenuous links between symptoms and aetiologies.

Included in the class of CBS are disorders which conform to this definition.

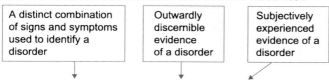

| A distinct combination of signs and symptoms used to identify a disorder | Outwardly discernible evidence of a disorder | Subjectively experienced evidence of a disorder |

Culture-bound **syndrome**: a collection of **signs** and **symptoms** (excluding notions of cause) that is restricted to a limited number of cultures, primarily by reason of their psychosocial features

Excluded from the class of CBS are disorders that:

(a) **are due to regional dietary or geographical peculiarities**, e.g. *pellagra*, a wasting disease marked by abnormal behaviour, found in regions where maize is a staple food
(b) **have local names but are similar to other recognised syndromes**, e.g. *bebainen*, a combination of weeping, tinnitus and abdominal pain, occurring in Bali and under other names in India and Puerto Rico
(c) **appear in different demographic groups in different regions**, e.g. *bebainen* often occurs in young Balinise females, but appears in other age groups elsewhere.

Figure 9.6 Prince and Tcheng-Laroche's criteria for CBS

Arguably, then, a more straightforward way of establishing whether an illness is a CBS is to skip the aetiological details and stick to tangible, observable signs and symptoms. Only culturally unique sets of signs and symptoms are awarded CBS status. This way, better communication between practitioners in different cultures is more likely. Using their cause-free definition of CBS as a starting point, these writers aim to set out clearer criteria for inclusion and exclusion of disorders in the category of CBS. To illustrate the practical application of these criteria they analyse a disorder from Japan, *taijin-kyofu-sho* (TKS) (Figure 9.7) and consider its CBS status.

Does TKS meet Prince and Tcheng-Laroche's 'tight' criteria for CBS status? Two factors are considered in relation to this question. First, TKS is more common in Japan than elsewhere, yet selected signs and symptoms have been identified in other places (Beary & Cobb, 1981 (England); Del Carlo-Giannini and Giannini, 1975 (Italy)). However, the full syndrome has not appeared outside Japan. Second, TKS is unlike traditional social phobia (as recognised in Europe and North America) in that unlike phobics, TKS patients do not recognise their fears to be excessive or unreasonable.

Prince and Tcheng-Laroche suggest that according to their own definition, TKS should be granted CBS status. While it is similar to some disorders seen outside Japan, in its totality it does seem peculiarly

Often glossed as	Social phobia or olfactory reference syndrome
Most likely to be diagnosed are	Young (adolescent, early 20s) Japanese males
Symptoms include	Fear of losing others' approval due to one's perceived shortcomings, e.g. blushing, intensity of gaze, awkwardness, body odour. Patients do not regard their fear as excessive

Figure 9.7 *Taijin-kyofu-sho* (TKS)

Japanese. All of this demonstrates that even a more stringent, 'symptom only' approach can recognise certain syndromes as unique to a particular cultural setting.

Universalists and relativists clearly react differently to syndromes that at first glance appear region-specific. The former prefer (etically) to assimilate them into established western classifications. The latter would rather judge them (emically) from within the meaning systems of their host culture. While the first approach holds out high hopes for an internationally recognised system for comparison and classification, relativists are arguably better prepared to view illness and health from a non-western viewpoint. Increasingly too, psychiatrists worldwide are acknowledging the influence of cultural factors when making diagnoses. The WHO and APA both now incorporate culture as a factor in the application of their respective international disease classifications (known as the *International Classification of Diseases* in the case of the WHO). For example, DSM-IV (American Psychiatric Association, 1994) encourages clinicians to acknowledge cultural differences between themselves and clients when making diagnoses (Paniagua, 1998). This acknowledgement of the role of culture in diagnosis has been largely welcomed by the psychiatric community (Sumathipala & Siribaddana, 2004). Following mainstream recognition of culture's influence on definitions of psychopathology, CBSs will continue to feature in the literature for some time to come, with newly identified syndromes continuing to be so labelled (Lee, 2001).

The long and diverse history of the culture-bound syndrome serves as an illustration of the inextricable link between culture and psychopathology. Aboud (1998) articulates this link eloquently, arguing that all cultures apparently distinguish between normal and abnormal behaviour and that furthermore common cross-cultural elements appear to exist between behaviours that are deemed to be abnormal. Inevitably, these symptoms manifest themselves differently according to the culturally unique influences of local values and meaning systems. In other words, there is arguably a culture-bound element to all abnormal syndromes.

Limitations of culture-bound syndrome research

1 *Universalists and relativists both have their weaknesses.* The debate between universalists (who see the value of classifying culturally diverse syndromes according to their diagnostic similarities) and relativists (who regard all diseases as uniquely bound to their own cultures) reflects broader disputes between distinct approaches to global psychology (Kleinman, 1987b). Universalists are allied to *cross-cultural* psychology (see Chapter 1), wherein the search is on for aspects of behaviour and experience that are common across cultures. Relativists take a more ethnographic viewpoint, similar to that of cultural psychology (see Chapter 5). Here the emphasis is on examining all behaviour, including aspects of psychological illness, in relation to its unique cultural context.

Considering the allegiances of universalists and relativists in the debate about culture-bound syndromes, it should be evident that protagonists on both sides suffer the limitations of their theoretical origins: universalists are always likely to ride roughshod over the local nuances of indigenous syndromes (Bhugra *et al.*, 1997); relativists are unlikely to aid the development of globally applicable systems for the classification of disease.

2 *What use is the CBS concept?* The very worth of the concept of the CBS is questioned from various perspectives. Western psychiatry highlights similarities between so-called 'exotic' syndromes and established conditions, thus casting doubt on the need for a distinct class of unique or exotic illnesses (Yap, 1969). *Latah*, for example, may be likened to a 'primary fear reaction' in western parlance. *Amok* may be seen as an example of a 'rage reaction'. On the other hand, those who argue that all psychopathologies are only fully comprehensible within their own contexts might assert that there is little need for a discrete category of culture-bound syndromes. After all, if culture is recognised as influencing all disorders then maybe all of them are effectively culture-bound (Sumathipala & Siribaddana, 2004). Oddly enough, on this evidence it appears that western psychiatrists and cultural relativists could both make a case for the abandonment of the CBS concept as a discrete category.

We have learned so far that psychopathology cannot be understood without some sensitivity to cultural contexts. As we are about to find out, the treatment of atypical behaviour also reflects diverse cultural traditions.

REFLECTIVE EXERCISE 35

Amok, **anorexia nervosa**, *latah* and **TKS** are disorders that have been referred to as culture-bound syndromes. On the diagram below, fill in the name of each of these disorders to indicate where they are most likely to be diagnosed.

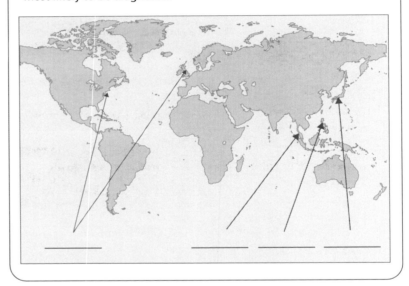

Culture, psychotherapy and healing

Ought we to expect a therapy that aids psychological well-being in one location to be similarly effective elsewhere? Questions regarding the universal effectiveness of psychotherapy understandably tax practitioners and researchers who concern themselves with the relationship between culture and abnormality. Arguably, one positive advertisement for the global applicability of psychotherapy is its historical rate of export, primarily from Europe and the US to Asia and other developing regions. Freudian psychoanalysis, for example, originally developed in twentieth-century Europe, is now used in China and South-East Asia (Zhang *et al.*, 2002). Yet we should note that such therapies have not been exported in unadulterated form. As we will learn later in this section, their effectiveness relies on their incorporation of and fusion with indigenous cultural elements.

Another way of investigating the cultural universality of psycho-therapy comes from those who have tracked their success rates across culturally and ethnically diverse groups. Does therapy work equally well for everyone, irrespective of culture? One American study suggested not, showing that psychotherapy was relatively unsuccessful in African American groups in the US in comparison with success rates among the white population (Sue et al., 1994). Another study revealed Latinos in Los Angeles to respond more effectively than their counterparts from other ethnic groups (Sue et al., 1994). Elsewhere, a research project conducted longitudinally in India among participants who had been diagnosed with schizophrenia recorded rates of recovery among clients from Madras that were 'much better' than those in developed nations (Thara, 2004).

It seems, then, that while data on the relative effects of therapy among different cultural groups are relatively scarce (Matsumoto & Juang, 2004), they do suggest a discernible level of cultural variation in response rates. This indicates that culture may be a factor in the efficacy of treatments.

The link between culture and the effectiveness of psychotherapy has not escaped the notice of the psychiatric profession. Indeed, the American Psychiatric Association acknowledges the influence of culture on both diagnosis and treatment. Since 2002 its members have been issued with guidelines to help them negotiate the challenges associated with delivering therapy to clients from diverse cultural backgrounds.

It seems we would be naïve to regard psychotherapy as a culture-free phenomenon, serving all humans equally well. Rather, the effectiveness of psychotherapy as a global tool may depend not just on clients' values or place of residence, but on how well the therapy adapts to those values and to diverse belief systems, perhaps for example by incorporating spiritual or religious elements that are meaningful in diverse contexts. Before we ask how therapies might make such adaptations, let us first consider more closely the nature of culture's influence on the effectiveness of psychotherapy.

Factors influencing the effectiveness of psychotherapy across cultures

Several factors are likely to influence how well clients from different ethnic or cultural groups are served by psychotherapy. These factors illustrate that psychotherapy's effectiveness depends partly on the values held by the clients and practitioners who take part in the therapeutic process.

Conceptual factors: ideas about health and illness

When client and a therapist hold similar views about what constitutes psychological health and illness, treatment is likely to be more effective. This is more likely to be the case where therapist and client share similar cultural backgrounds. Yet besides the influence of their cultural background, a therapist's views on abnormality or pathology will also be influenced by values instilled in them during training, perhaps due to their adherence to a particular therapeutic tradition. For example, where a Freudian psychoanalyst (following a European-based paradigm that interprets neurosis in terms of repressed sexual energy) treats a client from a cultural group whose belief system regards illness as arising from spiritual concerns, there may be a lack of understanding and empathy between the two parties. After all, it is culturally sanctioned in many regions to conceptualise illness within a spiritual belief system, rather than within the medical paradigm favoured by western psychiatry. For example, a Taoist interpretation of anxiety might seek solutions in unselfish conduct, in line with Taoist religious teachings (Zhang *et al.*, 2002). Similarly, Ayuverdic yogic healing, based on Indian Vedic scriptures dating back to 5000 BC, represents a religious or spiritual approach to illness and health (Fernando, 2002). For clients whose value system is informed by spirituality, the most appropriate therapy might seek to incorporate religious or spiritual features, perhaps in combination with a medical, scientific approach.

There is a growing acceptance of the local effectiveness of religion-based healing systems, and Jilek (1993) identifies a move towards the acceptance of some of these healing techniques. Practitioners in Europe and North America are now increasingly likely to incorporate, say, acupuncture or yogic remedies when seeking to promote health and balance.

A notable (though not yet mainstream in the west) example of a religion-based psychotherapy is *possession trance* (Bourguignon, 1984). Interestingly, some critics have debated whether this practice is a therapy at all, or just another pathological state (see key concept). This dispute aside, arguably the incorporation of religion-based therapies into the gamut of available treatments illustrates that even where a therapist represents a different cultural group from his or her client, identification with his or her belief system bodes well for the cross-cultural effectiveness of treatment (Atkinson, 2002).

KEY CONCEPT

Possession trance: a religious psychotherapy

Also known as	An **altered state of consciousness** (ASC), or spirit possession
ASCs are	**Experienced as periods (several hours, maximum) of disrupted emotion and cognition, loss of bodily control, hyper-suggestibility, even rejuvenation.** Exaggerated motor movements are a common feature. Some states are curative, when practised by healers; others are regarded as pathological (Berry *et al.*, 2002).
Originates from	African and American religions, notably voodoo, which combines aspects of West African, Roman Catholic and Haitian belief systems

Therapy or pathology?

While voodoo practitioners regard it as a positive force with the power to cure ills, some observers have dismissed it as superstition or, as one physician put it, signifying 'mental instability' (Dorsainvil, 1931). More recently some writers have suggested a compromise. They distinguish between two varieties of possession trance: first, as part of a voodoo system for curing neuroses; second, as part of a condition that may warrant a place in international disease classifications (Jilek, 1993). In the former variety the phenomenon may be at once theatre, therapy and prophylactic (against disease or attack from evil spirits), sanctioned by the community in which it is staged. In the latter variety it is merely an individual's maladjusted response (Cardenas, 1992); specifically, an example of a dissociative disorder (involving disorganised identity, consciousness and cognitive function) that should be included in international disease classifications (possession trance disorder has featured in the WHO's *ICD*). However, more evidence of the therapeutic potential of ASCs comes from their use in numerous locations: the Caribbean (Wittkower *et al.*, 1964), Malawi (Peltzer, 1987), North America and South-East Asia (Jilek, 1993).

Religious psychotherapy

Often used alongside other therapies such as herbal remedies and scientific medicine, possession trance rituals are an example of religious belief and indigenous medicine combining to treat mental illness. As well as solving individual ills, religion-based healing can help answer existential questions about its origins, life and death. Such questions are arguably culturally universal, although ways of answering them vary in different settings (Peters & Price-Williams, 1983).

A perfectly normal therapy – in some places

In Haiti the success of voodoo healing is no more remarkable than that of, say, psychoanalysis in Europe, where *its* ideas are culturally sanctioned (Berry *et al.*, 2002). Jilek (1993) argues that first-world commentators have often neglected the healing potential of ASCs, preferring instead to read them as pathologies. Arguably, this is an error arising out of a Eurocentric failure to recognise the mainstream nature of these systems of healing within their cultural contexts. Jilek generally highlights the effectiveness of indigenous healing, while at the same time reminding us that some ritual exorcisms (involving violence and bodily restraint) may in themselves be almost as traumatic as the conditions they seek to alleviate.

Interpersonal factors: at the client–therapist interface

Shared values about illness and health by no means guarantee effective treatment. With or without a shared belief system, diverse codes of interpersonal conduct and communication can also have a profound effect on the success of therapy. Like the values we hold about illness and health, these codes can differ from one cultural group to another. Where a client consults a therapist from another cultural group, there may be a lack of appreciation of these differing codes. For example, Arab clients have reportedly found direct eye-contact disrespectful during consultations, and this has adversely affected the success of diagnosis and treatment (Al-Krenawi & Graham, 2000).

Cultural differences also emerge in perceptions of status and power relations between clients and therapists. In some regions a therapist is more likely to be regarded as a 'fixer', an authority figure blessed with powers to lead the therapeutic process. While Arab American groups have been found to favour such proactivity from therapists (Al-Krenawi & Graham, 2000), more democratic, client-centred expectations may be held by Puerto Rican and First Nation American clients (Atkinson *et al.*, 1984). It has been suggested that a preference for more directive therapy may appeal to groups who are traditionally accustomed to seeking healing within their own families or communities, so that where these measures fall short the recruitment of a professional outsider represents a search for a last-resort solution (Lin *et al.*, 1992). Whether we are dealing with diverse communication styles or differing interpretations of status, it seems clear that the most effective therapists will be those who are prepared to engage with their clients on their own interpersonal terms.

Material factors: access to treatment

Before ending this discussion of factors influencing the cross-cultural effectiveness of therapy, we should acknowledge the key influence of material and economic factors. Wherever you are when you read this, ask yourself how long it would take you to walk to the nearest provider of psychotherapy. Answers to this question (measured in minutes, hours, days even) will vary wildly. For example, it is estimated that in Ethiopia the client–psychotherapist ratio is approximately 1 to 8 million, while in the US the comparable figure stands at 1 to 10,000 – a figure becoming still more favourable for city dwellers (Hopper *et al.*, 2007).

Clearly, economic prosperity and place of residence have an influence on access to psychotherapy. We should remember, though, that figures reflecting access to professional therapeutic services do not tell the whole story. As already hinted, in many regions, largely in the developing world, healing is the province of the extended family or community. Consequently, even though one may live miles from the nearest qualified provider, healing remains available 'on the doorstep'. It is to these varieties of indigenous healing that we now turn.

Indigenous therapies

It has already been suggested that the successful export of psychotherapy from the west depends to some extent on how well these practices incorporate values that are prevalent in the regions where they are introduced. So where European and North American techniques are able to integrate with locally existing indigenous therapeutic remedies, the overall effect is likely to be positive. Likewise, there is an increasing reciprocal tendency for therapies that are indigenous to developing countries to be applied more globally, in effect being exported to the west. So, what are the broad characteristics of healing practices that have operated in and emerged from the developing world?

After carrying out a meta-analysis of such practices across sixteen developing nations, Lin *et al.* (1992) characterised non-western indigenous therapies as:

- utilising expertise from family or community networks, rather than from professionally trained experts
- focusing on the reintegration of wayward or troubled individuals into the community, rather than on improving individual well-being

TABLE 9.1
Indigenous therapies from around the world

Indigenous therapy	Therapeutic approach
Sri Lankan spiritual healing	Aimed at exorcising malevolent spirits or counteracting sorcery, this approach addresses spiritual aspects of human existence at times of anxiety. While analogous to western psychotherapy, the spiritual tradition is based on deepening self-knowledge by meditation (Kakar, 1984). The therapy itself may also include astrology or exorcism rituals to relieve possession, during which masked actors may perform dances depicting demons and agents who are charged with their expulsion. These practices are likely to take place at temples or shrines (Kapferer, 1997).
Tibetan psychiatry	A system of addressing psychological distress which is based on Tibetan Buddhism. A fusion of religion and psychology, Tibetan psychiatry is often combined with herbal and dietary treatments. The aim is to tackle imbalances in the mind and body which may arise from a lack of self-awareness or unhealthy cravings (analogous to addictions). By adhering to the teachings of Buddha in everyday life (the dharma), the individual attempts to retain holistic balance. Treatments are tailored to an individual's particular feelings of imbalance, but may involve yogic practice, breath control, dietary restrictions. The ultimate aim is to lead a life that is not counter to one's inherent disposition, or to Buddhist teachings (Fernando, 2002).
Yoruba incantations in West Africa	Based on attempting to capture an individual's 'vital force' or 'inner self', perhaps by use of incantations (spells), which are spoken by a specialist spiritual healer or medicine man (Ayoade, 1979). Incantations help to dispel fear and drive out spirits that are in possession of the client's soul. Healing involves a combined treatment of the body and soul, by herbal medication as well as spiritual methods, in order to restore the balance of the body and soul.

- incorporating religious or spiritual elements as well as or instead of scientific, medical principles
- taking place in community settings such as churches, homes or other non-medical communal spaces.

Some examples of non-western, indigenous healing techniques from Asia and Africa are outlined in Table 9.1 (see also the key concept above, illustrating a Haitian practice). It has been noted that increasingly, clients who consult spiritual healers across Asia and Africa are likely to seek medical consultations simultaneously (Fernando, 2002) where these are available. Interestingly, then, in many regions indigenous therapies are not regarded as alternatives to western treatments, but as their complements.

Limitations of research on therapy and culture

1 *Limited samples*. While it is informative to learn about the therapeutic choices of clients that recognise varying philosophical traditions, it has been noted that the vastly greater part of research on the topic overall comes from Europe and North America (Fernando, 2002). We await more research on therapeutic choices made by participants from the developing world.

2 *The hidden therapies*. Traditional indigenous therapies from outside Europe and North America, often being religion-based, are by their very nature less formal than their western counterparts. They do not require formal training and take place within the home in many cases. They are not documented by professional bodies or medical councils. Consequently, their prevalence remains difficult to document effectively, other than with the use of small-scale or ethnographic and qualitative research. We therefore lack a reliable quantitative appreciation of the breadth of indigenous healing, thus limiting our own appreciation of its global uptake. This limitation appears to be inherent in the use of informal (what are often termed 'folk') remedies.

Recent developments in culture and psychotherapy: Multiculturalism, globalisation and healing

Beginning in the eighteenth century, the worldwide export of European medicine showed that colonialists and religious missionaries were very much on a mission to replace what they saw as superstitious indigenous 'folk' healing with newfound scientific insights (Frank & Stollberg, 2004). Subsequently, there has been no let-up in the traffic of medical knowledge and therapeutic practice to the developing world. Indeed, today's pharmaceutical industry and biomedical researchers ensure that medical practice continues to spread from west to east (Frank & Stollberg, 2004).

Yet recent history reveals an increasing global movement of medical and therapeutic knowledge along a two-way street. This of course reflects a more general trend towards **globalisation** (defined as the global integration and sharing of culturally, socially and internationally diverse ideas). For example, treatments originating in Asia are increasingly exported, with Chinese acupuncture and Indian Ayurvedic treatments becoming ever more popular in Europe and North America.

KEY TERM

Globalisation. The global integration and sharing of culturally, socially and internationally diverse ideas.

Such treatments provide patients in many countries with alternatives to those that are conventionally available. They offer ideas about diagnosis and treatment (of physical and psychological problems) that are distinct from those historically favoured by western psychiatrists (Lin *et al.*, 1992).

Recent research suggests that the cross-trafficking of treatments between east and west yields a global scenario wherein western and non-western treatments happily coexist within societies. This illustrates a general trend towards multiculturalism (wherein people from diverse ethnic and cultural groups coexist in society) in both therapeutic practice and wider society. For example, in many developing countries local healers and western-trained medics are often consulted simultaneously (Ademuwagun *et al.*, 1979; Weiss, 1982). Also, Healy and Aslam (1990) found Asian patients living England regularly consulting GPs as well as *hakims* (Ayurvedic healers trained in India or Pakistan). Similarly, Dein and Sembhi (2001) asked whether (and how) traditional South Asian treatments for psychological ills were being used by psychiatric patients in England. They uncovered a tendency to consult traditional South Asian healers during their psychiatric illness, while simultaneously consulting psychiatrists (where affordable).

The simultaneous use of healthcare from multiple traditions shows that clients have few reservations about using psychiatrists and non-western healers in tandem. Indeed, there is a strong belief among some clients that Ayurvedic treatments address the underlying causes of illness, with western treatments often not seen as treating the root causes (Dein & Sembhi, 2001).

The idea that clients favour the simultaneous use of therapies from different traditions is well supported. Karmi (1985) found that 22% of a sample of Sikhs living in London consulted a *hakim* ahead of seeing their GP. In Scotland, while a minority of South Asians preferred Ayurvedic treatments, some used them while also consulting their GPs (Bhopal, 1986).

Frank and Stollberg (2004) looked at the growing popularity of acupuncture and Ayurvedic treatments in Germany. They suggest that their introduction illustrates a process of hybridisation. In other words, as treatments enter a European setting from outside they undergo an adaptation process, with European and South Asian elements combining to produce a hybrid therapy. For example, GPs were found to use Ayurvedic ideas in their diagnoses, while South Asian healers incorporated biomedical procedures. Further evidence of a fusion of two traditions comes from Tovey (1997), who noted a growing sympathy of some European GPs for imported treatments.

These recent developments give the lie to the image of western medicine as a dominant worldwide movement, steamrollering all indigenous traditional treatments that stand in its way. Traditional healing, it seems, can thrive both indigenously and as an export to Europe. Arguably, these treatments, and the diverse belief systems that underpin them, have a key role to play in preserving the cultural identity of communities who themselves have undergone movements across continents. Indeed, the movement of healing between west and east reflects the simultaneous movement of people in today's world. It also shows that successful therapies in a globalised world are those that can adapt to a populace that values both the scientific and the spiritual.

Summary

Chapter 9 puts definitions, classifications and treatments of abnormality in a cultural context. Not surprisingly, how we define normal behaviour is not standard worldwide. Correspondingly, behaviours that are deemed pathological and requiring treatment vary from place to place too. Our discussion assesses some examples of culturally relative definitions and diagnoses. Yet extensive research has been carried out which suggests that some disorders, for example schizophrenia, have common core symptoms cross-culturally. This case for schizophrenia as a universal syndrome is discussed here. However, the influence of culture on the diagnosis of psychopathology is widely recognised, especially in the case of the so-called culture-bound syndromes (disorders that are recognised and diagnosed only in specific cultural contexts). The implications of these syndromes, along with several examples, are examined.

Finally, examples of culturally diverse psychotherapies are reviewed, especially in relation to their nature and relative effectiveness across cultures. This discussion covers both western psychotherapies and indigenous treatments. In this context there is also an assessment of the increasing cross-migration of treatments between east and west, illustrating the globalised nature of healing.

REFLECTIVE EXERCISE 36

Match up the definitions on the right with the terms on the left (see p. 229 for answers)

Terms	Definitions
Culture-bound syndrome	*A pattern of psychotic features including thought disturbances, bizarre delusions, hallucinations (usually auditory), disturbed sense of self and loss of reality testing*
Schizophrenia	*Syndrome including jumpiness, tics, echolalia (copying speech), echopraxia (copying actions), automatic obedience*
Latah	*A culture-specific disorder that tends to be undiagnosed or misunderstood elsewhere*
Drapetomania	*An initial period of solitary depressive brooding, followed by furious violent outbursts*
Amok	*Syndrome diagnosed among slaves, involving 'the uncontrollable urge to escape'*
Anorexia nervosa	*Syndrome involving weight loss, self-induced vomiting, binge eating and appetite loss*
Altered state of consciousness	*Periods of temporarily disrupted emotion and cognition, loss of bodily control, hyper-suggestibility, even rejuvenation*
Taijin-kyofu-sho	*Social phobia or olfactory reference syndrome*

FURTHER READING

- Fernando, S. (2002) *Mental Health, Race and Culture*, Basingstoke, UK: Palgrave.
- Prince, R. & Tcheng-Laroche, F. (1987) Culture-bound syndromes and international disease classifications, *Culture, Medicine and Psychiatry*, 2 (1), 3–21.
- World Health Organization (1979) *Schizophrenia: An International Follow-up Study*, New York: Wiley.

Concluding thoughts, future directions 10

No time for conclusions

It would be unrealistic to attempt anything as glib as 'a conclusion' from the diversity of material to have featured in the previous nine chapters. We have learned a great deal about the relationship between culture and behaviour in areas of life as wide-ranging as cognition (Chapter 6), sociality (Chapter 7), childrearing (Chapter 8) and abnormality (Chapter 9). We have learned too about the history of global psychology (Chapter 2), about the meaning and ramifications of culture itself (Chapter 3), about controversies surrounding ethnocentrism in psychology (Chapter 4) and about the values and methodological preferences of the subject's various theoretical approaches (Chapters 1 and 5). Inevitably then, diverse discussions such as these defy overarching or snappy conclusions. Nevertheless, I would argue that throughout our exploration of cultural issues past and present, certain themes and ongoing debates have been constant and discernible.

It would appear that in global psychology, as in the bigger tent of psychology as a whole, certain defining debates recur, from which emerge a clutch of alternative paradigms, each with its own ideas about the nature and scope of the subject. I refer in part here to well-documented (in this book and in others) alternative paradigms such as cross-cultural psychology (see Chapter 1) and cultural psychology (see Chapter 5). Some who align themselves with one or other of these alternatives habitually favour the existence of culturally universal human psychological capacities or behaviour patterns (see Chapter 1). Others emphasise cultural diversity in human behaviour (see Chapter 5).

Yet while such differences in approach are evident in the literature concerning cultural issues in psychology, it has to be said that for many practitioners in the field, these differences are reconcilable. In other words, many global psychologists appreciate the strengths of both universalism and relativism. Rather than veering towards one or other approach, they might be inclined to build theoretical and methodological bridges between what were once perhaps seen as incompatible stand-points. Let us now consider this more conciliatory view.

Bridging alternative paradigms

Perhaps the most keenly contested debate in global psychology, as reflected in all the major introductory volumes on the subject, is the one concerning universalism and relativism. The debate hinges on whether practitioners should search for evidence of cultural universals in psychological capacities, or whether the priority should be to uncover diversities in thought and behaviour that are effectively inseparable from the cultural contexts in which they are found (see Chapter 5). Yet this doesn't have to be an either-or – universalist versus relativist – debate. Rather than facing a theoretical and methodological choice between conducting universalist-oriented (etic) or relativist-oriented (emic) research (see Chapter 4), some global researchers prefer to draw on elements of both approaches. Such a conciliatory approach may for instance involve searching for behavioural diversity by using ethnographic methods, while also seeking out uniformity in behaviour across cultures using cross-cultural research methods (Berry *et al.*, 2002).

Combining the strengths of universalism and relativism is actually nothing new. It echoes Berry's (1989) so-called derived etic model of global research (see the 'Two concepts borrowed from linguistics' key concept in Chapter 4) and has gained in popularity in recent years. Poortinga (1997), for example, promotes the importance of theoretical bridge-building, pooling the resources of alternative paradigms, when investigating the relationship between culture and behaviour. The challenge global psychology faces, he argues, is to find a unified method that allows for the uncovering of psychological phenomena that occur across cultures (cultural universals), while also acknowledging culture's role in distinguishing peoples of the world from each other (cultural variation).

Yet obstacles stand in the way of this enterprise, especially in the form of the long-held theoretical assumptions held by researchers who align themselves with alternative approaches. Historical demarcations between researchers from different disciplines (and indeed factions within disciplines) are well documented. As you may recall, the history of the study of culture and behaviour (see Chapter 2) reveals serious divisions between practitioners from the more relativistic field of cultural anthropology on one hand, and the more traditionally universalistic approach of psychology on the other. Yet we also learned in Chapter 2 of a conciliatory precedent that yielded the (albeit rather short-lived) sub-discipline of psychological anthropology (see the 'Psychological anthropology' key concept in Chapter 2).

Such past attempts at combining paradigms resonate in contemporary attempts to reconcile alternative approaches to the study of culture and behaviour. History has a funny way of repeating itself. Just as in the mid-twentieth century, Benedict (1946) and Fromm (1941) tried to find a middle way between psychology and anthropology, the modern era has yielded welcome suggestions for convergence between the paradigms of global psychology. Poortinga (1997) recognises an opportunity for convergence between emic and etic approaches, allowing the discipline as a whole to overcome the inherent limitations of each. Despite differing assumptions of universalism (psychic unity) and relativism (culture as inseparable from the mind), such convergence between approaches has produced studies that combine the strengths of cross-cultural psychology with those of cultural psychology. For example:

> Wassman and Dasen (1994) studied Yupna numbering, counting and classification systems in New Guinea using a combination of ethnographic and cross-cultural methods. This involved the detailed study of Yupna counting *in situ*, as a culturally situated phenomenon revealing the shared meanings and cognitive style of the Yupna community. Meanwhile, more replicable aspects of the study allowed researchers to compare cognitive performance with that of other cultural groups in relation to cultural variables such as schooling and childrearing.

It appears, then, that without disturbing the integrity of universalist and relativist studies of culture and behaviour, convergent research can allow the flourishing of projects that to some extent make the most of the advantages of the two approaches while minimising their limitations.

The bigger picture: Culture, constraints, choices

A willingness among global psychologists to combine alternative paradigms represents a compromise between parties with differing views about the behaviour of individuals in their cultural context. But if we take a broader view of this scenario, such conciliation also offers us a bird's-eye vantage point of the relationship between cultures and humanity. We can view the convergence between (and complementary nature of) relativism and univeralism in relation to a bigger picture that encapsulates human behaviour, history, biology and culture.

One way of doing this is to see historical, biological and cultural influences on human action as a set of constraints. After all, our ancestry, our DNA, our upbringing all place limits on how we behave. In other words, phylogeny (how the human species has evolved), genetics (biologically inherited behavioural predispositions) and culture (learned and inherited norms and values that distinguish social groups from each other – see Chapter 3) – all set limits to our behavioural potential. This is a theme that recalls Berry *et al.*'s (2002) eco-cultural model of cultural transmission (see Chapter 3), and arguably such constraints can be viewed beneficially from both universalist and relativist perspectives. For example, the evolution of humans by natural selection is common to all cultural groups, yet it is also mediated by environmental and ecological variables. Likewise we know that cultural norms and values are transmitted to all cultural groups by universal processes of socialisation and enculturation (see Chapter 3), yet how these norms and values manifest themselves in diverse circumstances is mediated by contextual, ecological and climatic factors. It seems, then, that history, biology and culture all impose both universal and diverse constraints.

Yet there is more to the influence of history, biology and culture than pure constraint. Beyond the limits imposed by all these forces, humans retain the power to make choices that shape their own lives and cultures. Despite inherited biological, environmental and cultural constraints, individuals and groups are capable of developing new skills and technologies that power the development and evolution of culture itself. We have previously learned that choices made at the level of intentionality (see Chapter 5) produce intellectual and technological expansions that propel the human species forward, despite a host of constraining forces.

People in diverse places make different choices about how to adapt to their peculiar environmental, social and individual circumstances. By selecting one way of behaving they necessarily reject a host of others. Living nomadically means not setting up a long-term settlement. Living by Buddhist principles means rejecting Catholicism. As we have seen in this volume, global psychologists perpetually encounter people in different cultural settings who are making particular behavioural choices from much wider ranges of possible alternatives, defying the constraints imposed on them by biology and cultural inheritance. Responding to diverse circumstances, all of us stumble through life making behavioural selections that conceal innumerable rejected ways of thinking and acting. Each one of these rejections (not speaking

Japanese, not playing the piano, not joining the priesthood) provides a glimpse of our lives as they might otherwise have been.

To put it more positively, the things we avoid doing are often accepted with relish elsewhere, by other people, in the face of other circumstances, in other cultural settings. These are the glimpses of diversity that are sought and often caught by global psychologists. In a paradoxical sense, then, you could say that even the choices we make impose limits of their own. Every choice (learning to speak French) rather than another (learning Arabic) narrows down our available repertoire of thoughts, actions and experiences: futures, even. This process is nicely illustrated by this piece of research into speech perception:

> Werker (1989) describes how four-month-old English-speaking infants are able to detect phonemic contrasts that are peculiar to Hindu language (differences in sounds in Hindu speech that don't appear in English), while their parents are unable to do so. The suggestion here is that as infants we are blessed with speech perception abilities that we lose as we grew older, since they fall obsolete from lack of use.

We can be in only one place at a time, so the choices we make necessitate only a fraction of our ambitions being realised. This process of narrowing down our options for thinking, acting and experiencing owes a lot to where we happen to be located, culturally. Cultural variations like these contribute to the mind-boggling breadth of human diversity. It is this narrowing-down process, by which humans adapt to their cultural settings – changing it and being changed by it in the process – that occupies the thoughts and actions of global psychologists. I hope and trust that their time could not have been better spent doing something else instead.

Future directions

In the course of this volume we have examined the historical currents that led to the emergence of the discipline of global psychology. There has also been extensive coverage of the key debates that have characterised the field during the twentieth century and the first years of the twenty-first. It may now be fitting to make some informed speculations about the future course of the study of behaviour and culture. We might, for example, ask what changes are afoot in the research agendas of global psychologists, and indeed what theoretical and methodological trends are likely to take centre stage in the years to come.

1. An increase in applied global research

The emergence of indigenous psychological traditions (see Chapter 5) has been a major recent theme in global research. Specifically, there has been a proliferation of research projects rooted in localised, problem-solution scenarios. Such growth in research with an applied agenda stems partly from a critique of the cross-cultural, theory-testing tendencies of western-based replication research, which have been perceived by some as overly theoretical, lacking relevance to real-life issues (Sinha, 1997).

To add support to this critique, Poortinga (1997) cites an instance wherein a sample of cross-cultural psychologists were asked to decide whether on the whole cross-cultural psychology tends to produce research findings that (1) add to our knowledge but are not especially useful, (2) are conducive to becoming useful with extra input from practitioners or (3) are already applicable. Among this sample it was found that option (3) was relatively uncommon. Arguably, then, the predicted continued future development of applied indigenous research bodes well for bucking this trend and for the growth of applied global psychology. *Overall it is predicted that the proportion of global research projects with applied aspects will rise in relation to those that are merely theoretical.*

2. Changing dynamics in a globalised world

Predictably, the impact of globalisation on the research agenda of global psychologists has been considerable – and this is set to continue. In an increasingly interconnected world, communication between groups of global researchers is likely to become both greater in volume and qualitatively different in dynamic.

At least three changing dynamics are clearly decipherable. As more international partnerships between psychologists are forged, these are likely to become (1) more egalitarian, as the indigenous psychology movement spreads worldwide and psychology departments in the developing world become more established; (2) more collaborative, with an increasing number of research projects involving psychologists from the developed world working in diverse global locations in collaboration with local practitioners who have specialised knowledge of both their research field and their own community; and (3) more reciprocal, with developing-world researchers now more likely than ever before to export their ideas and concepts into the developed world (see Chapter 9, especially Frank & Stollberg, 2004; Dein & Sembhi, 2001).

A good example of collaborative research between global psychologists saw Connors and Maidman (2001) design a study to reinvigorate the parenting styles and the sense of ethnic identity of Canadian First Nations communities. The programmes are designed from an emic standpoint, with the participation of indigenous practitioners, and for the benefit of the local community. *Overall it is predicted that in an increasingly globalised world, partnerships between researchers from different continents will proliferate and become increasingly egalitarian, collaborative and reciprocal.*

3. Global consciousness replaces regional parochialism

Research into culture and behaviour has traditionally dealt with questions of identity in what could perhaps be seen as a rather parochial fashion. As we saw in Chapter 7, self-construal and identity are portrayed in many influential theories as being inextricably linked with membership of certain designated 'in-groups' (my nation, my ethnicity, my age-cohort). However, this is a moment in history when the importance of nationhood is arguably receding, when boundaries between nation states are becoming more permeable, less permanent. It is perhaps likely, then, that the perceived importance of such parochial sources of identity will wither.

In the twenty-first century we are concerned more than ever before with global issues, not matters of national rivalry or east–west splits which are throwbacks to the Cold War of the 1960s, 1970s and 1980s. Global warming, international recession, wars waged on 'ideas' (extremism, consumerism, terrorism) rather than states, are all phenomena that unite people from all continents and arguably require co-operation and a unified sense of global identity in order to have any hope of success. Maybe this rise in global consciousness will be reflected in the research agendas of global psychology. We might legitimately expect to see more studies focusing on our membership of the ultimate larger social group (humanity as a whole); on common, superordinate goals that unite divided factions, on the promotion of tolerance and reduction of prejudice between divided groups.

An example of the kind of research we might expect to proliferate in a more globally conscious world is Niens *et al.*'s (2003) study of contact and conflict resolution in Northern Ireland. *Overall it is predicted that a deepening sense of global consciousness will usher in more research into global identity, conflict resolution and the reduction of prejudice.*

4. New global samples and populations for psychological research

A well-worn critique of mainstream psychological research rightly contends that a disproportionately high number of research samples is selected from a narrow demographic that extends only to white, middle-class undergraduates from the US. For too long psychology has committed a sampling error wherein people from diverse ethnic, economic and cultural groups are excluded from the research laboratories of behavioural science. Inevitably this compromises psychology's intention of applying its findings to humanity as a whole (see Chapter 4).

However, this situation is changing. Demographic shifts (migration, enculturation, international studentships) dictate that even within the US undergraduate population, participants for research are now far more ethnically diverse. Furthermore, increased global electronic communication and the development of online databases mean that access to geographically and culturally diverse samples worldwide is easier than ever before. Reliance on participants from the US is in any case counterproductive when you consider that this group is unusually monolingual and so represents, cognitively speaking, an unrepresentative sample of the global population.

For all these reasons the disproportionate use of white US undergraduates for research is now less necessary and less viable than ever before. *Overall it is predicted that culturally diverse samples will increasingly become available within single nation states (such as the US), and that opportunities for access to globally diverse samples will continue to increase due to technological development and globalisation.*

Summary

Chapter 10 resists the temptation to draw overarching conclusions, as many of the debates covered in the previous chapters are ongoing and ever changing. Rather, this final chapter opts to consider the case for reconciliation between alternative (cross-cultural and cultural, universalist and relativist) perspectives that dominate so much of the literature on cultural issues in psychology.

Ways forward in the form of theoretical and methodological bridge building are considered, perhaps with a view to combining the best of cross-cultural and cultural approaches. To this end, there is a peek into the future of the discipline of global psychology, revealing some predicted new research directions for psychologists the world over.

Answers to reflective exercises

ANSWERS TO REFLECTIVE EXERCISE 4

Cross-cultural psychology	Translating the research text or instructions from the original language (A) to that of the comparison group (B), then translating it back from language B to language A to see if the original meaning is preserved
'Transport and test' research	Psychometric measures of how attitudes, norms, values and behaviours vary across cultures
Global psychologists	An original study is repeated, or replicated, in different cultural settings to see if the same results emerge
Back-translation	Aspects of behaviour and experience common to all cultural settings
Dimensions of cultural variability	Where two cultural groups are treated in an equivalent manner throughout a study and are drawn from equivalent populations that differ only with respect to their cultural background
Cultural universals	Psychologists with a special interest in placing psychology in a global context
Cultural equivalence	Underlying our cultural variations is a set of psychic (memory, perceptual capacities) structures that all humans share
Cultural differences	Behaviours or experiences that manifest themselves differently in different cultures
Psychic unity	A branch of global psychology that compares the behaviour and experience of people from different cultures in order to understand the extent of culture's influence on psychological functioning

ANSWERS TO REFLECTIVE EXERCISE 8

Projective test

Cultural anthropology

Indigenous psychologies

Race

Social Darwinism

Evolutionary thinking

Eugenics

Psychological anthropology

National character

Ethnography

A brand of ethnocentrism which assumes that one's own group is the ideal towards which others will presently develop

The notion that people from the same nation share certain personality traits

The idea that some societies grow stronger, more complex and are better at maintaining themselves over time, while others may fall by the wayside

The collection of data for descriptive purposes by using fieldwork techniques, focusing on a single cultural setting

Controlling inheritance by selective breeding

A term used to distinguish a relatively large division of persons from another. It refers to how groups with distinct ancestries differ from each other in terms of appearance

Psychological traditions within cultures

Anthropological investigations that make use of psychological concepts and methods

Test designed to provide insight about personality traits

The study of the complex social structures that make up communities, societies and nations

ANSWERS TO REFLECTIVE EXERCISE 12

Cultural determinism

Socialisation

Circumstantial variables

Dual influence

Culture-level analysis

Enculturation

Ethnicity

Culture

Parallel individual analyses

Ecological fallacy

Acculturation

Nation

Assumption that findings that are demonstrated at the culture level of analysis will be replicated within cultural groups

Norms, values, behaviours and other psychological characteristics are passed on via a variety of agencies (family, media, peers, church), often by formal instruction

Actions and psychological characteristics of individuals are deemed to vary according to their membership of one cultural group

Sovereign state, with precise geographical boundaries that are internationally recognised, if subject to change

The people around us and the things emanating from them (encompassing objects, institutions, beliefs, opinions, customs, norms of behaviour)

Circumstances that prevail to a greater or lesser extent out there in the world

Informal process wherein individuals adopt the norms, values and behaviours of their cultural group into their repertoires

The view that human behaviour is primarily shaped by cultural factors

The subjective experience of feeling different from people from other social groups

Cultural transmission by contact with other groups

The notion that biology and culture both work according to the evolutionary principles of selection and adaptation

Strategy to ensure that concepts and variables which are used in culture-level analyses are meaningful to all the cultural groups involved

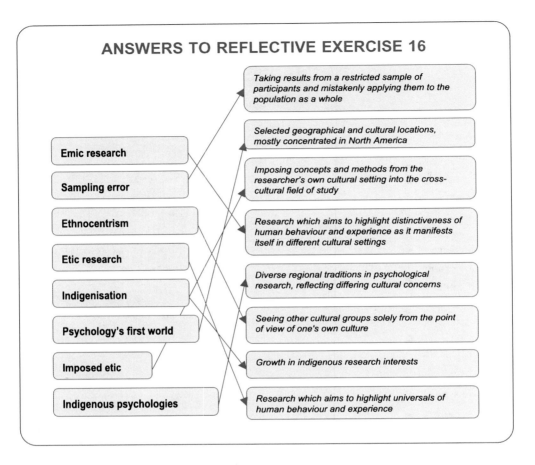

ANSWERS TO REFLECTIVE EXERCISE 16

ANSWERS TO REFLECTIVE EXERCISE 20

Action research	Study of the relationship between people and their multiple (physical and social) environments
Ethnography	States of affairs, persons, objects and behaviours that form everyday contexts
Located experiment	Paradigm in global psychology that challenges the consensus that research should focus on culturally universal behaviour and experience
Ecological psychology	Experimental method in which research questions and testing procedures are modelled on participants' everyday practices
Cultural psychology	View about the discipline's proper subject matter and the best method for studying it
Paradigm	Method for collecting data for descriptive purposes, focusing on a particular culture or setting
Life space	Degree to which research findings have relevance in the outside world
Ecological validity	Ongoing record of observations, events and conversations
Field notes	Paradigm in global psychology that conducts goal-directed research with the aim of transforming situations of oppression
Critical psychology	Studies that help develop an understanding of phenomena so that practical solutions can be found to local and global problems

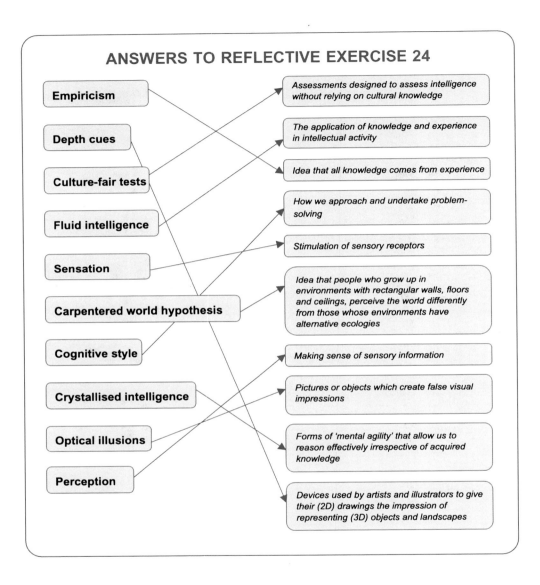

ANSWERS TO REFLECTIVE EXERCISE 24

Empiricism	*Assessments designed to assess intelligence without relying on cultural knowledge*
Depth cues	*The application of knowledge and experience in intellectual activity*
Culture-fair tests	*Idea that all knowledge comes from experience*
Fluid intelligence	*How we approach and undertake problem-solving*
Sensation	*Stimulation of sensory receptors*
Carpentered world hypothesis	*Idea that people who grow up in environments with rectangular walls, floors and ceilings, perceive the world differently from those whose environments have alternative ecologies*
Cognitive style	*Making sense of sensory information*
Crystallised intelligence	*Pictures or objects which create false visual impressions*
Optical illusions	*Forms of 'mental agility' that allow us to reason effectively irrespective of acquired knowledge*
Perception	*Devices used by artists and illustrators to give their (2D) drawings the impression of representing (3D) objects and landscapes*

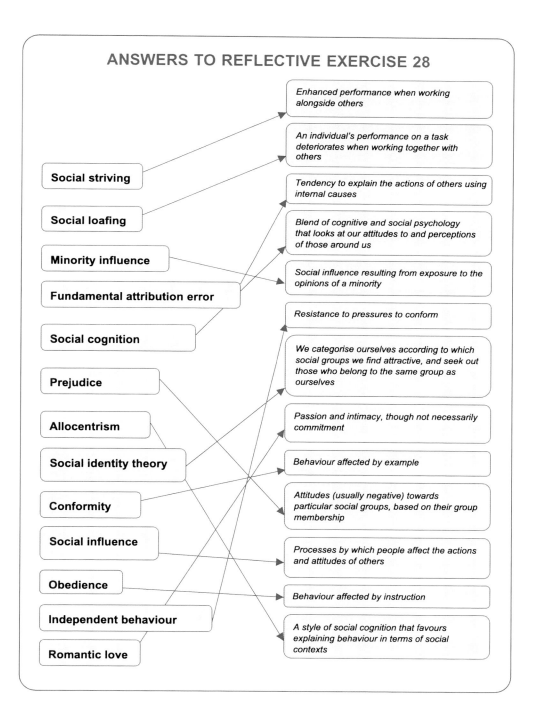

ANSWERS TO REFLECTIVE EXERCISE 28

Social striving

Social loafing

Minority influence

Fundamental attribution error

Social cognition

Prejudice

Allocentrism

Social identity theory

Conformity

Social influence

Obedience

Independent behaviour

Romantic love

Enhanced performance when working alongside others

An individual's performance on a task deteriorates when working together with others

Tendency to explain the actions of others using internal causes

Blend of cognitive and social psychology that looks at our attitudes to and perceptions of those around us

Social influence resulting from exposure to the opinions of a minority

Resistance to pressures to conform

We categorise ourselves according to which social groups we find attractive, and seek out those who belong to the same group as ourselves

Passion and intimacy, though not necessarily commitment

Behaviour affected by example

Attitudes (usually negative) towards particular social groups, based on their group membership

Processes by which people affect the actions and attitudes of others

Behaviour affected by instruction

A style of social cognition that favours explaining behaviour in terms of social contexts

ANSWERS TO REFLECTIVE EXERCISE 32

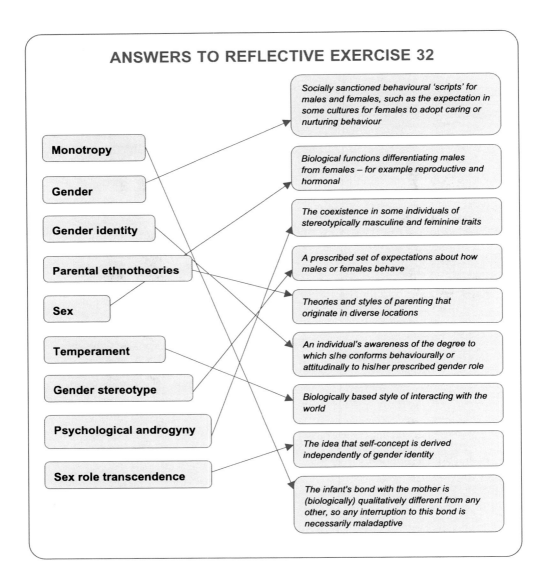

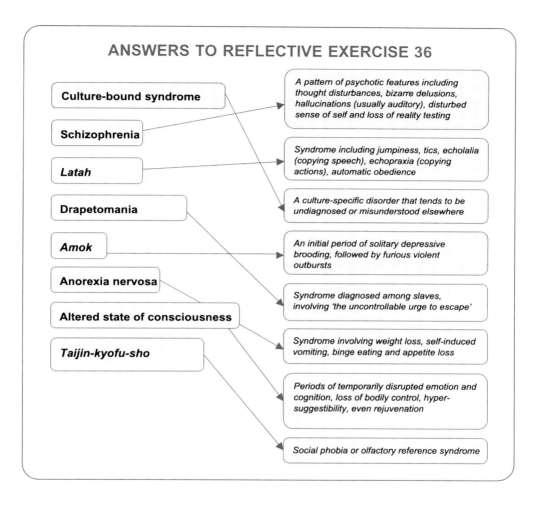

ANSWERS TO REFLECTIVE EXERCISE 36

Culture-bound syndrome

Schizophrenia

Latah

Drapetomania

Amok

Anorexia nervosa

Altered state of consciousness

Taijin-kyofu-sho

A pattern of psychotic features including thought disturbances, bizarre delusions, hallucinations (usually auditory), disturbed sense of self and loss of reality testing

Syndrome including jumpiness, tics, echolalia (copying speech), echopraxia (copying actions), automatic obedience

A culture-specific disorder that tends to be undiagnosed or misunderstood elsewhere

An initial period of solitary depressive brooding, followed by furious violent outbursts

Syndrome diagnosed among slaves, involving 'the uncontrollable urge to escape'

Syndrome involving weight loss, self-induced vomiting, binge eating and appetite loss

Periods of temporarily disrupted emotion and cognition, loss of bodily control, hyper-suggestibility, even rejuvenation

Social phobia or olfactory reference syndrome

Glossary

Action research. Studies that help develop an understanding of phenomena so that practical solutions can be found to local and global problems.

Allocentrism. Style of social cognition that favours explaining behaviour in terms of contexts for action.

Attachment patterns. Emotional ties between people.

Attributions. Inferences we make to explain behaviour.

Back-translation. Translating the research text or instructions from the original language (A) to that of the comparison group (B), then translating it back from language B to language A to see if the original meaning is preserved.

Circumstantial variables. Circumstances that prevail to a greater or lesser extent.

Cognitive style. How we approach and undertake problem-solving.

Conformity. Behaviour affected by example.

Critical psychology. Paradigm in global psychology that conducts goal-directed research with the aim of transforming situations of oppression.

Cross-cultural psychology. A branch of global psychology that compares the behaviour and experience of people from different cultures in order to understand the extent of culture's influence on psychological functioning.

Cross-cultural replication research. An original study is replicated in different cultural settings to see if the same results emerge.

Crystallised intelligence. The application of knowledge and experience in intellectual activity.

Cultural anthropology. The study of the complex social structures that make up communities, societies and nations.

Cultural determinism. The view that human behaviour is primarily shaped by cultural factors.

Cultural differences. Behaviours or experiences that manifest themselves differently in different cultures.

Cultural equivalence. Where two (or more) groups are treated in an *equivalent* manner throughout the study and are drawn from *equivalent* populations that differ only with respect to their cultural background.

Cultural psychology. A paradigm in global psychology that challenges the consensus that research should focus on culturally universal behaviour and experience.

Cultural universals. Aspects of behaviour and experience that are common to all cultural settings.

Culturally constructed. Having different meanings in different cultural settings.

Culture. The people around us and the things emanating from them (encompassing objects, institutions, beliefs, opinions, customs, norms of behaviour).

Culture-bound syndrome. A culture-specific disorder that tends to be undiagnosed or misunderstood elsewhere.

Culture-fair tests. Tests designed to assess intelligence without relying on cultural knowledge.

Culture-level analyses. The actions and psychological characteristics of individuals are deemed to vary according to their membership of one cultural group or another.

Dimensions of cultural variability. Psychometric measures of how attitudes, norms, values and behaviours vary across cultures.

Ecological fallacy. The assumption that findings which are demonstrated at the culture level of analysis will be replicated within cultural groups.

Ecological psychology. The study of the relationship between people and their multiple (physical and social) environments.

Ecological validity. The degree to which research findings have relevance in the outside world.

Emic research. Research that aims to highlight distinctiveness of human behaviour and experience as it manifests itself in different cultural settings.

Empiricism. The idea that all knowledge comes from our experiences.

Ethnicity. A sense of belonging to a social group, the subjective experience of feeling different from other groups.

Ethnocentrism. Seeing other cultural groups solely from the point of view of one's own culture.

Ethnographies. The collection of data for descriptive purposes by using fieldwork techniques, focusing on a single cultural setting.

Etic research. Research that aims to highlight universals of human behaviour and experience.

Eugenics. Controlling inheritance by selective breeding.

Evolutionary psychology. A branch of psychology focusing on genetic and biological antecedents of behaviour.

Evolutionary thinking. A brand of ethnocentrism which assumes that one's own group is the ideal towards which others will presently develop.

Fluid intelligence. Forms of 'mental agility' that allow us to reason effectively irrespective of acquired knowledge.

Fundamental attribution error. Tendency to explain the actions of others using internal causes.

Gender schemas. Ideas about appropriate behaviours for males and females.

Global psychology. A branch of psychology with a special interest in placing psychology in a global context.

Globalisation. The global integration and sharing of culturally, socially and internationally diverse ideas.

Imposed etic. Imposing concepts and methods from the researcher's own cultural setting into the cross-cultural field of study.

Independent behaviour. Resistance to pressures to conform.

Indigenous psychologies. Diverse regional traditions in psychological research, reflecting differing cultural concerns.

Instincts. Biological predispositions to act.

Life space. The states of affairs, persons, objects and behaviours that form everyday contexts.

Located experiment. An experimental method in which research questions and testing procedures are modelled on participants' everyday practices.

Meta-analysis. A review of findings from a large number of investigations into a similar research question.

Monotropy. The infant's bond with the mother is (biologically) qualitatively different from any other, so any interruption to this bond is necessarily maladaptive.

Motherese. Vocal intonation patterns directed towards infants that are characterised by raising the pitch of the voice, exaggerated variations in sound.

Nation. Sovereign state, with geographical boundaries, which incorporates many cultures and ethnicities.

National character. The notion that people from the same nation share certain personality traits.

Nature–nurture debate. Dispute about the relative contributions of biological inheritance (nature) and environmental influence (nurture) to our behavioural repertoire.

Obedience. Behaviour affected by instruction.

Optical illusions. Pictures or objects that create false visual impressions.

Paradigm. View about the discipline's proper subject matter and the best method for studying it.

Parallel individual analysis. A strategy to ensure that concepts and variables which are used in culture-level analyses are meaningful to all the groups involved.

Parental ethnotheories. Theories and styles of parenting that originate in diverse locations.

Perception. How we make sense of sensory information.

Prejudice. Attitudes (usually negative) towards particular social groups, based on their group membership.

Projective techniques. Tests designed to provide insight about personality traits.

Psychic unity. A set of psychic structures (mind, memory capacity, perceptual processes) that all humans share.

Psychological anthropology. Anthropological investigations that make use of psychological concepts and methods.

Psychometrics. Measuring psychological abilities.

Psychopathology. Psychological state without normal functioning, requiring treatment.

Race. How groups with distinct ancestries differ from each other in terms of appearance, including skin colour, blood group, hair texture.

Romantic love. Passion and intimacy though not necessarily commitment.

Rorschach test. A clinical technique by which an analyst uncovers aspects of a client's personality from their perception of a series of ambiguous black and coloured shapes (inkblots).

Sampling error. Taking results from a restricted sample of participants and mistakenly applying them to the population as a whole.

Schizophrenia. A pattern of psychotic features including thought disturbances, bizarre delusions, hallucinations (usually auditory), disturbed sense of self and loss of reality testing.

Sensation. Stimulation of sensory receptors.

Social cognition. Blend of cognitive and social psychology that looks at our attitudes and our perceptions of those around us.

Social constructivism. The view that there is no such thing as a knowable objective truth or reality since all truth is generated in cultural contexts.

Social Darwinism. The idea that some societies grow stronger, more complex and are better at maintaining themselves over time, while others may fall by the wayside.

Social identity theory. Asserts that we categorise ourselves according to which social groups we find attractive, and seek out those who belong to the same group as ourselves.

Social influence. Processes by which people affect the actions and attitudes of others.

Social loafing. When an individual's performance on a task deteriorates when working together with others.

Temperament. Biological predisposition to behave in certain ways.

Transformative research. Research that investigates how disadvantaged individuals or groups can achieve social justice by bringing about change in their material and political circumstances.

References

Aboud, F. (1998) *Health Psychology in Global Perspective*, Thousand Oaks, CA: Sage.

Adair, J. (1995) The research environment in developing countries: contributions to the national development of the discipline, *International Journal of Psychology*, 30, 643–662.

Adair, J., Coelho, A. & Luna, J. (2002) How international is psychology? *International Journal of Psychology*, 37 (3), 160–170.

Ademuwagun, Z., Ayoade, J., Harrison, I., & Warren, D. (eds.) (1979) *African Therapeutic Systems*, Waltham, MA: Crossroads Press.

Ager, A. (1993) *Mental health issues in refugee populations: a review*, Working paper for the Harvard Centre for the Study of Culture and Medicine, Boston: Harvard Medical School.

Ager, A. (1996) Children at war, in Carr, S. & Schumaker, J. (eds.), *Psychology and the Developing World*, London: Praeger.

Ahmadu, F. (2000) Rites and wrongs: an insider/outsider reflects on power and excision, in Shell-Duncan, B. & Hernlund, Y. (eds.), *Controversy and Change*, Boulder, CO: Lynne Rienner.

Ainsworth, M., Blehar, M., Waters, E. & Wall, S. (1978) *Patterns of Attachment*, Hillsdale, NJ: Lawrence Erlbaum Associates.

Alexander, Y. (2002) *Palestinian Religious Terrorism: Hamas and Islamic Jihad*, Ardsley, NY: Transnational.

Al-Issa, I. & Tousignant, M. (1997) *Ethnicity, Immigration and Psychopathology*, New York: Plenum.

Al-Krenawi, A. & Graham, J. (2000) Culturally sensitive social work: practice with Arab clients in mental health settings, *Health & Social Work*, 25, 9–22.

Allison, J. & Wrightsman, L. (1993) *Rape: The Misunderstood Crime*, Newbury Park, CA: Sage.

Allport, G. (1954) *The Nature of Prejudice*, Reading, MA: Addison-Wesley.

Allport, G. & Pettigrew, T. (1957) Cultural influences on the perception of movement: the trapezoidal illusion among Zulus, *Journal of Abnormal and Social Psychology*, 55, 104–113.

Allwood, M. (2005) Psychology in a global world: locally relevant but globally ignored? *The Psychologist*, February, 18 (2), 84–86.

American Psychiatric Association (1994) *Diagnostic and Statistical Manual of Mental Disorders (DSM-IV)* (4th ed.), Washington: APA.

Ancona, L. & Pareyson, R. (1968) Contributo allo studio della aggressione: la dinamica della obbedienze distinctiva, *Archivio di Psicologia Neurologia e Psichiatria*, 29, 340–372.

Anwar, S. (1997) Jilted Bangladeshis take brutal revenge, *Ottawa Citizen*, May 12, p. A12.

Aptekar, L. & Stocklin, D. (1997) Children in particularly difficult circumstances, in Berry, J., Poortinga, Y. & Pandey, J. (eds.) *Handbook of Cross-cultural Psychology* (2nd ed., Vol. 2), Boston: Allyn & Bacon.

Arbesman, M., Kahler, L. & Buck, G. (1993) Assessment of the impact of female circumcision on the gynaecological, genitourinary and obstetrical health problems of women from Somalia, *Women and Health*, 20 (3), 27–42.

Ardrey, R. (1966) *The Territorial Imperative*, New York: Atheneum.

Arieti, S. (ed.) (1959) *American Handbook of Psychiatry* (Vol. 1), New York: Basic Books.

Arnett, J. (2002) The psychology of globalisation, *American Psychologist*, 57, 774–783.

Asch, S. (1955) Opinions and social pressure, *Scientific American*, 193, 31–35.

Atkinson, D. (2002) *Counseling Diverse Populations*, New York: McGraw-Hill.

Atkinson, D., Ponce, F. & Martinez, F. (1984) Effects of ethnic, sex and attitude similarity on counsellor credibility, *Journal of Counselling Psychology*, 31 (40), 588–590.

Atkinson, R. & Shiffrin, R. (1968) Human memory, in Spence, K. & Spence, J. (eds.), *The Psychology of Learning and Motivation* (Vol. 2), London: Academic Press.

Atkinson, R.L., Atkinson, R.C., Smith, E. & Bem, D. (1990) *Introduction to Psychology* (10th ed.), San Diego, CA: Harcourt Brace Jovanovich.

Atsumi, T. & Sugiman, T. (1990) Group decision process by majority and minority: decision and implementation, *Japanese Journal of Experimental Social Psychology*, 30, 15–23.

Attran, S. (2003) Genesis of suicide terrorism, *Science*, 299, 1534–1539.

Attran, S. (2004) Mishandling suicide terrorism, *The Washington Quarterly*, 27 (3), 67–90.

Aycicegi, A. (1993) *The effects of the mother training program*, published master's training program, Bogazici University, Istanbul, Turkey.

Ayoade, J. (1979) The concept of inner essence in Yoruba traditional medicine, in Ademuwagun, A., Ayoade, J., Harrison, I. & Warren, D. (eds.), *African Therapeutic Systems* (pp. 49–55), Waltham, MA: Crossroads Press.

Bandura, A., Ross, D. & Ross, S. (1961) Transmission of aggression through imitation of aggressive models, *Journal of Abnormal and Social Psychology*, 63, 575–582.

Banister, P., Burman, E., Parker, I., Taylor, M. & Timdall, C. (1997) *Qualitative Methods in Psychology*, Buckingham, UK: Open University Press.

Banton, M. (1987) *Racial Theories*, Cambridge, UK: Cambridge University Press.

Banyard, P. (1999) *Controversies in Psychology*, London: Routledge.

Banyard, P. & Grayson, A. (2000) *Introducing Psychological Research*, Basingstoke, UK: Palgrave.

Barfield, T. (ed.) (1997) *The Dictionary of Anthropology*, Oxford, UK: Blackwell.

Barker, P. (1996) *The Regeneration Trilogy*, London: Viking.

Baron, R. & Byrne, D. (1994) *Social Psychology: Understanding Human Interaction* (7th ed.), Boston: Allyn & Bacon.

Bartlett, F. (1932) *Remembering*, Cambridge, UK: Cambridge University Press.

Baumrind, D. (1971) Current patterns of parental authority, *Developmental Psychology Monographs*, 75, 43–88.

Bauserman, R. (1997) International representation in the psychological literature, *International Journal of Psychology*, 32, 107–112.

Beard, G. (1878) Remarks at American Neurological Association meeting, *Journal of Nervous and Mental Disease*, 5, 526.

Beard, G. (1880) Experiments with the 'Jumpers' or 'Jumping Frenchmen' of Maine, *Journal of Nervous and Mental Disease*, 7, 487–490.

Beary, M. & Cobb, J. (1981) Solitary psychosis – three cases of monosymptomatic delusion of alimentary stench treated with behavioural psychotherapy, *British Journal of Psychiatry*, 138, 64–66.

Beiser, M. (1987) Commentary on 'Culture-bound syndromes and international disease classifications', *Culture, Medicine and Psychiatry*, 2 (1), 29–35.

Beiser, M., Dion, R., Gotowiec, A., Hyman, I. & Vu, N. (1995) Immigrant and refugee children in Canada, *Canadian Journal of Psychiatry*, 40, 67–72.

Bem, S. (1974) The measurement of psychological androgyny, *Journal of Consulting and Clinical Psychology*, 42, 155–162.

Benedict, R. (1934) *Patterns of Culture*, New York: Mentor.

Benedict, R. (1946) *The Chrysanthemum and the Sword*, Boston, MA: Houghton Mifflin.

Berkeley, G. (1927) *Three Dialogues Between Hylas and Philonious*, Chicago: Open Court (originally published in 1713).

Berlin, B. & Kay, P. (1968) *Basic Colour Terms*, Los Angeles: University of California Press.

Berry, J. (1969) On cross-cultural comparability, *International Journal of Psychology*, 4 (2), 119–128.

Berry, J. (1983) The sociogenesis of social sciences: an analysis of the cultural relativity of social psychology, in Brain, B. (ed.), *The Sociogenesis of Language and Human Conduct* (pp. 449–458), New York: Plenum.

Berry, J. (1989) Imposed etics-emics-derived etics: the operationalisation of a compelling idea, *International Journal of Psychology*, 24, 721–735.

Berry, J. & Bennett, J. (1989) Syllabic literacy and cognitive performance among the Cree, *International Journal of Psychology*, 24, 429–450.

Berry, J., Poortinga, Y., Segall, M. & Dasen, P. (1992/2002) *Cross-cultural Psychology: Research and Applications* (1st and 2nd eds.), Cambridge, UK: Cambridge University Press.

Best, D. & Ruther, N. (1994) Cross-cultural themes in developmental psychology: an examination of texts, handbooks and reviews, *Journal of Cross-cultural Psychology*, 25, 54–77.

Beveridge, W. (1935) Racial differences in phenomenal regression, *British Journal of Psychology*, 26, 59–62.

Bhopal, R. (1986) The inter-relationship of folk, traditional and western medicine with an Asian community in Britain, *Social Science and Medicine*, 22, 99–105.

Bhugra, D., Leff, J., Mallett, R., Der, G., Corridan, B. & Rudge, S. (1997) Incidence and outcome of schizophrenia in whites, African-Caribbeans and Asians in London, *Psychological Medicine*, 27, 791–798.

Biesheuvel, S. (ed.) (1969) *Methods for Measurement of Psychological Performance*, Oxford, UK: Blackwell.

Billig, M. (1978) *Fascists: A Social Psychological View of the National Front*, London: Academic Press.

Billig, M. (1984) Political ideology: social psychological aspects, in Tajfel, H. (ed.), *The Social Dimension* (pp. 446–470), Cambridge, UK: Cambridge University Press.

Binet, A. & Simon, T. (1905) Methodes nouvelles pour le diagnostic du niveau intellectual des anormaux, *L'Annee Psychologique*, 11, 191–244.

Birch, A. & Hayward, S. (1994) *Individual Differences*, Basingstoke, UK: Macmillan.

Bissilat, J. *et al.* (1967) The concept of lakal in Djerma-Songhai culture, *Psychopathologie Africaine*, 26 (3), 342–359.

Blanden, J., Gregg, P. & Macmillan, L. (2007) Accounting for intergenerational income persistence: non-cognitive skills, ability and education, *Economic Journal*, conference volume, C43–C60.

Blass, T. (ed.) (2000) *Obedience to Authority: Current Perspectives*, Hillsdale, NJ: Lawrence Erlbaum Associates.

Blau, Z. (1981) *Black Children–White Children: Competence, Socialization, and Social Structure*, New York: Free Press.

Bleuler, M. (1961) Bewusstseinsstoerungen in der Psychiatrie, in Staub, H. & Thoelen, H. (eds.), *Bewusstseinsstoerungen* (pp. 199–213), Stuttgart, Germany: Thieme.

Blum, R., Harmon, B., Harris, L. & Resnick, M. (1992) American Indian–Alaskan native youth health, *Journal of the American Medical Association*, 267, 1637–1644.

Blumenbach, J. (1865) *The Anthropological Treatises*, London: Anthropological Society of London.

Boas, F. (1911) *The Mind of Primitive Man*, New York: Macmillan.

Bochner, S. (1994) Cross-cultural differences in the self-concept, *Journal of Cross-cultural Psychology*, 25, 273–283.

Bock, P. (1980) *Continuities in Psychological Anthropology: An Historical Introduction*, San Francisco: Freeman.

Bodde, D. (1953) Harmony and conflict in chinese philosophy, in Wright, A. (ed.) *Studies in Chinese Thought*, Chicago: University of Chicago Press.

Boddy, J. (1996) Violence embodied?, in Dobash, R. & Dobash, R. (eds.), *Rethinking Violence Against Women*, Thousand Oaks, CA: Sage.

Bond, R. & Smith, P. (1996) Culture and conformity: a meta-analysis of studies using Asch's line judgement task, *Psychological Bulletin*, 111, 119–137.

Booth, K. & Dunne, T. (2002) *Worlds in Collision: Terror and the Future Global Order*, New York: Palgrave.

Boothby, N. (1992) Children of war: survival as a collective act, in McCallin, M. (ed.), *The Psychological Well-being of Refugee Children* (pp. 169–184), Geneva, Switzerland: International Catholic Child Bureau.

Boram, R. (2004) *Psychology of Terrorism*, Tampa, FL: University of South Florida.

Boring, E. (1923) Cited in Birch, A. & Hayward, S. (1994), *Individual Differences*, Basingstoke, UK: Palgrave.

Bornstein, M., Tamis-LeMonda, C., Pecheux, M., & Rahn, C. (1968) Mother and infant activity and interaction in Japan and in the U.S.: II: a comparative mocroanalysis of naturalistic exchanges focused on the organization of infant attention, *International Journal of Behavioural Development*, 13, 289–308.

Bornstein, M., Haynes, O., Azuma, H., Galperin, C., Maital, S., Ogino, M. *et al.* (1998) A cross-national study of self-evaluations and attributions in parenting: Argentina, Belgium, France, Israel, Italy, Japan and the U.S., *Developmental Psychology*, 34 (4), 662–676.

Bouchard, T. & McGue, M. (1981) Familial studies of intelligence: a review, *Science*, 22, 1059.

Bourguignon, E. (1976) *Possession*, Corte Madera, CA: Chandler & Sharp.

Bourguignon, E. (1984) Belief and behaviour in Haitian folk healing, in Pederson, P., Sartorius, N. & Marsella, A. (eds.), *Mental Health Services: The Cross-cultural Context* (pp. 242–266), New Delhi, India: Sage.

Bourguignon, E. & Evascu, T. (1977) Altered states of consciousness within a general evolutionary perspective: a holocultural analysis, *Behaviour Science Research*, 12, 197–216.

Bowlby, J. (1951) *Child Care and the Growth of Love*, Harmondsworth, UK: Penguin.

Bowlby, J. (1969) *Attachment*, New York: Basic Books.

Boyd, R. & Richerson, P. (1985) *Culture and the Evolutionary Process*, Chicago: University of Chicago Press.

Bradley, L. (2000) *This Reggae Music: The Story of Jamaica's Music*, London: Penguin.

Brazelton, T. (1972) Implications of infant development among the Mayan Indians of Mexico, *Human Development*, 15, 90–111.

Bremmer, M. (1985) The practice of arithmetic in Liberian schools, *Anthropology and Education Quarterly*, 16, 177–186.

Brewer, K. (2001) *Clinical Psychology*, New York: Heinemann.

Brislin, R. (1970) Back-translation for cross-cultural research, *Journal of Cross-cultural Research*, 1, 185–216.

Brislin, R. & Keating, C. (1976) Cultural differences in the perception of a three dimensional Ponzo Illusion, *Journal of Cross-cultural Psychology*, 7, 397–411.

Bronfenbrenner, U. (1979) *The Ecology of Human Development*, Cambridge, MA: Harvard University Press.

Browning, C. (1992) *Ordinary Men: Reserve Police Battalion 101 and the Final Solution in Poland*, New York: HarperCollins.

Bruner, F. (1908) The hearing of primitive people. *Archives of Psychology*, 11, 1–13.

Brunswik, E. (1943) Orgasmic achievement and environmental probability, *Psychological Review*, 50, 255–272.

Brunswik, E. (1956) *Perception and Representative Design of Psychological Experiments*, Berkeley: University of California Press.

Burley, P. & McGuinness, J. (1977) Effects of social intelligence on the Milgram paradigm, *Psychological Reports*, 40, 767–770.

Burt, C. (1937) *The Backward Child*, London: University of London Press.

Burton, M. (2004) Viva Nacho! Liberating psychology in Latin America, *The Psychologist*, 17 (10), 584–587.

Buss, D. (1989) Sex differences in human mate preferences: evolutionary hypothesis tested in 37 cultures, *Behavioural and Brain Sciences*, 12, 1–49.

Buss, D., Shackelford, T. & LeBlanc, G. (2000) Number of children desired and preferred spousal age difference: context specific mate preference patterns across 37 cultures, *Evolution and Human Behaviour*, 21, 323–331.

Cardenas, E. (1992) Trance and possession as dissociative disorders, *Transcultural Psychiatric Research Review*, 29 (4), 287–299.

Cardwell, M. (2004) *Psychology AS, the Exam Companion*, London: Nelson Thorn.

Carr, S. & Schumaker, J. (1996) *Psychology and the Developing World*, London: Praeger.

Carraher, T. (1986) From drawings to buildings: working with mathematical scales, *International Journal of Behavioural Development*, 9, 527–544.

Carraher, T., Carraher, D. & Schliemann, A. (1985) Mathematics in the streets and in schools, *British Journal of Developmental Psychology*, 3, 21–29.

Cartwright, S. (1851) Report on the diseases and peculiarities of the Negro races, *New Orleans Medical and Surgical Journal*, 691–715, Reading, MA: Addison Wesley.

Cattell, R. (1971) *Abilities: Their Structure, Growth and Action*, Boston: Houghton Mifflin.

Cattell, R. & Cattell, H. (1973) *Measuring Intelligence with the Culture Fair Tests*. Champaign, IL: Institute for Personality and Ability Testing.

Cavalcanti, C. & Duarte, R. (1980) *A Procura de Espaci na Economia Urbana: O Setor Informal de Forteleza*, Recife, Brazil: SUDENE/FUNDAJ.

Cavanaugh, J. & Blanchard-Fields, F. (2006) *Adult Development and Aging* (5th ed.). Belmont, CA: Wadsworth Publishing/Thomson Learning.

Chan, H. (2004) *The relationship between societal factors and universal mate selection*, unpublished thesis, University of Hong Kong.

Chen, X., Liu, M., Li, B., Cen, G., Chen, H. & Wang, L. (1997) Authoritative and authoritarian parenting practices and social and school performances in

Chinese children, *International Journal of Behavioural Development*, 21 (4), 855–873.

Chesler, P. (1989) *Women and Madness*, New York: Harcourt Brace Jovanovich.

Cheung, F. & Leung, K. (1998) Indigenous personality measures, Chinese examples, *Journal of Cross-cultural Psychology*, 29, 233–248.

Cheung, F., Cheung, S., Wada, S. & Zhang, J. (2003) Indigenous measures of personality assessment in Asian countries, *Psychological Assessment*, 15, 280–289.

Cheyne, G. (1733) *The English Malady*, London: Strahan and Leake.

Chieuw, S. (1983) Ethnicity and national integration: the evolution of a multi-ethnic society, in Chen, P. (ed.) *Singapore: Development and Trends* (pp. 29–64), Singapore: Oxford University Press.

Chinese Culture Connection (1987) Chinese values and the search for culture-free dimensions of culture, *Journal of Cross-cultural Psychology*, 18, 143–164.

Clammer, J. (1983) Chinese ethnicity and political culture in Singapore, in Gosling, P. and Lim, L. (eds.), *Chinese Ethnicity and Economy in Southeast Asia*, Ann Arbor, MI: Centre for Southeast Asian Studies.

Coalition to Stop Child Soldiers (2004) *Child Soldiers Global Report 2004*, London: Amnesty International.

Cogan, J., Bhalla, S., SefaDedeh, A. & Rothblum, E. (1996) A comparison study of U.S. and African students on perceptions of obesity and thinness, *Journal of Cross-cultural Psychology*, 27, 98–113.

Cole, M. (1978) Ethnographic psychology of cognition – so far, in Spindler, G. (ed.), *The Making of Psychology Anthropology* (pp. 614–631), Berkeley: University of California Press.

Cole, M. (1992) Culture in development, in Bornstein, M. & Lamb, M. (eds.), *Developmental Psychology: An Advanced Textbook* (3rd ed.), London: Lawrence Erlbaum Associates.

Cole, M. (1998) *Cultural Psychology: A Once and Future Discipline*, London: Harvard University Press.

Cole, M., Gay, J., Glick, J. & Sharpe, D. (1971) *The Cultural Context of Learning and Thinking*, New York: Basic Books.

Coleman, V. (1994) Lesbian battering: the relationship between personality and the perpetuation of violence, *Violence and Victims*, 9 (2), 139–152.

Condorcet, M. (1794) *Equisse d'un tableau historique des progres de l'esprit humain*, Paris : Editions Sociales.

Connors, E. & Maidman, F. (2001) A circle of heating: family wellness in aboriginal communities, in Prilleltensky, I., Nelson, G. & Peirson, L. (eds.), *Promoting Family Wellness and Preventing Child Maltreatment: Fundamentals for Thinking and Action*, Toronto, Canada: University of Toronto Press.

Conroy, M., Hess, H., Azuma, H. & Kashiwagi, K. (1980) Maternal strategies for regulating children's behaviour, *Journal of Cross-cultural Psychology*, 11 (2), 153–172.

Constable, P. (2000) In Pakistan, women pay the price of honour, *Washington Post*, May 8, A1, A16.

Coogan, T. (2002) *The IRA*, New York: Palgrave.

Cook, N. & Kono, S. (1977) Black psychology: the third great generation, *Journal of Black Psychology*, 3, 18–28.

Cooper, J., Kendell, R., Gurland, B., Sharpe, L., Copeland, J. & Simon, R. (1972) *Psychiatric Diagnosis in New York and London*, Maudsley Monograph no. 20, London: Oxford University Press.

Crandon, L. (1983) Why Susto? *Ethnology*, 22, 153–167.

Cranshaw, R. (1983) The object of the centrefold, *Block*, 9, 26–33.

Crenshaw, M. (1981) The causes of terrorism, *Comparative Politics*, 13, 379–399.

Crittenden, K. (1991) Asian self-effacement or feminine modesty? Attributional patterns of women university students in Taiwan, *Gender and Society*, 5, 98–117.

Crittenden, P. (2000) A dynamic maturational exploration of the meaning of security and adaptation, in Crittenden, P. & Claussen, A. (eds.), *The Organization of Attachment Relationships* (pp. 358–383), Cambridge, UK: Cambridge University Press.

Crump, T. (1978) Money and number: the Trojan horse of language, *Man*, 13, 503–508.

Cunningham, H. (2006) *The Invention of Childhood*, London: BBC.

Cunningham, M., Roberts, A., Barbee, A., Druen, P. & Wu, C. (1995) Their ideas of beauty are, on the whole, the same as ours: consistency and variability in the cross-cultural perception of female physical attractiveness, *Journal of Personality and Social Psychology*, 68, 261–279.

Daibo, I., Murasawa, H. & Chuo, Y. (1994) Attractive faces and affection of beauty: a comparison of preference of feminine facial beauty in Japan and Korea, *Japanese Journal of Research in Emotions*, 1 (2), 101–123.

Darley, J. (1992) Social organisation for the production of evil, *Psychological Inquiry*, 3, 199–218.

Darwin, C. (1859) *On the Origin of Species*, London: Penguin.

Darwin, C. (1871) *The Descent of Man*, London: John Murray.

Darwin, C. (1872) *The Expression of the Emotions in Man and Animals*, London: John Murray.

Darwin, C. (1940) *The Voyage of the Beagle*, New York: Bantam.

Dasen, P. (1972) Cross-cultural Piagetian research: a summary, *Journal of Cross-cultural Psychology*, 7, 75–85.

Dasen, P. (1977) *Piagetian Psychology: Cross-cultural Contributions*, New York: Gardner.

Dasen, P., Dembele, B., Ettien, K., Kabran, K., Kamagate, D., Koffi, D. *et al.* (1985) N'glouele: intelligence among the Ivory Coast Baoule, *Archives de Psychologie*, 53, 293–324.

Dasgupta, S. (1977) *Hindu Ethos and the Challenge of Change*, New Delhi, India: Arnold-Heinemann.

Dawes, A. & Donald, D. (1994) *Childhood and Adversity: Psychological Perspectives from South African Research*, Cape Town, South Africa: David Phillip

Deconchy, J. (1984) Rationality and social control in orthodox systems, in Tajfel, H. (ed.), *The Social Dimension* (pp. 446–470), Cambridge, UK: Cambridge University Press.

Dein, S. & Sembhi, S. (2001) The use of traditional healing in Asian patients in the UK, *Transcultural Psychiatry*, 38(2), 243–257.

Del Carlo-Giannini, G. & Giannini, A. (1975) Anthropophenomenological approach to dysmorphopohobia, in Arieti, S. & Chrzanowski, G. (eds.), *New Dimensions in Psychiatry: A World View*, New York: Wiley.

Demarath, N. (1942) Schizophrenia among primitives, *American Journal of Psychiatry*, 98, 703–707.

Denham, S., Renwick, S. & Holt, R. (1997) Working and playing together: prediction of pre-school social emotional competence from mother-child interaction, *Child Development*, 62 (2), 242–249.

Denzin, N. & Lincoln, Y. (eds.) (2000) *Handbook of Qualitative Research* (2nd ed.), Thousand Oaks, CA: Sage.

Deregowski, J. (1968) Difficulties in pictorial depth perception in Africa, *British Journal of Psychology*, 59, 195–204.

Deregowski, J. (1972) Pictorial perception and culture, *Scientific American*, 227, 82–88.

Deregowski, J. & Bentley, A. (1986) Perception of pictorial space by Bushmen, *International Journal of Psychology*, 21, 743–752.

Deregowski, J., Muldrow, E. & Muldrow, W. (1972) Pictorial recognition in a remote Ethiopian population, *Perception*, 1, 417–425.

Derksen, B. & Nelson, G. (1995) Partnerships between community residents and professionals: issues of power and social class across the lifespan of neighbourhood organisations, *Canadian Journal of Community Mental Health*, 14 (1), 61–77.

DeVries, M. (1989) Difficult temperament: a universal and culturally embedded concept, in Carey, W. & McDevitt, S. (eds.), *Clinical and Educational Applications of Temperament Research* (pp. 81–85), Amsterdam: Swets & Zeitlinger.

Diener, E., Diener, M. & Diener, C. (1995) Factors predicting subjective well-being of nations, *Journal of Personality and Social Psychology*, 69, 851–864.

DiNicola, V. (1990) Anorexia multiform: self starvation in historical and cultural context, *Transcultural Psychiatric Research Review*, 27, 245–286.

Dion, K. & Dion, K. (1993) Gender and ethnocultural comparisons in styles of love, *Psychology of Women Quarterly*, 17, 463–473.

Dirie, M. & Lindmark, R. (1991) Female circumcision in Somalia and women's motives, *Acta Obstetricia Gynecologica Scandinavia*, 70, 581–585.

Dobles Oropeza, I. (2000) A Central American voice, in Sloan, T. (ed.), *Critical Psychology* (pp. 125–135), Basingstoke, UK: Palgrave.

Doi, T. (1973) *The Anatomy of Dependence*, Tokyo: Kodansha.

Donaldson, M. (1982) Conservation: what is the question? *British Journal of Psychology*, 73, 199–207.

Doob, L. (1960) *Becoming More Civilized*, New Haven, CT: Yale University Press.

Dorsainvil, J. (1931) *Vodou et Névrose*, Port-au-Prince, Haiti: Imprimerie la Presse.

Dove, A. (1971) The 'Chitling' Test, in Aiken, L., Jr. (ed.), *Psychological and Educational Testings*, Boston: Allyn and Bacon.

Drew, N. (2000) Psychological testing with indigenous people in Australia, in Dudgeon, P., Garvey, D. & Pickett, H. (eds.), *Working with Indigenous Australians: A Handbook for Psychologists* (pp. 325–334), Perth, Australia: Gunada Press.

Drew, N., Sonn, C., Bishop, B. & Contos, N. (1990) Is doing good just enough? Enabling practice in a disabling discipline, in Sloan, T. (ed.), *Critical Psychology: Voices for Change* (pp. 171–184), Basingstoke, UK: Palgrave.

DuBois, C. (1944) *The People of Alor*, New York: Harper and Row.

Duncan, H., Gourlay, N. & Hudson, W. (1973) *A Study of Pictorial Perception among Bantu and White Primary School Children in South Africa*, Johannesburg, South Africa: Witwatersand University Press.

Dutton, D. & Strachan, C. (1987) Motivational needs for power and spouse-specific assertiveness in assaultive and nonassaultive men, *Violence and Victims*, 2 (3), 145–156.

Eagleton, T. (2000) *The Idea of Culture*, Oxford, UK: Blackwell.

Earley, P. (1993) East meets West meets Mideast: further explorations of collectivistic versus individualistic work groups, *Academy of Management Journal*, 36, 319–348.

Eckensberger, L. (1996) Agency, action and culture: 3 basic concepts for cross-cultural psychology, in Pandey, J., Sinha, D. & Bhawuk, D. (eds.), *Asian Contributions to Cross-cultural Psychology*, New Delhi, India: Sage.

Edgerton, R. (1974) Cross-cultural psychology and psychological anthropology: one paradigm or two? *Review in Anthropology*, 1, 52–65.

Ehrenreich, B. (2002) *Nickel and Dimed: Undercover in Low-wage America*, London: Granta.

Ekman, P. (1971) Universals and cultural differences in facial expressions of emotions, in Cole, J. (ed.), *Nebraska Symposium on Motivation* (Vol. 19, pp. 207–282), Lincoln, NE: University of Nebraska Press.

Ekman, P. & Freisen, W. (1969) The repertoire of non-verbal behaviour: categories, origins, usage and coding, *Semiotica*, 1, 49–98.

Ekman, P. & Freisen, W. (1971) Constants across cultures in the face and emotion, *Journal of Personality and Social Psychology*, 17, 124–129.

Ekman, P., Friesen, W., O'Sullivan, M., Chan, A., Diacovanni-Tarlatzis, I., Heider, K., *et al.* (1987) Universals and cultural differences in the judgements of facial expressions of emotions, *Journal of Personality and Social Psychology*, 53, 712–717.

Ekman, P., Sorensen, E. & Friesen, W. (1969) Pan-cultural elements in facial displays of emotions, *Science*, 164 (3875), 86–88.

Elliot, C. (1986) *British Ability Scales: Test Administration Manual*, Slough, UK: NFER Nelson.

Ellis, W. (1893) The amok of the Malays, *Journal of Mental Science*, 43, 325–338.

Ellis, W. (1897) Latah: a mental malady of the Malays, *Journal of Mental Science*, 43, 32–40.

El-Sheikh, M. and Klaczynski, P. (1993) Cross-cultural variability in stress and control: an investigation of Egyptian middle-class, countryside and inner-city girls, *Journal of Cross-cultural psychology*, 24 (1), 181–198.

Eltringham, P. & McNeil, J. (1999) *Central America*, London: The Rough Guides.

Enriquez, V. (1993) Developing a Filipino psychology, in Kim, U. & Berry, J. (eds.), *Indigenous Pychologies Research and Experience in Cultural Context* (pp. 152–169), Thousand Oaks, CA: Sage.

Errington, F. & Gewertz, D. (1987) *Cultural Alternatives and a Feminist Anthropology*, Cambridge, UK: Cambridge University Press.

Espino, C. (1991) Trauma and adaptation: the case of Central American children, in Ahearn, F. & Athey, J. (eds.), *Refugee Children: Theory, Research and Services* (pp. 92–105), Baltimore, MD: Johns Hopkins University Press.

Estioko-Griffen, A. & Griffen, P. (1981) Woman the hunter: the Agta, in Dahlberg, F. (ed.), *Woman the Gatherer* (pp. 121–152), New Haven, CT: Yale University Press.

Eysenck, H. (1991a) The learning theory model of neurosis, *Behaviour Research and Therapy*, 14, 251–267.

Eysenck, H. (1991b) Introduction, in Pearson, R. (ed.), *Race, Intelligence and Bias in Academe* (pp. 16–55), Washington, DC: Scott-Townsend.

Eysenck, H. & Eysenck, S. (1975) *Manual of the Eysenck Personality Questionnaire*, London: Hodder and Stoughton.

Fals Borda, O. (1988) *Knowledge and People's Power: Lessons with Peasants in Nicaragua, Mexico and Colombia*, New Delhi, India: Indian Social Institute.

Feather, N. (1995) National identification and ingroup bias in majority and minority groups: a field study, *Australian Journal of Psychology*, 47, 129–136.

Feingold, A. (1992) Good looking people are not what we think, *Psychological Bulletin*, 111 (2), 304–341.

Fejes, F. (1992) Masculinity as fact: a review of empirical mass communication and research on masculinity, in Craig, S. (ed.), *Men, Masculinity and the Media* (pp. 9–22), Thousand Oaks, CA: Sage.

Fernando, S. (2002) *Mental Health, Race and Culture*, Basingstoke, UK: Palgrave.

Fields, J. (2001) Living arrangements of children, in U.S. Bureau of the Census, *Current Population Reports* (pp. 70–74), Washington, DC: Government Printing Office.

Firth, R. (1972) Anthropological background to work, in Bryant, C. (ed.) *The Social Dimensions of Work*, Englewood Cliffs, NJ: Prentice Hall.

Fisher, A. (1988) *The Logic of Real Arguments*, Cambridge, UK: Cambridge University Press.

Fitzgerald, R. (1923) A thesis on two tropical neuroses (amok and latah) peculiar to Malaya, in the *Far Eastern Association for Tropical Medicine: Transactions of the Fifth Biennial Congress, Singapore*, London: John Bale Sons and Danielson Ltd.

Fleming, J. (1975) Fear of success imagery in urban Kenya, *Kenya Educational Review*, 2 (2), 121–129.

Fletcher, W. (1908) Latah and crime, *Lancet*, 175, 254–255.

Frager, R. (1970) Conformity and anti-conformity in Japan, *Journal of Personality and Social Psychology*, 15, 203–210.

Frank, R. & Stollberg, G. (2004) Conceptualizing hybridization, *International Sociology*, 19 (1), 71–78.

Freedman, D. (1974) *Human Infancy: An Evolutionary Perspective*, Hillsdale, NJ: Lawrence Erlbaum Associates.

Freeman, D. (1983) *Margaret Mead and Samoa: The Making and Unmaking of an Anthropological Myth*, Cambridge, MA: Harvard University Press.

Freire, P. (1971) *Pedagogy of the Oppressed*, Harmondsworth, UK: Penguin.

Freire, P. (1974) *Pedagogia del Oprimido*, Mexico City, Mexico: Siglo Veintiuno Editores.

Freire, P. (1975) Cultural action for freedom, *Harvard Educational Review Monograph*, Series 1 revised ed.

Freud, A. & Burlingham, D. (1943) *War and Children*, New York: Willard.

Freud, S. (1909) Analysis of a phobia of a five year old boy, in *The Pelican Freud Library* (1977, Vol. 8, pp. 169–306).

Friedländer, S. (1997) *Nazi Germany and the Jews: Vol. 1: The Years of Persecution 1933–9*, New York: HarperCollins.

Fromm, E. (1941) *Escape from Freedom*, New York: Farrar and Rinehart.

Fu, X. & Jing, Q. (1994) The relation between psychology and the development of economy, science and technology, *Acta Psychologica Sinica*, 26 (2), 208–218.

Fuchs, D. (2005) British pair found dead in Mallorca, *The Guardian*, p. 13 (August 20).

Furnham, A. (1984) Value systems and anomie in three cultures, *International Journal of Psychology*, 19, 565–579.

Furnham A., Moutafi, J. & Baguma, P. (2002) A cross-cultural study on the role of weight and waist to hip ratio on female attractiveness, *Personality and Individual Differences*, 32, 729–745.

Gabrenya, W., Wang, Y. & Latané, B. (1985) Social loafing on an optimising task: cross cultural differences among Chinese and Americans, *Journal of Cross-cultural Psychology*, 16, 223–242.

Galton, F. (1869) *Hereditary Genius: An Inquiry into its Laws and consequences*, London: Macmillan.

Garbarino, J., Kostelny, K. & Dubrow, N. (1991) *No Place for a Child; Growing up in a War Zone*, Lexington, MA: Lexington Books.

Garcia Coll, C. (1990) Developmental outcomes of minority infants: a process oriented look at our beginnings, *Child Development*, 61, 270–289.

Gardner, H. (1983) *Theory of Multiple Intelligences*, London: Heinemann.

Garner, D. & Garfinkel, P. (1980) Socio-cultural factors in the development of anorexia nervosa, *Psychological Medicine*, 10, 747–756.

Gay, J. & Cole, M. (1976) *The New Mathematics and an Old Culture: A Study of Learning among the Kpelle of Liberia*, New York: Holt, Rinehart and Winston.

Geertz, C. (1973) *The Interpretation of Cultures*, New York: Basic Books.

Geiger, L. (1880) *Contribution to the History of the Development of the Human Race*, London: Tubner.

Gelfand, M. (2004) Cultural tightness-looseness: a multi-level theory, *Theoretical and Methodological Issues in Cross-cultural Psychology*, available online at: www.bsos.umd.edu/psyc/gelfand/theoretical.html (accessed January 25, 2007).

Georgas, J., Berry, J., Fons, J., Cigdem, K., Ype, H. & Fons, J. (eds.) (2005) *Families across Cultures: A 30 Nation Psychological Study*, Cambridge, UK: Cambridge University Press.

Gergen, K. (1973) Social psychology as history, *Journal of Personality and Social Psychology*, 26, 309–320.

Gesell, A. (1940) *The First Five Years of Life* (9th ed.), New York: Harper and Row.

Gibbons, J., Stiles, D. & Shkodriani, G. (1991) Adolescents' attitudes towards family and gender roles: an international comparison, *Sex Roles*, 25 (11–12), 625–643.

Gibson, J. (1966) *The Senses Considered as Perceptual Systems*, Boston, MA: Houghton Mifflin.

Gilbert, M. (1993) *Atlas of the Holocaust*, New York: William Morrow.

Gill, R. & Keats, D. (1980) Elements of intellectual competence: judgement by Australian and Malay university students, *Journal of Cross-cultural Psychology*, 11, 233–243.

Gilroy, P. (1993) *Small Acts: Thoughts on the Politics of Black Cultures*, London: Serpent's Tail.

Gladstone, W. (1858) *Studies on Homer and the Homeric Age*, London: Oxford University Press.

Goldhagen, D. (1996) *Hitler's Willing Executioners: Ordinary Germans and the Holocaust*, New York: Knopf.

Gombrich, E. (1977) *Art and Illusion: A Study in the Psychology of Pictorial Representation* (5th ed.), Oxford, UK: Phaidon.

Good, B. (1994) *Medicine, Rationality and Experience*, Cambridge, UK: Cambridge University Press.

Goodale, S. (1971) *Tiwi Wives*, Seattle, WA: University of Washington Press.

Goodwin, R. & Lee, L. (1994) Taboo topics among Chinese and English friends, *Journal of Cross-cultural Psychology*, 25 (3), 335–338.

Gordon, R. (2001) Eating disorders East and West: a CBS unbound, in Nasser, M. & Katzman, M. (eds.), *Eating Disorders and Cultures in Transition* (pp. 1–16), New York: Routledge.

Gorer, G. & Rickman, J. (1949) *The People of Great Russia*, London: Cresset.

Gould, S. (1981) *The Mismeasure of Man*, London: Penguin.

Gould, S. (1995) Curveball, in Fraser, S. (ed.), *The Bell Curve Wars*, New York: Basic Books.

Graitcer, P. & Youssef, Z. (1993) Cited in Koss, *et al.* (1994).

Grassivaro-Gallo, P. (1986) Female circumcision in Somalia: some psychological aspects, *Genus*, 41, 133–147.

Greenfield, P. (1997) Culture as process: empirical methods for cultural psychology, in Berry, J., Poortinga, Y. & Pandey, J. (eds.), *Theory and Method, Vol. 1 of Handbook of Cross-cultural Psychology* (2nd ed.), Boston, MA: Allyn & Bacon.

Grimsley, K. (1996) In court, women felt harassed again, *Washington Post*, pp. A1, A12 (October 27).

Gross, R. (1992) *Psychology: The Science of Mind and Behaviour*, London: Hodder and Stoughton.

Gross, R. (1994) *Key Studies in Psychology*, London: Hodder and Stoughton.

Grossman, K. & Grossman, K. (1990) The wider concept of attachment in cross-cultural research, *Human Development*, 33, 31–47.

Gruenbaum, E. (1996) The cultural debate over female circumcision: the Sudanese are arguing this one out for themselves, *Medical Anthropology Quarterly*, 10 (4), 455–475.

Gudykunst, W. & Lee, C. (2003) Assessing the validity of self-construal scales: a response to Levine et al, *Human Communication Research*, 29, 253–274.

Gwako, E. (1995) Continuity and change in the practice of clitoridectomy in Kenya: a case study of the Abagusii, *Africana*, 33, 331–338.

Hacker, F. (1983) Dialectical interrelationships of personal and political factors in terrorism, in Freedman, L. & Alexander, Y. (eds.), *Perspectives on Terrorism*, Wilmington, DE: Scholarly Resources.

Haidt, J. and Keltner, D. (1999) Culture and facial expression: open-ended methods find more expressions and a gradient of recognition, *Cognition and Emotion*, 13, 225–266.

Hallpike, C. (1986) *The Principles of Social Evolution*, Oxford, UK: Clarendon.

Harkness, S. & Super, C. (1995) *Parents' Cultural Belief Systems: Their Origins, Expressions and Consequences*, New York: Guilford.

Harrison, A., Stewart, R., Myambo, K. & Teveraishe, C. (1995) Perceptions of social networks among adolescents from Zimbabwe and the United States, *Journal of Black Psychology*, 21(4), 382–407.

Harrison, G., Glazebrook, C., Brewin, J., Cantwell, R., Dalkin, T., Fox, R. *et al.* (1997) Increased incidents of psychotric disorders in migrant from the Caribbean to the UK, *Psychological Medicine*, 27, 799–806.

Hart, K. (1998) *The place of the 1898 Cambridge Anthropological Expedition to the Torres Straits (CAETS) in the history of British social anthropology*, lecture given in the opening session of a conference held at St John's College, Cambridge, UK, 'Anthropology and psychology: the legacy of the Torres Strait expedition, 1898–1998', 10–12 August 1998.

Haslam, A. & Reicher, S. (2003) A tale of two prison experiments, *Psychology Review*, 9, 2–6.

Hassan, N. (2001) An arsenal of believers: talking to the human bombs, *The New Yorker*, 77 (36), 36–41.

Hate, C. (1969) *Changing Status of Women in Post-Independence India*, New York: Paragon.

Hayes, N. (2000) *Foundations of Psychology*, London: Thomson.

Healy, M. & Aslam, M. (1990) *The Asian Community: Medicines and Traditions*, London: Silver Link.

Hefner, R., Rebecca, M. & Oleshansky, B. (1975) Development of sex-role transcendence, *Human Development*, 18, 142–158.

Heider, K. (1984) *Emotion: inner state v. interaction*, paper presented at the meeting of the American Anthropological Association, Denver, CO.

Heise, L., Pitanguy, J. & Germain, A. (1993) *Violence against Women: The Hidden Health Burden*, Washington, DC: World Bank.

Herrnstein, R. & Murray, C. (1994) *The Bell Curve: Intelligence and Class Structure in American Life*, New York: Free Press.

Herskovits, M. (1948) *Man and His Works, the Science of Cultural Anthropology*, New York: Knopf.

Hewlett, B. (1991) *Intimate Fathers: The Nature and Context of Aka Pygmy Paternal Infant Care*, Ann Arbor: University of Michigan Press.

Hewstone, M., Stroebe, W. & Stephenson, G. (eds.) (1996) *Introduction to Social Psychology: A European Perspective* (2nd ed.), Oxford, UK: Blackwell.

Hewstone, M. & Ward, C. (1985) Ethnocentrism and causal attribution in Southeast Asia, *Journal of Personality and Social Psychology*, 48 (3), 614–623.

Hodes, M., Jones, C. & Davies, H. (1996) Cross-cultural differences in maternal evaluations of children's body shapes, *International Journal of Eating Disorders*, 19, 257–263.

Hodges, R. & French, L. (1980) The effect of class and collection labels on cardiality, conservation and class inclusion tasks, *Child Development*, 59, 354–374.

Hofstede, G. (1980) *Culture's Consequences*, Beverly Hills, CA: Sage.

Hofstede, G. (1983) Dimensions of national cultures in fifty countries and three regions, in Deregowski, J., Dzuirawiec, S. & Annis, R. (eds.), *Explications in Cross-cultural Psychology*, Lisse, Switzerland: Swets and Zeitlinger.

Hogan, J. (1995) International psychology in the next century, *World Psychology*, 1, 9–25.

Hogg, M. & Vaughan, G. (1995) *Social Psychology: An Introduction*, Hemel Hempstead, UK: Prentice Hall.

Honda, Y. (1983) DSM III in Japan, in Spitzer, R., Williams, J. & Skodol, A. (eds.), *International Perspectives on DSM III*, Washington, DC: American Psychiatric Association.

Hopper, K., Harrison, G., Janca, A. & Sartorius, N. (2007) *Recovery from Schizophrenia: An International Perspective*, New York: Oxford University Press.

Horgan, J. & Taylor, M. (2003) *The Psychology of Terrorism*, London: Frank Cass.

Horner, M. (1969) Fail: bright women, *Psychology Today*, 3, 36–38.

Howitt, D. & Owusu-Bempah, J. (1995) *The Racism of Psychology*, London: Harvester.

Hsu, F. (1961) *Educational Anthropology*, Homewood, IL: Dorsey.

Hudson, W. (1960) Pictorial depth perception in sub-cultural groups in Africa, *Journal of Social Psychology*, 52, 183–208.

Hui, C., Triandis, H. & Yee, C. (1995). The relationship between individualism-collectivism and satisfaction at the work place, *Applied Psychology*, 44, 276–282.

Hui, K., Fock, M. & Au, K. (2004) Empowerment effects across cultures, *Journal of International Business Studies*, 35 (1), 46–60.

Hulme, P. (2001) *Ethnographic origins: St Vincent and Tasmania*, paper presented at the Australian Association for Caribbean Studies conference, Canberra, February.

Hume, D. (1784/1894) *Essays Literary, Moral and Political*, London: Routledge.

Huston, A. (1983) Sex-typing, in Hetherington, E. (ed.), *Handbook of Child Psychology* (Vol. 4), New York: Wiley.

Hwang, K. (2005) The third wave of cultural psychology: the indigenous movement, *The Psychologist*, 18 (2), 80–83.

Icheiser, G. (1943) Misunderstandings of personality in everyday life and the psychologist's frame of reference, *Character and Personality*, 12, 145–160.

Inglehart, R. & Baker, W. (2000) Modernization, culture change and the persistence of traditional values, *American Sociological Review*, 65, 19–51.

International Union of Psychological Science (1998) survey, cited in Pawlik, K. & Rosenzweig, M.R. (2000) *International Handbook of Psychology*, London: Sage.

Iskander, T. (1970) *Kamus Dewan*, Kuala Lumpur, Malaysia: Dewan Bahasa don Pustaka.

Izard, C. (1971) *The Face of Emotion*, New York: Appleton-Century-Crofts.

Jablensky, A., Sartorius, N., Ernberg, G., Anker, M., Korten, A., Cooper, J. *et al.* (1992) Schizophrenia: manifestations, incidence and course in different cultures, *Psychological Medicine Monograph*, Supplement, 20, 1–97.

Jackson, J., Brown, K., Brown, T. & Marks, B. (2001) Contemporary immigration policy orientations among dominant group members in Western Europe, *Journal of Social Issues*, 57, 431–456.

Jahoda, G. (1971) Retinal pigmentation, illusion susceptibility and space perception, *International Journal of Psychology*, 6, 199–208.

Jahoda, G. (1984) Do we need a concept of culture? *Journal of Cross-cultural Psychology*, 15, 139–152.

Jahoda, G. & Krewer, B. (1997) History of cross-cultural psychology and cultural psychology, in Berry, J., Poortinga, Y. & Panday, J. (eds.), *Handbook of Cross-cultural Psychology. Vol. 1: Theory and Method*, Boston: Allyn & Bacon.

Jain, A. (2005) Psychology in India, *The Psychologist*, 18 (4), 206–208.

Jankowiak, W. & Fischer, E. (1992) A cross cultural perspective on romantic love, *Ethology*, 32, 149–156.

Jensen, A. (1969) How much can we boost IQ and scholastic achievement?, *Harvard Educational Review*, 39, 1–123.

Jensen, A. (1981) *Straight Talk about Mental Tests*, London: Methuen.

Jepson, T., Lee, P. & Smith, T. (1998) *Canada: The Rough Guide*, London: The Rough Guides.

Jilek, W. (1993) Traditional medicine relevant to psychiatry, in Sartorius, N., de Girolamo, G., Andrews, G., German, G.A. & Eisenberg, L. (eds.), *Treatment of Mental Disorders: A Review of Effectiveness* (pp. 341–390), Washington, DC: American Psychiatric Press.

Jilek-Aall, L. (1979) *Call Mama Doctor/African Notes of a Young Woman Doctor*, Saanichton, Canada: Hancock House.

Johnson, T. (1987) Premenstrual syndrome as a western culture-specific disorder, *Culture, Medicine & Psychiatry*, 11, 337–356.

Johnston, P. (1983) *Native Children and the Child Welfare System*, Toronto Canada: James Lorimer & Co.

Jones, J.S. (1981) How different are human races? *Nature*, 293, 188–190.

Jones, S. (2000) *The Language of the Genes* (revised), London: Flamingo.

Junod, H. (1927) *The Life of a South African Tribe*, New York: University Books.

Kagan, J. (1994) *Galen's Prophecy: Temperament in Human Nature*, New York: Basic Books.

Kagitcibasi, C. (1996) The autonomous-relational self: a new synthesis, *European Psychologist*, 1, 180–186.

Kakar, S. (1984) *Shamans, Mystics and Doctors*, London: Unwin.

Kao, H., Chen, C.C. & Chang, T.M. (1997) The effect of calligraphy practice on character recognition reaction time among children with ADHD, in Roth, P. (ed.), *Psychologists Facing the Challenge of a Global Culture with Human Rights and Mental Health* (pp. 45–9), Proceedings of 55th Annual Convention of the Council of Psychologists, July 14–18, Graz, Austria.

Kapferer, B. (1997) *The Feast of the Sorcerer*, Chicago: University of Chicago Press.

Kaplan, H. & Dove, H. (1987) Infant development among the Ache of Paraguay, *Developmental Psychology*, 23, 190–98.

Karau, S. & Williams, K. (1993) Social loafing: a meta-analytic view of social integration, *Journal of Personality and Social Psychology*, 65, 681–707.

Karmi, G. (1985) *Traditional Asian Medicine in Britain*, Wisbeck, UK: Menas Press.

Kashima, Y. & Triandis, H. (1986) The self-serving bias in attributions as a coping strategy, *Journal of Cross-cultural Psychology*, 17, 83–97.

Keith, S., Regier, D. & Rae, D. (1991) Schizophrenic disorders, in Robins, L. & Robins, D. (eds.), *Psychiatric Disorders in America* (pp. 33–52), New York: Free Press.

Kelly, G. (1955) *The Psychology of Personal Constructs* (1 and 2), New York: Norton.

Kelvin, P. (1984) The historical dimension of social psychology: the case of unemployment, in Tajfel, H. (ed.), *The Social Dimension* (pp. 446–470), Cambridge, UK: Cambridge University Press.

Kendell, R. (1973) Psychiatric diagnoses: a study of how they are made, *British Journal of Psychiatry*, 122, 437–445.

Kendell, R., Pichot, P. & von Cranach, M. (1974) Diagnostic criteria of English, French and German psychiatrists, *Psychological Medicine*, 4, 187–195.

Kendler, K. (1991) The genetic epidemiology of bulimia nervosa, *American Journal of Psychiatry*, 148, 1627–1637.

Kessen, W. (1979) The American child and other cultural inventions, *American Psychologist*, 34, 815–820.

Kessler, C. (1977) Conflict and sovereignty in Kelantanese Malay spirit seances, in Crapanzano, V. & Garrison, V. (eds.), *Case Studies in Spirit Possession*, New York: Wiley.

Kettl, P. (1993) Homicide in Alaska natives, *Alaska Medicine*, 35, 168–172.

Kiev, A. (1961) Folk psychiatry in Haiti, *Journal of Nervous and Mental Disorders*, 132, 260–265.

Kilham, W. & Mann, L. (1974) Level of destructive obedience as a function of transmitter and executant roles in the Milgram obedience paradigm, *Journal of Personality and Social Psychology*, 29, 696–702.

Kinzie, J. & Sack, W. (1991) Severely traumatized Cambodian children, in Ahearn, F. & Athey, J. (eds.), *Refugee Children: Theory, Research and Services* (pp. 92–105), Baltimore, MD: Johns Hopkins University Press.

Kitayama, S., Markus, H. & Matsumoto, H. (1995) Culture, self and emotion: a cultural perspective on 'self-conscious' emotions, in Tangney, J. and Fischer, K. (eds.), *Self-conscious Emotions: The Psychology of Shame, Guilt, Embarrassment and Pride*, New York: Guilford.

Klappenbach, H. (2004) Psychology in Argentina, in Stevens, M. & Wedding, D. (eds.) *Handbook of International Psychology*, New York: Brunner-Routledge.

Klein, R., Freeman, H., Spring, B., Nerlove, S. & Yarbrough, C. (1976) Cognitive test performance and indigenous conceptions of intelligence, *Journal of Psychology*, 93, 273–279.

Kleinman, A. (1987a) Culture and clinical reality: commentary on 'Culture-bound syndromes and international disease classifications', *Culture, Medicine and Psychiatry*, 2 (1), 49–53.

Kleinman, A. (1987b) Depression, somatization and the new cross-cultural psychiatry, *Social Science & Medicine*, 11 (3), 3–10.

Kline, N. (1963) Psychiatry in Indonesia, *American Journal of Psychiatry*, 119, 809–815.

Kluckhohn, F. & Strodtbeck, F. (1961) *Variations in Value Orientation*, Evanston, IL: Row, Peterson.

Kohlberg, L. (ed.) (1984) *Essays on Moral Development* (Vol. 1), San Francisco: Harper and Row.

Konner, M. (1972) Aspects of the developmental ethology of a foraging people, in Blurton-Jones, N. (ed.), *Ethological Studies of Child Behaviour*, Cambridge, UK: Cambridge University Press.

Konner, M. (1981) Evolution of human behaviour development, in Munroe, R.H., Munroe, R.L. & Whiting, B. (eds.), *Handbook of Cross-cultural Human Development* (pp. 3–51), New York: Garland.

Koseki, Y. (1989) A study of influence of a deviant minority on visual judgements within a small group, *Japanese Psychological Research*, 31 (4), 149–160.

Koss, M., Heise, L. & Russo, N. (1994) The global health burden of rape, *Psychology of Women Quarterly*, 18 (4), 509–537.

Kostarova-Unkovska, L. (ed.) (1993) *Children Hurt by War*, Skopje, Macedonia: General Consulate of the Republic of Macedonia.

Kraepelin, E. (1920) Patterns of mental disorder, in Hirsch, S. & Shepherd, M. (eds.), *Themes and Variations in European Psychiatry*, Bristol, UK: John Wright, 1974, pp. 3–6.

Kramer, D.A. & Woodruff, D.S. (1986) Relativistic and dialectical thought in three adult age-groups, *Human Development*, 29, 280–290.

Kroeber, A. & Kluckhohn, C. (1952) *Culture: A Critical Review of Concepts and Definitions* (Vol. 47), Cambridge, MA: Peabody Museum.

Kunkle, E. (1967) The 'Jumpers of Maine': a re-appraisal, *Archives of International Medicine*, 119, 355–358.

Kuper, A. (1994) *The Chosen Primate*, Cambridge, MA: Harvard University Press.

Landis, D. & O'Shea, W. (2000) Cross-cultural aspects of passionate love: an individual differences analysis, *Journal of Cross-cultural Psychology*, 31 (6), 752–777.

Lane, S. & Rubenstein, R. (1996) Judging the other: responding to traditional female genital surgeries, *Hastings Centre Report*, 26, 31–40.

Lane, S. & Sawaia, B. (1991) Community social psychology in Brazil, *Applied Psychology*, 40, 119–142.

LaPiere, R. (1934) Attitudes vs. actions, *Social Forces*, 14, 230–237.

Larose, S. (1977) The meaning of Africa in Haitian Vodu, in Lewis, I. (ed.), *Symbols and Sentiments: Cross-cultural Studies in Symbolism*, London: Academic.

Larsen, U. & Yan, S. (2000) Does female genital circumcision affect infertility and fertility? A study of the Central African Republic, Cote d'Ivoire and Tanzania, *Demography*, 37, 313–321.

Latané, B. and Darley, J. (1968) Group inhibition of bystander intervention in emergencies, *Journal of Personality and Social Psychology*, 10, 215–221.

Latané, B., Williams, K. & Harkins, S. (1979) Many hands make light the work: causes and consequences of social loafing, *Journal of Personality and Social Psychology*, 37, 822–832.

Lave, J. (1977) Tailor-made experiments and evaluating the intellectual consequences of apprenticeship training, *Quarterly Newsletter of the Journal of Human Comparative Cognition*, 1, 1–3.

Lave, J. & Wenger, E. (1991) *Situated Learning*, Cambridge, UK: Cambridge University Press.

Leach, E. (1972) The influence of the cultural context on non-verbal communication in man, in Hinde, R. (ed.), *Nonverbal Communication* (pp. 315–344), London: Cambridge University Press.

Lee, M. & Seligman, M. (1997) Are Americans more optimistic than the Chinese? *Personality & Social Psychology Bulletin*, 23, 32–40.

Lee, S. (2001) From diversity to unity: the classification of mental disorders in 21st century China, *Cultural Psychiatry: International Perspectives*, 24 (3), 421–431.

Lee, Y. & Ottati, V. (1995) Perceived in-group homogeneity as a function of group salience and stereotype threat, *Personality and Social Psychology Bulletin*, 21, 610–619.

Leff, J. (1973) Cultural and the differentiation of emotional states, *British Journal of Psychiatry*, 123, 299–306.

Leff, J. (1977a) International variations in the diagnosis of psychiatric illness, *British Journal of Psychiatry*, 131, 329–338.

Leff, J. (1977b) The cross-cultural study of emotions, *Culture, Medicine and Psychiatry*, 1, 317–350.

Lehmann, H. (1967) Unusual psychiatric disorders and atypical psychoses, in Freedman, A. and Kaplan, H. (eds.), *Comprehensive Textbook of Psychiatry*, Baltimore, MD: Williams and Wilkins.

Leung, K. (1987) Some determinants of reactions to procedural models for conflict resolution: a cross-cultural study, *Journal of Personality and Social Psychology*, 53, 898–908.

Levenson, R., Ekman, P., Heider, K. & Friesen, W. (1992) Emotion and autonomic nervous system activity in the Minangkabau of West-Sumatra, *Journal of Personality and Social Psychology*, 62, 972–988.

Levin, S., Henry, P., Pratto, F. & Sidanius, J. (2003) Social dominance and social identity in Lebanon: implications for support of violence against the west, *Group Processes and Inter-group Relations*, 6, 353–368.

Levine, R., Levine, S., Dixon, S., Richman, A., Leiderman, P., Keefer, C., *et al.* (1996) *Child Care and Culture: Lessons from Africa*, Cambridge, UK: Cambridge University Press.

Levine, R., Sato, S., Hashimoto, T. & Verma, J. (1995) Love and marriage in eleven cultures, *Journal of Cross-cultural psychology*, 26 (5), 554–571.

Lewin, K. (1936) *Principles of Topological Psychology*, New York: McGraw-Hill.

Lifton, R. (1986) *The Nazi Doctors: Medical Killing and the Psychology of Genocide*, New York: Basic Books.

Lightfoot-Klein, H. (1989) *Prisoners of Ritual: An Odyssey into Female Genital Circumcision in Africa*, New York: Harrington Park.

Lin, K., Inui, T., Kleinman, A. & Womack, W. (1992) Socio-cultural determinants of the help-seeking behaviour of patients with mental illness, *Journal of Nervous and Mental Disease*, 170, 78–85.

Lincoln, Y. & Guba, E. (2000) Paradigmatic controversies, contradictions and emerging conflicts, in Denzin, N. & Lincoln, Y. (eds.), *Handbook of Qualitative Research* (2nd ed.), Thousand Oaks, CA: Sage.

Linnaeus, C. (1759) *Systema Naturae per Regina Tria Naturae* (10th ed.), Stockholm: Laurentius Salius.

Linssen, H. & Hagendoorn, L. (1994) Social and geographic factors in the explanation of European nationality stereotypes, *British Journal of Social Psychology*, 33, 165–182.

Linton, R. (1936) *The Study of Man: An Introduction*, New York: Appleton.

Lips, H. (2005) Violence against women: a worldwide problem, in Lips, H., *A New Psychology of Women: Gender, Culture and Ethnicity* (3rd ed.), Boston: McGraw-Hill.

Littlewood, R. (1996) Cultural comments on culture bound syndromes: 1, in Mezzich, J., Kleinman, A., Fabrega, H. & Parron, D. (eds.), *Culture and Psychiatric Diagnosis: A DSM–IV Perspective* (pp. 309–312), Washington, DC: American Psychiatric Association.

Littlewood, R. & Lipsedge, M. (1986) The culture-bound syndromes of the dominant culture, in Cox, J. (ed.), *Transcultural Psychiatry*, London: Croom Helm.

Liu, J., Lawrence, B., Ward, C. & Abraham, S. (2003) Social representations of history in Malaysia and Singapore, *Asian Journal of Social Psychology*, 5, 3–20.

Lloyd, G. (1990) *Demystifying Mentalities*, Cambridge, UK: Cambridge University Press.

Lonner, W. (1979) Issues in cross-cultural psychology, in Marsella, A., Thorp, R. & Ciborowski, T. (eds.), *Perspectives in Cross-cultural Psychology*, New York: Academic Press.

Lonner, W. & Berry, J. (eds.) (1986) *Field Methods in Cross-cultural Research*, London: Sage.

Lorenz, K. (1966) *On Aggression*, New York: Harcourt, Brace and World.

Loring, M. & Powell, B. (1988) Gender, race and DSM-III: a study of the objectivity of psychiatric diagnostic behaviour, *Journal of Health and Social Behaviour*, 29: 1–22.

Low, B. (1989) Cross-cultural patterns in the training of children: an evolutionary perspective, *Journal of Comparative Psychology*, 103, 311–319.

Luria, A. (1976) *Cognitive Development: Its Cultural and Social Foundations*, Cambridge, MA: Harvard University Press.

Lutsky, N. (1995) When is 'obedience' obedience? *Journal of Social Issues*, 51 (3), 55–65.

Macario, J. (1991) Young children's use of colour classification: foods and canonically coloured objects. *Cognitive Development*, 6, 17–46.

Macfarlane, A. (1977) *The Psychology of Childbirth*, Cambridge, MA: Harvard University Press.

Mackie, G. (1996) Ending footbinding and infibulation: a convention account, *American Sociological Review*, 61: 999–1017.

Maidman, F. (1996) *Mooka'am Children's Circle Program: an evaluation*, unpublished manuscript.

Malinowski, B. (1931) Introduction, in Aldrich, C.R., *The Primitive Mind and Modern Civilization*, New York: AMS Press.

Maloney, P., Wilkof, J. & Dambrot, F. (1981) Androgyny across two cultures: United States and Israel, *Journal of Cross-cultural Psychology*, 12, 95–102.

Mandel, D. (1998) The obedience alibi: Milgram's account of the Holocaust reconsidered, *Analyse & Kritik*, 20, 74–94.

Mandler, J., Scribner, S., Cole, M. & de Forest, M. (1980) Cross-cultural invariance in story recall, *Child Development*, 51, 19–26.

Manson, S., Shore, J. & Bloom, J. (1985) The depressive experience in American Indian communities, in Kleinman, A. & Good, B. (eds.), *Culture & Depression*, Berkeley, CA: University of California Press.

Mantell, D. (1971) The potential for violence in Germany, *Journal of Social Issues*, 27, 101–112.

Maracek, J. (1979) Social change, positive mental health and psychological androgyny, *Psychology of Women Quarterly*, 3 (3), 241–247.

Markus, H. & Kitayama, S. (1991a) Cultural variation in self-concept, in Goethals, G. & Strauss, J. (eds.), *Multidisciplinary perspectives on the self* (pp. 18–48), New York: Springer-Verlag.

Markus, H. & Kitayama, S. (1991b) Culture and the self: implications for cognition and motivation, *Psychological Review*, 98, 224–253.

Markus, H. & Kitayama, S. (2003) Culture, self and the reality of the social, *Psychological Inquiry*, 14, 277–283.

Mars, L. (1947) *La lutte conte la folie*, Port-au-Prince, Haiti: Imprimerie de l'etat.

Marsden, P. & Attia, S. (2005) A deadly contagion? *The Psychologist*, 18 (3), 152–155.

Marshall, G. (ed.) (1998) *Oxford Dictionary of Sociology*, Oxford, UK: Oxford University Press.

Martin-Baró, I. (1994) *Writings for a Liberation Psychology*, Cambridge, MA: Harvard University Press.

Martin-Baró, I. (1996) Toward a liberation psychology, in Aron, A. & Corne, S. (eds.), *Writings for a Liberation Psychology* (pp. 17–32), New York: Harvard University Press.

Maslow, A. (1970) *Motivation and Personality* (2nd ed.), New York: Harper and Row.

Masten, A. & Coatsworth, M. (1998) The development of competence in favourable and unfavourable environments, *American Psychologist*, 53, 205–220.

Matchett, W. (1972) Repeated hallucinatory experiences as part of the mourning process among Hopi women, *Psychiatry*, 35, 185–194.

Matsumoto, D. (1992) American-Japanese cultural differences in the recognition of universal facial expressions, *Journal of Cross-cultural Psychology*, 23, 72–84.

Matsumoto, D. & Juang, L. (2004) *Culture and Psychology* (3rd ed.), New York: Wadsworth.

Matsumoto, K. (1991) *The Rise of the Japanese Corporate System: The Inside View of a Miti Official*, London: Kegan Paul.

McAndrew, F., Akande, A., Bridgstock, R., Mealey, L. (2001) A multicultural study of stereotyping in English-speaking countries, *Journal of Social Psychology*, 140, 487–502.

McCormick, G. (2003) Terrorist decision making, *Annual Review of Political Science*, 6, 473–507.

McDougall, W. (1908) *An Introduction to Social Psychology*, London: Methuen.

McElroy, A. & Townsend, K. (1989) *Medical Anthropology in Ecological Perspective* (2nd ed.), Boulder, CO: Westview Press.

McGrew, A. (1992) 'A Global Society' in Hall, S., Held, D. & McGrew, A. (eds.), *Modernity and its Future* (pp. 61–102), Cambridge, UK: Polity Press.

McKenzie, B. & Morrissette, V. (1993) *Aboriginal child and family services in Manitoba*, paper presented to 6th conference on social welfare policy, St John's, Newfoundland, Canada.

Mead, M. (1928) *Coming of Age in Samoa*, New York: Morrow.

Mead, M. (1935) *Sex and Temperament in Three Primitive Societies*, London: Routledge.

Mead, M. (1949) *Male and Female*, New York: William Morrow.

Mead, M. (1972) *Blackberry Winter*, New York: Simon & Schuster.

Mead, M. (1975) Review of *Darwin and Facial Expression*, in Ekman, P. (ed.), *Journal of Communication*, 25 (1), 209–213.

Medicine, B. (2002) Directions in gender research in American Indian societies: two spirits and other categories, in Lonner, W.J., Dinnel, D.L., Hayes, S.A. & Sattler, D.N. (eds.), *Online Readings in Psychology and Culture* (Unit 3, Chapter 2), Washington, DC: Center for Cross-Cultural Research, Western Washington University, Bellingham, available online at www.wwu.edu/~culture.

Meeus, W. & Raaijmakers, Q. (1986) Administrative obedience: carrying out orders to use psychological-administrative violence, *European Journal of Social Psychology*, 16, 311–324.

Metraux, A. (1959) *Vodou in Haiti*, New York: Oxford University Press.

Milgram, S. (1963) Behavioural study of obedience, *Journal of Abnormal Psychology*, 67, 371–378.

Milgram, S. (1974) *Obedience to Authority: An Experimental View*, New York: Harper & Row.

Miller, J. (1984) Culture and the development of everyday social explanation, *Journal of Personality and Social Psychology*, 46, 961–978.

Millman, M. (1974) *Such A Pretty Face: Being Fat in America*, New York: Norton.

Miranda, F., Caballero, R., Gomez, M. & Zamorano, M. (1981) Obediencia a la autoridad, *Psiquis*, 2, 212–221.

Mischel, W. (1968) *Personality and Assessment*, New York: Wiley.

Mishra, R., Sinha, D. & Berry, J. (1996) *Ecology, Acculturation and Adaptation: A Study of Adivasi in Birhar*, New Delhi, India: Sage.

Moghaddam, F. (1987) Psychology in three worlds, *American Psychologist*, 42 (10), 919–920.

Moghaddam, F. (1990) Modulative and generative orientations in psychology, *Journal of Social Issues*, 46 (3), 21–41.

Moghaddam, F. (2005) The staircase to terrorism: a psychological exploration, *American Psychologist*, 60 (2), 161–169.

Montepare, J. & Zebrowitz, L. (1993) A cross-cultural comparison of impressions created by age-related variations in gait, *Journal of Non-verbal Behaviour*, 17, 55–68.

Montero, M. (ed.) (1991) *Accion y Discurso: Problemas de psicologia politica en America Latina*, Caracas, Venezuela: Eduven.

Moore, M. (2001) In Turkey, a matter of conviction, *Washington Post*, A1 (May 21).

Morelli, G., Rogoff, B., Oppenheim, D. & Goldsmith, D. (1992) Cultural variations in infant sleeping arrangements, *Developmental Psychology*, 28, 604–613.

Morison, L., Scherf, C., Ekpo, G., Paine, K., West, B., Coleman, R. *et al.* (2001) The long-term reproductive health consequences of female genital cutting in rural Gambia, *Tropical Medicine and International Health*, 6 (8): 643–653.

Morris, M. & Peng, K. (1994) Culture and cause: American and Chinese attributions for social and physical events, *Journal of Personality and Social Psychology*, 67 (6), 949–971.

Morrison, R. & Wilson, C. (1995) *Native Peoples: The Canadian Experience*, Toronto, Canada: McClelland & Stewart.

Moscovici, S. (1976) *Social Influence and Social Change*, London: Academic Press.

Moscovici, S. (1981) On social representation, in Forgas, J. (ed.), *Social Cognition: Perspectives on Everyday Life*, London: Academic Press.

Moscovici, S. & Personnaz, B. (1980) Studies in social influence: minority influence and conversion behaviour in a perceptual task, *Journal of Experimental Social Psychology*, 16, 270–282.

Mpofu, E. (1994) Children's interpretive strategies for class inclusion tasks, *British Journal of Educational Psychology*, 64, 77–89.

Mpofu, E. (2001) *Psychology in sub-Saharan Africa: challenges, prospects and promises*, keynote address to the International Society for the Study of Behavioural Development (Africa region) conference, Kampala, Uganda, September.

Mukherjee, S., Shukla, S., Woodle, J., Rosen, A. & Olaste, S. (1983) Misdiagnosis of schizophrenia in bipolar patients: a multi-ethnic comparison, *American Journal of Psychiatry*, 140: 1571–1574.

Mule, P. & Barthel, D. (1992) The return to the veil: individual autonomy and social esteem, *Sociological Forum*, 7 (2), 323–333.

Mullen, B., Brown, R. & Smith, C. (1992) Ingroup bias as a function of salience, relevance and status: an integration, *European Journal of Social Psychology*, 22, 103–122.

Mummendey, A. & Schreiber, H. (1984) 'Different' just means 'better': some obvious and some hidden pathways to ingroup favouritism, *British Journal of Psychology*, 23, 363–368.

Munroe, R.L. and Munroe, R.H. (1986) Fieldwork in cross-cultural psychology, in Lonner, W. and Berry, J. (eds.), *Field Methods in Cross-cultural Research*, London: Sage.

Munster, S. (1544) *Cosmographia*, Basle, Switzerland: Petri.

Murdock, G. (1975) *Outline of World Cultures* (5th ed.), New Haven, CT: HRAF.

Murdock, G., Ford, C. & Hudson, A. (1971) *Outline of Cultural Materials* (4th ed.), New Haven, CT: HRAF.

Murphy, H. (1971) History and evolution of syndromes, in Hammer, M., Salzinger, K. & Sutton, S. (eds.), *Psychopathology: Contributions from the Social, Behavioral and Biological Sciences*, New York: Wiley Interscience.

Murphy, H. (1982a) *Comparative Psychiatry*, New York: Springer-Verlag.

Murphy, H. (1982b) Culture and schizophrenia, in Al-Issa, I. (ed.), *Culture and Psychopathology* (pp. 221–249), Baltimore, MD: University Park Press.

Murphy, J. (1976) Psychiatric labelling in cross-cultural perspective, *Science*, 191, 1019–1028.

Muzaffar, C. (1983) *Has the communal situation in Malaysia worsened over the last decade?* Paper presented at the Conference on Modernisation and National Cultural Identity, Kuala Lumpur, Malaysia.

Mwamwenda, T. & Mwamwenda, B. (1989) Sequence of transitivity, conservation and class inclusion, in an African culture, *Journal of Cross-cultural Psychology*, 20 (4), 416–430.

Myers, D. (1996) *Social Psychology* (5th ed.), New York: McGraw-Hill.

Nadel, S. (1937) Experiments in culture psychology, *Africa*, 10, 421–425.

Nakamura, H. (1985) *Ways of Thinking of Eastern Peoples: India, China, Japan*, Honolulu, HI: East-West Center Press.

Nangolo, L. & Peltzer, K. (2003) Violence against women and its mental health consequences in Namibia, *Gender & Behaviour*, 1, pp. 16–34.

Narasimhan, S. (1990) *Sati: Widow Burning in India*, New York: Anchor.

Narroll, R., Michik, G. & Narroll, F. (1980) Holocultural research methods, in Triandis, H. & Berry, J. (eds.), *Handbook of Cross-cultural Psychology* (Vol. 2), Boston: Allyn & Bacon.

Neft, N. & Levine, A. (1997) *Where Women Stand: An International Report on the Status of Women in 140 Countries*, New York: Random House.

Nenty, H. (1986) Cross-cultural bias analysis of Cattell culture fair intelligence test, *Perspectives in Psychological Researches*, 9 (1), 1–16.

Newman, H., Freeman, F. & Holzinger, K. (1937) *Twins: A Study of Heredity and Environment*, Chicago: University of Chicago Press.

Niemi, M. (2004) *Popular Music*, London: Harper.

Niens, U., Cairns, E. & Hewstone, M. (2003) *Contact and Conflict in Northern Ireland*, Coleraine, UK: University of Ulster.

Nisbett, R. (2003) *The Geography of Thought: How Asians and Westerners Think Differently . . . and Why*, London: Nicholas Brealey.

Nissani, M. (1990) A cognitive reinterpretation of Stanley Milgram's observations on obedience to authority, *American Psychologist*, 45, 1384–1385.

Nobles, W. (1976) Extended self: rethinking the so-called Negro self-concept, *Journal of Black Psychology*, 2, 15–24.

Nsamenang, B. (1992) *Human Development in Cultural Context: A Third World Perspective*, Newbury Park, CA: Sage.

Nsamenang, B. (1996) Cultural organisation of human development within the family context, in Carr, S. & Schumaker, J. (eds.), *Psychology and the Developing World*, London: Praeger.

Nsamenang, B. (2000) Critical psychology: a sub-Saharan African voice from Cameroon, in Sloan, T. (ed.), *Critical Psychology: Voices for Change* (pp. 91–103), Basingstoke, UK: Palgrave.

Obermeyer, C. (1999) Female genital surgeries: the known, the unknown and the unknowable, *Medical Anthropology Quarterly*, 13: 79–106.

Oishi, S., Diener, E., Lucas, R. & Suh, E. (1999) Cross-cultural variations in predictors of life satisfaction: perspectives from needs and values, *Personality and Social Psychology Bulletin*, 25, 980–990.

Okie, S. (1993) The boys 'only wanted to rape them', *Washington Post*, p. A24, February 17.

Oliver, R. (1932) The musical talents of natives in East Africa, *British Journal of Psychology*, 22, 333–334.

Oxley, J. (1849) Malay amoks, *Journal of the Indian Archipelago*, 3, 532–533.

Paniagua, F. (1998) *Assessing and Treating Culturally Diverse Clients: A Practical Guide*, Newbury Park, CA: Sage.

Panok, V., Pavlenko, V. & Korallo, L. (2006) Psychology in the Ukraine, *The Psychologist*, 19: 12.

Pape, R. (2003) The strategic logic of suicide terrorism, *American Political Science Review*, 97, 343–361.

Papousek, H. & Papousek, M. (1997) Preverbal communication in humans and the genesis of culture, in Segerstrale, C. & Molnar, P. (eds.), *Nonverbal Communication: Where Nature Meets Culture* (pp. 87–107), Hillsdale, NJ: Lawrence Erlbaum Associates.

Pawlik, K. & Rosenzweig, M. (2000) *International Handbook of Psychology*, London: Sage.

Peabody, D. (1985) *National Characteristics*, Cambridge, UK: Cambridge University Press.

Pearson, K. (1901) *National Life from the Standpoint of Science*, London: A and C Black.

Pearson, K. & Moul, M. (1925) The problem of alien immigration into Britain illustrated by an examination of Russian and Polish Jewish children, *Annals of Eugenics*, 1, 5–127.

Pelto, P. (1968) The differences between 'tight' and 'loose' societies, *Transaction*, April, 37–40.

Pelto, P. and Pelto, J. (1981) *Anthropological Research*, Cambridge, UK: Cambridge University Press.

Peltzer, K. (1987) *Some Contributions of Traditional Healing Practices towards Psychosocial Health Care in Malawi*, Frankfurt: Fachbuchhandlung für Psychologie.

Peng, K. & Nisbett, R. (1999) Culture, dialectics and reasoning about contradiction, *American Psychologist*, 54 (9), 741–754.

Pennell, J. & Burford, G. (1997) Family group decision making: after the conference – progress in resolving violence and promoting well-being, St John's, Newfoundland: Memorial University of Newfoundland School of Social Work.

Perrin, S. & Spencer, C. (1981) Independence or conformity in the Asch experiment as a reflection of cultural and situational factors, *British Journal of Social Psychology*, 20, 205–210.

Peters, L. & Price-Williams, D. (1983) A phenomenological overview of trance, *Transcultural Psychiatric Research Review*, 20, 5–39.

Pettigrew, T. & Tropp, L. (2000) Does intergroup contact reduce prejudice? Recent meta-analytical findings, in Oskamp, S. (ed.), *Reducing prejudice and discrimination* (pp. 93–114), Mahwah, NJ: Lawrence Erlbaum Associates.

Pfeiffer, W. (1982) Culture-bound syndromes, in Al-Issa, I. (ed.), *Culture and Psychopathology*, Baltimore, MD: University Park Press.

Piaget, J. (1952) *The Origins of Intelligence in Children*, New York: International Universities Press.

Piaget, J. (1966) Need and significance of cross-cultural studies in genetic psychology, in Berry, J. & Dasen, P. (eds.), *Culture and Cognition: Readings in Cross-cultural Psychology*, London: Methuen.

Piaget, J. (1973) *The Psychology of Intelligence*, Totowa, NJ: Littlefield and Adams.

Piaget, J. (1977) *The Origin of Intelligence in the Child*, Harmondsworth, UK: Penguin.

Pick, A. (1980) Cognition: psychological perspectives, in Triandis, H. and Lonner, W. (eds.), *Handbook of Cross-cultural Psychology* (Vol. 3), Needham Heights, MA: Allyn and Bacon.

Pike, K. (1967) *Language in Relation to a Unified Theory of the Structure of Human Behaviour*, The Hague, The Netherlands: Mouton.

Plomin, R. (1990) *Nature and Nurture: An Introduction to Human Behavioral Genetics*, Pacific Grove, CA: Brooks/Cole.

Pollitt, K. (1999) Whose culture?, in Cohen, J., Howard, M. & Nussbaum, M. (eds.), *Is Multiculturalism Bad for Women?*, Princeton, NJ: Princeton University Press.

Poole, M. (1982) Social class sex contrasts in patterns of cognitive style: a cross-cultural replication, *Psychological Reports*, 50, 19–26.

Poortinga, H. (1989) Equivalence of cross-cultural data: an overview of basic issues, *International Journal of Psychology*, 24, 737–756.

Poortinga, Y. (1997) Towards convergence?, in Berry J., Segall, M. & Kagitcibasi, C., *Handbook of Cross-cultural Psychology* (2nd ed., Vol. 1), London: Allyn & Bacon.

Posada, G., Gao, Y., Wu, F., Posada, R., Tascon, M., Schoelmerich, A., et al. (1995) The secure base phenomenon across cultures, in Waters, E., Vaughn, B., Posada, G. & Kondo-Ikemura, K. (eds.), *Caregiving, Cultural and Cognitive Perspectives on Secure Base Behaviour and Working Models, Monographs of the Society for Research on Child Development*, 60 (2–3), 27–48.

Post, J. (1984) Notes on a psychodynamic theory of terrorist behaviour, *Terrorism*, 7, 241–256.

Potter, J. & Wetherell, M. (1987) *Discourse and Social Psychology*, London: Sage.

Pratto, F., Liu, J., Levin, S., Sidanius, J., Shih, M., Bachrach, H., *et al.* (2000) Social dominance orientation and the legitimization of inequality across cultures, *Journal of Cross-cultural Psychology*, 31, 369–409.

Price-Williams, D. (1975) *Explorations in Cross-cultural Psychology*, San Francisco: Chandler and Sharp.

Price-Williams, D., Gordon, W. & Ramirez, M. (1969) Skill and conservation: a study of pottery-making children, *Developmental Psychology*, 1, 769.

Prichard, J. (1843) *The Natural History of Man*, London: Bailliere.

Prilleltensky, I. (1993) The immigration experience of Latin American families: research and action on perceived risk and protective factors, *Canadian Journal of Community Mental Health*, 12 (2), 101–116.

Prilleltensky, I. & Nelson, G. (2002) *Doing Psychology Critically*, Basingstoke, UK: Palgrave.

Prilleltensky, I., Nelson, G. & Peirson, L. (2001) *Promoting Family Wellness and Preventing Matreatment*, Toronto, Canada: University of Toronto Press.

Prince, R. & Tcheng-Laroche, F. (1987) Culture-bound syndromes and international disease classifications, *Culture, Medicine and Psychiatry*, 2 (1), 3–21.

Pryse-Phillips, W. (1971) An olfactory reference syndrome, *Acta Psychiatrica Scandinavica*, 47, 484–510.

Puig-Casauranc, M. (1977) Personality and interest characteristics of females in traditional and non-traditional fields of academic study and their relationship to psychological androgyny, *Dissertation Abstracts International*, 37A, 5001 (University Microfilms no. 77–2895).

Punetha, D., Giles, H. & Young, L. (1987) Ethnicity and immigrant values: religion and language choice, *Journal of Language and Social Psychology*, 6, 229–241.

Rabinovitch, R. (1965) An exaggerated startle reflex resembling a kicking horse, *Canadian Medical Association Journal*, 93, 130.

Rao, V. & Rao, V. (1985) Sex-role attitudes across two cultures: U.S. and India, *Sex Roles*, 13 (11–12), 607–624.

Raundalen, M. & Dyregrov, A. (1991) War experiences and psychological impact on children, in Dodge, C. & Raundalen, M. (eds.), *Reaching Children in War* (pp. 21–38), Bergen, Norway: Sigma Forlag.

Ravinder, S. (1987) Androgyny: is it really a product of educated, middle class western societies? *Journal of Cross-cultural Psychology*, 18 (2), 208–220.

Rawnsley, K. (1968) An international diagnostic exercise, *Proceedings of the 4th World Congress of Psychiatry* (Vol. 4), Amsterdam: Excerpta Medica Foundation.

Ray, V. (1952) Techniques and problems in the study of human colour perception, *Southwestern Journal of Anthropology*, 8, 251–259.

Reader, J. (1998) *Africa*, London: Penguin.

Reber, A. (1997) *Penguin Dictionary of Psychology*, London: Penguin.

Redden, P. & Simons, J. (1986) *Manual for the Redden-Simons 'Rap' Test*, Ankeny, IO: Des Moines Area Community College.

Reed, H. & Lave, J. (1981) Arithmetic as a tool for investigating the relationship between culture and cognition, *American Ethnologist*, 6, 568–582.

Reed, T. & Jensen, A. (1993) Conduction velocity in a brain nerve pathway in normal adults correlates with intelligence levels, *Intelligence*, 16 (3–4), 259–272.

Ressler, E., Boothby, N. & Steinbock, D. (eds) (1998) *Unaccompanied Children*, New York: Oxford University Press.

Rhee, E., Uleman, J., Lee, H. & Roman, R. (1995) Spontaneous self-descriptions and ethnic identities in individualistic and collectivistic cultures, *Journal of Personality and Social Psychology*, 69, 142–152.

Rhoades, E., Marshall, M., Attneave, C., Echohawk, M., Bjork, J. & Beiser, M. (1980) Mental health problems of American Indians seen in outpatient facilities of the Indian Health Service, 1975, *Public Health Reports*, 96 (4), 329–335.

Richman, N. (1993) *Communicating with Children: Helping Children in Distress*, London: Save the Children.

Ritenbaugh, C. (1982) Obesity as a culture-bound syndrome, *Culture, Medicine & Psychiatry*, 6, 347.

Rivers, W. (1901) Vision, in *Physiology and Psychology*, Part 1: *Reports of the Cambridge Anthropological Expedition to Torres Straits* (Vol. 2), Cambridge, UK: Cambridge University Press.

Robertson, C. (1996) Grass-roots in Kenya: women, genital mutilation and collective action, 1920–1990, *Journal of Women in Culture and Society*, 21, 615–642.

Robin, R., Chester, B., Rasmussen, J., Jaranson, J. & Goldman, D. (1997) Prevalence and characteristics of trauma and Posttraumatic Stress Disorder in a southwestern American Indian community, *American Journal of Psychiatry*, 154, 1582–1588.

Robin, R., Long, J., Rasmussen, J., Chester, B., Jaranson, J. & Goldman, D. (1995) Comorbidity of alcoholism and other psychiatric disorders in a southwestern American Indian community, *Alcoholism: Clinical and Experimental Research*, April supplement, 92A.

Rodrigues, A. (1982) Replication: a neglected type of research in social psychology, *Interamerican Journal of Psychology*, 16, 91–109.

Rodriguez, A. & Seoane, J. (eds.) (1989) *Creencias, Actitudes y Valores*, Vol. 7 of Mayor, J. & Pinillos, J. (eds.), *Tratado de Psicologia General*, Madrid, Spain: Alhambra University Press.

Rohner, R. (1984) Towards a concept of culture for cross-cultural psychology, *Journal of Cross-cultural Psychology*, 15, 111–138.

Rokeach, M. (1973) *The Nature of Human Values*, New York: Free Press.

Rosaldo, M. & Lamphere, L. (eds.) (1974) *Woman, Culture and Society*, Stanford, CA: Stanford University Press.

Rosch-Heider, E. (1972) Universals in colour naming and memory, *Journal of Experimental Psychology*, 93, 10–20.

Rosenthal, R. & Jacobsen, L. (1968) Pygmalion in the classroom: teacher and pupils' intellectual development, New York: Holt, Rinehart & Winston.

Rosenzweig, M. (1999) Continuity and change in the development of psychology around the world, *American Psychologist*, 53, 252–259.

Ross, L. (1988) Situationist perspectives on the obedience experiments, *Contemporary Psychology*, 33, 101–104.

Rothbaum, F. & Tsang, B. (1998) Love songs in the U.S. and China: on the nature of romantic love, *Journal of Cross-cultural Psychology*, 29, 306–319.

Rousseau, J.-J. (1755) Discourse on political economy, in Diderot's *Encyclopédie*.

Royal Commission on Aboriginal Peoples (1995) *For Seven Generations*, Ottowa, Canada: Libraxus.

Rozée, P. (1993) Forgiven or forbidden? Rape in cross-cultural perspective, *Psychology of Women Quarterly*, 17 (4), 499–514.

Rus, V. & Pecjak, V. (2004) Psychology in Slovenia, *The Psychologist*, 17 (5), 266–271.

Rushdie, S. (2002) Anti-Americanism has taken the world by storm, *The Guardian*, February 6, 19.

Russell, J. (1991) Culture and the categorization of emotions, *Psychological Bulletin*, 110, 426–450.

Russell, J. (1994) Is there universal recognition of emotion from facial expression? *Psychological Bulletin*, 115, 102–141.

Rutter, M. (1981) *Maternal Deprivation Reassessed* (2nd ed.), Harmondsworth, UK: Penguin.

Ryle, J. (1999) Why must a child be forced to kill? *The Guardian*, January 25.

Sacks, O. (2007) *Musicophilia: Tales of Music and the Brain*, London: Picador.

Saco-Pollit, C. (1989) Ecocultural context and developmental risk, in Nugent, B., Lester, B. & Brazelton, T. (eds.), *The Cultural Context of Infancy* (Vol. 1, pp. 3–25), Norwood, NJ: Ablex.

Sageman, M. (2004) *Understanding Terror Networks*, Philadelphia: University of Pennsylvania Press.

Sager, L. (2000) The free exercise of culture: some doubts and distinctions, in Shweder, R., Markus, H., Minor M. & Kessel, F. (eds.), *The Free Exercise of Culture, Daedalus: Journal of the American Arts and Sciences*, Autumn 2000.

Sagi, A., Lamb, M., Lewkowicz, K., Shoham, R., Dvir, R. & Estes, D. (1985) Security of infant-mother, -father and metapelet attachments among kibbutz-reared Israeli children, in Bretherton, I. & Waters, E. (eds.), *Growing Point in Attachment Theory, Monographs of the Society for Research in Child Development*, 50 (1–2), 257–275.

Sahlins, M. (1976) Colours and culture, *Semiotica*, 16, 1–22.

Sahlins, M. & Service, E. (eds.) (1960) *Evolution and Culture*, Ann Arbor, MI: University of Michigan Press.

Sampath, B. (1974) Prevalence of psychiatric disorders in southern Baffin Island Eskimo settlement, *Canadian Psychiatric Association Journal*, 19, 363–367.

Sanchez, E. (1996) The Latin American experience in community psychology, in Carr, S. & Schumaker, J. (eds.), *Psychology and the Developing World*, London: Praeger.

Sanday, P. (1980) Margaret Mead's view of sex roles in her own and other societies, *American Anthropologist*, 82 (2), 340–348.

Sanday, P. (1981) *Female Power and Male Dominance*, Cambridge, UK: Cambridge University Press.

Sandifer, M., Hordern, A., Timbury, G. & Green, L. (1969) Similarities and differences in patient evaluation by US and UK psychiatrists, *American Journal of Psychiatry*, 126, 968–973.

Sapir, E. (1929) The status of linguistics as a science, *Language*, 5, 207–214.

Sapir, E. (1949) *Culture, Language and Personality*, Berkeley, CA: University of California Press.

Sartorius, N., de Girolamo, G., Andrews, G., German, A. & Eisenberg, L. (eds.) (1993) *Treatment of Mental Disorders: A Review of Effectiveness*, Washington, DC: American Psychiatric Press.

Saunders, B. (1992) *The Invention of Colour Terms*, Utrecht, The Netherlands: ISOR.

Saxe, G. (1982) Developing forms of arithmetical thought among the Oksapmin of Papua New Guinea, *Developmental Psychology*, 18 (4), 583–594.

Saxe, G. (1991) *Culture and Cognitive Development*, Hillsdale, NJ: Lawrence Erlbaum Associates.

Schachter, S., Nuttin, J., de Monchaux, C., Osmer, D., Duijker, H., Rommetveit, R. *et al.* (1954) Cross-cultural experiments on threats and rejection, *Human Relations*, 7, 403–439.

Schaffer, H. & Emerson, P. (1964) The development of social attachments in infancy, *Monographs of Social Research in Child Development*, 29, 94.

Schieffelin, E. (1985) The cultural analysis of depressive affect, in Kleinman, A. & Good, B. (eds.), *Culture and Depression* (pp. 101–133), Berkeley, CA: University of California Press.

Schlegel, A. (ed.) (1977) *Sexual Stratification: A Cross-cultural View*, New York: Columbia University Press.

Schmitt, D., Alcalay, L., Allik, J., Ault, L., Austers, I., Bennett, K. *et al.* (2003) Universal sex differences in the desire for sexual variety, *Journal of Personality and Social Psychology*, 85, 85–104.

Scholte, P., Van de Put, W. & De Smedt, J. (1994) *Proposal for a Psycho-social Programme in Rwandan Refugee Camps*, Ngara, Tanzania: MSF Holland.

Schurz, G. (1985) Experimentelle Uberprufung des Zusammenhangs zwischen personlichkeitsmerkmalen und der bereitschaft der destruktiven Gehorsam gegnuber Autoritaten, *Zeitschrift fur Experimentelle und Angewandte Psychologie*, 32, 160–177.

Schwartz, S. (1992) Universals in the content and structure of values, in Zanna, M. (ed.), *Advances in Experimental Social Psychology* (Vol. 25, pp. 1–65), New York: Academic Press.

Schwartz, S. (2002) *The Two Faces of Islam: The House of Sa'ud from Tradition to Terror*, New York: Doubleday.

Schwartz, S., Melech, G., Lehmann, A., Burgess, S. & Harris, M. (2001) Extending the cross-cultural validity of the theory of basic human values with a different method of measurement, *Journal of Cross-cultural Psychology*, 32, 519–542.

Schwartz, S. & Sagiv, L. (1995) Identifying culture specifics in the content and structure of values, *Journal of Cross-cultural Psychology*, 26, 92–116.

Scribner, S. (1975) Situating the experiment in cross-cultural research, in Riegel, K. and Meacham, J. (eds.), *The Developing Individual in a Changing World*, The Hague, The Netherlands: Mouton.

Scribner, S. & Cole, M. (1981) *The Psychology of Literacy*, Cambridge, MA: Harvard University Press.

Seaver, W. (1973) The effects of naturally induced teacher expectancies, *Journal of Personality and Social Psychology*, 28, 333–342.

Segall, M., Campbell, D., & Herskovits, M. (1963) Cultural differences in the perception of geometric illusions, *Science*, 139, 769–771.

Segall, M., Campbell, D., & Herskovits, M. (1966) *The Influence of Culture on Visual Perception*, Indianapolis, IN: Bobbs-Merrill.

Segall, M., Dasen, P., Berry, J. & Poortinga, V. (1990/1999) *Human behavior in global perspective* (1st/2nd ed.), Boston: Allyn & Bacon.

Sehl, M. (1987) *The creation of a multi-ethnic housing co-operative: a social intervention*, unpublished master's thesis, Wilfrid Laurier University, Waterloo, Canada.

Semblene, O. (2005) Village voice, *The Guardian Review*, May 14, 20.

Serpell, R. (1976) *Culture's Influence on Behaviour*, London: Methuen.

Seskar-Hencic, D. (1996) *Breaking the silence: new immigrant children affected by war trauma – community needs and resources assessment*, unpublished master's thesis, Wilfrid Laurier University, Waterloo, Canada.

Seul, J. (1999) 'Ours is the way of God': religion, identity and inter-group conflict, *Journal of Peace Research*, 36, 553–569.

Shanab, M. & Yahya, K. (1978) A cross-cultural study of obedience, *Bulletin of the Psychonomic Society*, 11, 267–269.

Shell-Duncan, B. & Hernlund, Y. (eds.) (2000) *Female Circumcision in Africa: Culture, Change and Controversy*, Boulder, CO: Lynn Rienner.

Shepherd, M., Brooke, E., Cooper, J. & Lin, T. (1968) An experimental approach to psychiatric diagnosis, *Acta Psychiatrica Scandinavica*, Suppl. 201.

Sherif, M. (1966) *Group Conflict and Co-operation: Their Social Psychology*, London: Routledge.

Shields, J. (1962) *MZ Twins Brought Up Apart and Brought Up Together*, Oxford, UK: Oxford University Press.

Shirikashi, S. (1985) Social loafing of Japanese students, *Hiroshima Forum of Psychology*, 10, 35–40.

Shore, J. & Manson, S. (1981) Cross-cultural studies of depression among American Indians and Alaskan natives, *White Cloud Journal*, 2 (2), 5–12.

Shouksmith, G. (1996) History of psychology in developing countries, in Carr, S. & Schumaker, J. (eds.), *Psychology and the Developing World*, London: Praeger.

Shouksmith, G. (2005) Psychology in New Zealand, *The Psychologist*, 18 (1), 14–16.

Shweder, R. (1991) *Thinking through Cultures*, London: Harvard University Press.

Shweder, R. (2003) *Why Do Men Barbecue? Recipes for Cultural Psychology*, London: Harvard University Press.

Sian, G. (1972) Measuring field dependence in Zambia, *International Journal of Psychology*, 7, 89–96.

Sidanius, J. & Pratto, F. (1999) *Social Dominance: An Intergroup Theory of Social Hierarchy and Oppression*, Cambridge, UK: Cambridge University Press.

Silke, A. (2003) *Terrorists, Victims and Society: Psychological Perspectives on Terrorism and Its Consequences*, Chichester, UK: Wiley.

Simmons, C., Koike, A. & Shimizu, H. (1986) Attitudes toward romantic love among American, German and Japanese students, *Journal of Social Psychology*, 126, 327–336.

Simons, R. (1980) The resolution of the Latah paradox, *Journal of Nervous and Mental Disease*, 171, 168–175.

Simons, R. (1987) A feasible and timely enterprise: commentary on 'Culture-bound syndromes and international disease classifications', *Culture, Medicine and Psychiatry*, 2 (1), 21–29.

Singelis, T., Bond, M., Sharkey, W. & Lai, C. (1999) Unpackaging culture's influence on self-esteem and embarrassability: the role of self-construals, *Journal of Cross-cultural Psychology*, 30, 315–341.

Singh, P., Huang, S. & Thompson, G. (1962) A comparative study of selected values, attitudes and person characteristics of American, Chinese and Indian students, *Journal of Social Psychology*, 57, 123–132.

Sinha, D. (1979) Perceptual style among nomads and transitional agriculturalist Birhors, in Eckensberger, L., Lonnes, W. & Poortinga, Y. (eds.), *Cross-cultural Contributions to Psychology* (pp. 83–93), Lisse, The Netherlands: Swets and Zeitlinger.

Sinha, D. (1986) *Psychology in a Third World Country: The Indian Experience*, New Delhi: Sage.

Sinha, D. (1997) Indigenous psychology, in Berry, J., Segall, M. & Kagiteibasi, C. (eds.), *Handbook of Cross-cultural psychology* (2nd ed., Vol. 1, pp. 129–169), Needham Heights, MA: Allyn & Bacon.

Skinner, B. (1953) *Science and Human Behaviour*, New York: Macmillan.

Sloan, T. (1996) Psychological research methods in developing countries, in Carr, S. & Schumaker, J. (eds.), *Psychology and the Developing World*, London: Praeger.

Sloan, T. (ed.) (2000) *Critical Psychology*, Basingstoke, UK: Palgrave.

Smith, P. (1980) Shared care of young children: alternatives to monotropism, *Merrill-Palmer Quarterly*, 26 (4), 371–389.

Smith, P. (2002) Levels of analysis in cross-cultural psychology, in Lonner, W., Dinnel, D., Hayes, S. & Sattler, D. (eds.), *Online Readings in Psychology and Culture* (Unit 2, Chapter 7), Bellingham, WA: Center for Cross-Cultural Research, Western Washington University.

Smith, P. & Bond, M. (1993/1998) *Social Psychology across Cultures*, London: Harvester.

Smith, P., Bond, M. & Kagitcibasi, C. (2006) *Understanding Social Psychology across Cultures*, London: Sage.

Snarey, J. (1985) Cross-cultural universality of social-moral development, *Psychological Bulletin*, 87, 202–232.

Soudijn, K., Hutschemaekers, G. & Van de Vijver, F. (1990) Culture conceptualizations, in Van de Vijver, F. & Hutschemaekers, G. (eds.), *The Investigation of Culture* (pp. 19–39), Tilburg, The Netherlands: Tilburg University Press.

Spearman, C. (1904) General intelligence, objectively determined and measured, *American Journal of Psychology*, 15, 201–293.

Stanley Hall, G. (1907) *Adolescence*, New York: D. Appleton.

Stark-Adamec, D., Graham, J. & Pyke, S. (1980) Androgyny and mental health: the need for a critical evaluation of the theoretical equation, *International Journal of Women's Studies*, 3 (5), 490–507.

Staub, E. (1989) The Roots of Evil: The Origins of Genocide and other Group Violence, New York: Cambridge University Press.

Steele, C. & Aronson, J. (1995) Stereotype threat and the intellectual test performance of African Americans, *Journal of Personality and Social Psychology*, 69, 797–811.

Steinberg, M., Pardes, H., Bjork, D. & Sporty, L. (1977) Demographic and clinical characteristics of black psychiatric patients in a private general hospital, *Hospital and Community Psychiatry*, 28, 128–132.

Stephan, W., Stephan, C., Abalakina, M., Ageyev, V., Blanco, A., Bond, M. *et al.* (1996) Distinctiveness effects in inter-group perceptions: an international study, in Grad, H., Blanco, A. & Georgas, J. (eds.), *Key Issues in Cross-cultural Psychology* (pp. 298–308), Lisse, The Netherlands: Swets & Zeitlinger.

Stephan, W., Diaz-Loving, R. & Duran, A. (2000) Integrated threat theory and intercultural attitudes: Mexico and the United States, *Journal of Cross-cultural Psychology*, 31, 240–249.

Sternberg, R.J. (2002) Cultural explorations of human intelligence around the world, in Lonner, W., Dinnel, D., Hayes, S. & Sattler D. (eds.), *Online Readings in Psychology and Culture* (Unit 5, Chapter 1), Bellingham, WA: Center for Cross-Cultural Research, Western Washington University.

Stevens, J. (1990) *An Observational Study of Skilled Memory in Waitresses*, New York: Laboratory for Cognitive Studies of Work, CUNY Graduate Centre.

Stevens, M. & Gielen, U. (eds.) (2007) *Toward a Global Psychology*, London: Lawrence Erlbaum Associates.

Stevens, M. & Wedding, D. (eds.) (2004) *Handbook of International Psychology*, New York: Brunner-Routledge.

Stewart, V. (1973) Tests of the 'carpentered world' hypothesis by race and environment in America and Zambia, *International Journal of Psychology*, 8, 83–94.

Stipek, D., Weiner, B. & Li, K. (1989) Testing some attribution-emotion relations in the People's Republic of China, *Journal of Personality and Social Psychology*, 56 (1), 109–116.

Stocking, G. (1983) *Observers Observed: History of Anthropology*, Vol. 1, Madison, WI: University of Wisconsin.

Stocking, G. (1995) *After Tylor: British Anthropology 1888–1951*, Madison, WI: University of Wisconsin.

Stouffer, S., Suchman, E., DeVinney, L., Star, S. & Williams, R. (1949) *The American Soldier: Adjustment during Army Life* (Vol. 1), Princeton, NJ: Princeton University Press.

Stratton, P. (1983) Biological programming of infant behaviour, *Journal of Child Psychology and Psychiatry*, 24 (2), 301–309.

Stropes-Roe, M. & Cochrane, R. (1990) The child rearing values of Asian and British parents and young people, *British Journal of Social Psychology*, 29, 149–160.

Strzelecki, A. (1989) The plunder of victims and their corpses, in Gutman, Y. & Berenbaum, M. (eds.), *Anatomy of the Auschwitz Death Camp* (pp. 246–266), Bloomington, IN: Indiana University Press.

Stuart, R. & Jacobsen, B. (1979) Sex differences in obesity, in Gomberg, E. & Franks, V. (eds.), *Gender and Disordered Behaviour*, New York: Brunner/ Mazel.

Stuvland, R. & Dodge, C. (1991) Internally displaced: a silent minority under stress, in Dodge, C. & Raundalen, M. (eds.), *Reaching Children in War* (pp. 21–38), Bergen, Norway: Sigma Forlag.

Sue, D. (1994) Asian American mental health and help-seeking behaviour: comment on Solberg *et al.* (1994), Tata & Leong (1994), and Lin (1994), *Journal of Counselling Psychology*, 41, 292–295.

Sue, S., Zane, N., Young, K., Bergin, A. & Garfield, S. (1994) Research on psychotherapy with culturally diverse populations, in Bergin, A. & Garfield, S. (eds.), *Handbook of Psychotherapy and Behaviour Change* (4th ed., pp. 428–466), New York: Wiley.

Sumathipala, A. & Siribaddana, S. (2004) Culture-bound syndromes: the story of *dhat* syndrome, *British Journal of Psychiatry*, 184, 200–209.

Super, C., Harkness S., van Tijen, N., van der Vlugt, E., Fintelman, M. & Dijkstra, J. (1996) The three R's of Dutch childrearing and the socialization of infant arousal, in Harkness, S. & Super, C. (eds.), *Parents' Cultural Belief Systems: Their Origins, Expressions and Consequences* (pp. 447–465), New York: Guilford.

Suryani, L. (1984) Culture and mental disorder: the case of Bebainen in Bali, *Culture, Medicine and Psychiatry*, 8, 95–113.

Sushruta (1963) *Susruta Samhita*, Bhisagratne, K. (ed.), Varanasi, India: Chowkambra Sanskrit Series Office.

Sveaass, N. (2000) Psychological work in a post-war context: experiences from Nicaragua, *Community Work and Family*, 3 (1), 37–64.

Swartz, L. (1985) Anorexia as a culture-bound syndrome, *Social Science & Medicine*, 20 (7), 725–730.

Tafarodi, R., Lo, C., Yamaguchi, S., Lee, W. & Katsura, H. (2004) The inner self in three countries, *Journal of Cross-cultural Psychology*, 35 (1), 97–117.

Tajfel, H. (1970) Experiments in intergroup discrimination, *Scientific American*, 223, 96–102.

Tajfel, H. (1981) *Human Groups and Social Categories*, Cambridge, UK: Cambridge University Press.

Takahashi, K. (1990) Are the key assumptions of the 'strange situation' procedure universal? *Human Development*, 33, 23–30.

Taylor, D. & Jaggi, V. (1974) Ethnocentrism and causal attribution in a South Indian context, *Journal of Cross-cultural Psychology*, 5, 162–171.

Taylor, P., Langley, P., Hasalambos, M., Pilkington, A. & Yeo, A. (2000) *Sociology in Focus*, Bath, UK: Causeway.

Taylor-Henry, S. & Hill, E. (1990) *Treatment and healing: an evaluation*, unpublished manuscript.

Thara, R. (2004) Twenty-year course of schizophrenia: the Madras Longitudinal Study, *Canadian Journal of Psychiatry*, 49 (8), 564–569.

Thomas, A. & Chess, A. (1977) *Temperament and Development*, New York: Brunner/Mazel.

Thomas, D. (1994) In search of solutions: women's police stations in Brazil, in Davies, M. (ed.), *Women and Violence: Realities and Responses Worldwide* (pp. 32–43), London: Zed.

Thouless, R. (1933) A racial difference in perception, *Journal of Social Psychology*, 4, 330–339.

Thurnwald, R. (1913) Ethno-psychologische Studie an Sudseevolkern: *Beihefte zur Zeitschrift fur angewandte Psychologie und psychologische Sammelforschung*, Vol. 6, Leipzig, Germany: Barth.

Thurstone, L. (1938) *Primary Mental Abilities*, Chicago: University of Chicago Press.

Tierney, P. (2001) *Darkness in El Dorado: How Scientists and Journalists Devastated the Amazon*, New York: Norton.

Tikkanen, T. (2004) *The European Diploma in Psychology and the future of the profession in Europe*, available online at: www.efpa.be/start.php (accessed January 4, 2005).

Tinburgen, N. (1952) *The Study of Instinct*, Oxford, UK: Oxford University Press.

Titchener, E. (1916) On ethnological tests of sensation and perception, *Proceedings of the American Philosophical Society*, 55, 204–236.

Titiev, M. (1972) *The Hopi Indians of Old Oraibi*, Ann Arbor, MI: University of Michigan Press.

Tobin, J., Wu, D. & Davidson, D. (1989) *Pre-school in Three Cultures*, New Haven, CT: Yale University Press.

Tovey, P. (1997) Contingent legitimacy: UK alternative practitioners and inter-sectorial acceptance, *Social Science and Medicine*, 45, 1129–1133.

Trew, K. (1986) Catholic-Protestant contact in Northern Ireland, in Hewstone, M. & Brown, R. (eds.), *Contact and Conflict in Intergroup Encounters* (pp. 93–106), Oxford, UK: Basil Blackstaff.

Triandis, H. (gen. ed.) (1980) *Handbook of Cross-cultural Psychology* (6 vols), Boston: Allyn & Bacon.

Triandis, H. (1994) *Culture and Social Behaviour*, New York: McGraw-Hill.

Triandis, H. (2002) Odysseus wandered for 10, I wondered for 50 years, in Lonner, W., Dinnel, D., Hayes, S. & Sattler D. (eds.), *Online Readings in Psychology and Culture* (Unit 2, Chapter 1), Bellingham, WA: Center for Cross-Cultural Research, Western Washington University.

Triandis, H., Brislin, R. & Hui, C. (1988) Cross-cultural training across the individualism-collectivism divide, *International Journal of Intercultural Relations*, 12, 269–289.

Trommsdorff, G. & Iwawaki, S. (1989) Student perception of socialization and gender role in Japan and Germany, *International Journal of Behavioural Development*, 12 (4), 485–493.

Tronick, E. & Morelli, G. (1992) The Efe forager infant and toddler's pattern of social relationships, *Developmental Psychology*, 28 (4), 568–577.

Tronick, E., Morelli, G. & Winn, S. (1987) Multiple caretaking of Efe (pygmy) infants, *American Anthropologist*, 89 (1), 96–106.

Tseng, W. & Hsu, J. (1970) Chinese culture, personality formation and mental illness, *International Journal of Social Psychology*, 16, 5–14.

Tyler, T. & Huo, Y. (2002) *Trust in the Law*, New York: Russell Sage.

Tylor, E. (1865) *Researches into the Early History of Mankind and the Development of Civilization* (Paul Bohannan, ed.), Chicago: University of Chicago Press, 1964.

Tylor, E. (1874) *Primitive Culture: Researches into the Development of Mythology, Philosophy, Religion, Language, Art and Custom*, London: Murray.

United Nations (2000) *The World's Women 2000: Trends and Statistic*, New York: UN.

United Nations Children's Fund (2000) Domestic violence against women and girls, *Innocenti Digest* (Vol. 6), Florence, Italy: Innocenti Research Centre.

United Nations Development Programme (2002) *Human Development Report: Deepening Democracy in a Fragmented World*, New York: UN.

Vanbeselaere, N. (1983) Mere exposure: a search for an explanation, in Doise, W. & Moscovici, S. (eds.), *Current Issues in European Social Psychology* (Vol. 1), Cambridge, UK: Cambridge University Press.

van de Koppel, J. (1983) *A Developmental Study of the Biaka Pygmies and the Bangandu*, Lisse, The Netherlands: Swets and Zeitlinger.

Van de Vijver, F. & Lueng, K. (1997) *Methods and Data Analysis for Cross-cultural Research*, Newbury Park, CA: Sage.

Van de Vliert, E. (2006) Autocratic leadership around the globe: do climate and wealth drive leadership culture?, *Journal of Cross-cultural Psychology*, 37 (1), 42–59.

van Ijzendoorn, M. (1995) Adult attachment representations, parental responsiveness, and infant attachment: a meta-analysis on the predictive validity of the adult attachment interview, *Psychological Bulletin*, 117, 387–403.

van Ijzendoorn, M. (1996) Attachment patterns and their outcomes: commentary, *Human Development*, 39 (4), 224–231.

van Ijzendoorn, M. & Sagi, A. (1999) Cross-cultural patterns of attachment: universal contextual dimensions, in Cassidy, J. & Shaver, P. (eds.), *Handbook of Attachment* (pp. 713–734), New York: Guilford.

Van Oudenhoven, J., Askevis-Leherpeux, F., Hannover, B., Jaarsma, R. & Dardenne, B. (2002) Asymmetric international attitudes, *European Journal of Social Psychology*, 32, 275–289.

van Wijk, H. (1959) A cross-cultural theory of colour and brightness nomenclature, *Bijdraden tot de Taal, Land, en-Volkenkinde*, 15 (2), 113–137.

Vico, G. (1725) *Scienza Nuova*. Published as *The New Science of Giambattista Vico* (trans. T. Bergin & M. Fixch), Ithaca, NY: Cornell University Press, 1968.

Volney, C. (1804) *A View of the Climate and Soil of the United States of America*, London: J. Johnson.

Vygotsky, L. (1978) *Mind in Society: The Development of Higher Psychological Processes*, Cambridge, MA: Harvard University Press.

Washburn, S. (1960) Tools and human evolution, *Scientific American*, 203, 63–73.

Wassman, J. & Dasen, P. (1994) Yupno number system and counting, *Journal of Cross-cultural Psychology*, 25, 78–94.

Weaver, D. (1974) *An intra-cultural test of empiricist vs. physiological explanations for cross-cultural differences in geometric illusion susceptibility using two illusions in Ghana*, unpublished doctoral dissertation, Northwestern University, Evanston, IL.

Weiss, C. (1982) Controlling domestic life and mental illness, *Culture, Medicine and Psychiatry*, 16, 237–271.

Werker, J. (1989) Becoming a native listener, *American Scientist*, 77, 54–59.

Werry, J. (1986) Physical illness, symptoms and allied disorders, in Quay, H. & Werry, J. (eds.), *Psychopathological Disorders of Childhood* (3rd ed.), New York: Wiley.

Westaby, J. (1995) Presence of others and task performance in Japan and the U.S.: a laboratory investigation, *International Journal of Psychology*, 30 (4), 451–460.

Westen, D. (1996) *Psychology: Mind, Brain and Culture* (2nd ed.), New York: Wiley.

Westermeyer, J. (1973) The epidemicity of amok violence, *Archives of General Medicine*, 28, 873–876.

Wetherell, M. (1982) Cross-cultural studies of minimal groups: implications for the social identity theory of intergroup relations, in Tajfel, H. (ed.), *Social Identity and Intergroup Relations*, Cambridge, UK: Cambridge University Press.

Wheeler, L. & Kim, Y. (1997) What is beautiful is culturally good, *Personality and Social Psychology Bulletin*, 23 (8), 795–800.

Whiting, J. (1974) A model for psychocultural research, *Annual Report*, Washington, DC: American Anthropological Association.

Whiting, J. (1981) Environmental constraints on infant care practices, in Munroe, R., Munroe, B. & Whiting, B. (eds.), *Handbook of Cross-cultural Human Development* (pp. 151–181), New York: Garland Press.

Whiting, J. (1994) Fifty years as a behavioural scientist, in Chasdi, E. (ed.) *Culture and Human Development* (pp. 14–41), New York: Cambridge University Press.

Whiting, R. (1989) *You Gotta Have Wa*, New York: Macmillan.

Whorf, B. (1956) *Language, Thought and Reality*, Carroll, J. (ed.), Cambridge, MA: MIT Press.

Willemsen, M. (1996) *Unhealthy Societies: The Affliction of Inequality*, London: Routledge.

Williams, J. & Best, D. (1982) *Measuring Sex Stereotypes: A Thirty Nation Study*, Beverly Hills, CA: Sage.

Williams, J. & Best, D. (1990) *Sex and Psyche: Gender and Self Viewed Cross-culturally*, Beverly Hills, CA: Sage.

Williams, J. & Best, D. (1994) Cross-cultural views of women and men, in Lonner, W. & Malpas, R. (eds.), *Psychology & Culture*, Boston: Allyn & Bacon.

Williams, L. & Sobieszczyk, T. (1997) Attitudes surrounding the continuation of female circumcision in the Sudan: passing the tradition to the next generation, *Journal of Marriage and the Family*, 59, 966–981.

Winder, R. (2004) *Bloody Foreigners*, London: Little, Brown.

Wing, J., Coopes, J. & Sartorius, N. (1974) *Measurement and Classification of Psychiatric Symptoms*, London: Cambridge University Press.

Winter, W. (1963) The perception of safety posters by Bantu industrial workers, *Psychologia Africana*, 10, 127–135.

Witkin, H. (1959) The perception of the upright, *Scientific American*, 200, 50–56.

Witkin, H. (1967) A cognitive style approach to cross-cultural research, *International Journal of Psychology*, 2, 233–250.

Witkin, H. & Berry, J. (1975) Psychological differentiation in cross-cultural perspective, *Journal of Cross-cultural Psychology*, 6, 4–87.

Witkin, H., Goodenough, D. & Oltman, P. (1979) Psychological differentiation: current status, *Journal of Personality and Social Psychology*, 37, 1127–1145.

Wittkower, E., Douyon, L. & Bijou, L. (1964) Spirit possession in Haitian vodun ceremonies, *Acta Psychoterapeutica et Psychosomatica*, 12, 72–80.

Wober, M. (1969) Distinguishing centri-cultural from cross-cultural tests and research, *Perceptual and Motor Skills*, 28, 488.

Wober, M. (1974) Towards an understanding of the Kiganda concept of intelligence, in Berry, J. & Dasen, P. (eds.), *Culture & Cognition*, London: Methuen.

Woodworth, R. (1910) Racial differences in mental traits, *Science*, 31, 171–186.

World Health Organization (1974) *The International Pilot Study of Schizophrenia*, Vol. 1, Geneva: WHO.

World Health Organization (1979) *Schizophrenia: An International Follow-up Study*, New York: Wiley.

World Population Bureau (2007) *World Population Data Sheet*, available online at www.prb.org/Publications/Datasheets.

Yamaguchi, S. (2004) Further clarification of the concept of Amae in relation to attachment and dependence, *Human Development*, 47, 28–33.

Yamashita, I. (1977) *Taijin-Kyofu*, Tokyo: Kanehara.

Yang, K. (2000) Mono-cultural and cross-cultural indigenous approaches: the royal road to the development of a balanced global psychology, *Asian Journal of Social Psychology*, 3, 241–263.

Yap, P. (1967) Classification of the culture-bound reactive syndromes, *Australian, New Zealand Journal of Psychiatry*, 1, 172–179.

Yap, P. (1969) The culture-bound reactive syndromes, in Cauldill, W. & Lin, T. (eds.), *Mental Health Research in Asia and the Pacific*, Honolulu, HI: East-West Centre Press.

Yap, P. (1974) *Comparative Psychiatry: A Theoretical Framework*, Lau, M. & Stokes, A. (eds.), Toronto, Canada: University of Toronto Press.

Yrizarry, N., Matsumoto, D. & Wilson-Cohn, C. (1998) American-Japanese differences in muscular intensity ratings of universal facial expressions of emotion, *Motivation and Emotion*, 22 (4), 315–327.

Zaguirre, J. (1957) Amuck, *Journal of Philippine Federation of Private Medical Practitioners*, 6, 1138–1149.

Zajonc, R. (1966) Social facilitation of dominant and subordinate responses, *Journal of Experimental Social Psychology*, 2 (2), 160–168.

Zajonc, R. (1968) Attitudinal effects of mere exposure, *Journal of Personality and Social Psychology*, 9 (suppl.), 1–27.

Zaslavsky, C. (1973) *Africa Counts*, Boston: Prindle, Weber and Schmidt.

Zhang, Y., Young, S., Lee, H., Zhang, Z., Xiao, W., Hao, Y., *et al.* (2002) Chinese Taoist cognitive psychotherapy in the treatment of generalised anxiety disorder in contemporary China, *Transcultural Psychiatry*, 39 (1), 115–129.

Zukow, P. (1989a) *Sibling Interaction across Cultures*, New York: Springer.

Zukow, P. (1989b) Communicating across disciplines, in Zukow, P. (ed.), *Sibling Interaction across Cultures*, New York: Springer.

Index